Brecht and Method

Brecht and Method

FREDRIC JAMESON

VERSO

London • New York

First published by Verso 1998
© Fredric Jameson 1998
All rights reserved

Verso
UK: 6 Meard Street, London W1V 3HR
USA: 180 Varick Street, New York NY 10014–4606

Verso is the imprint of New Left Books

ISBN 1–85984–809–5

British Library Cataloguing in Publication Data
A catalogue record for this book is available from the British Library

Library of Congress Cataloging-in-Publication Data
Jameson, Frederic.
　　Brecht and method / Fredric Jameson.
　　　　p.　　cm.
　　Includes bibliographical references.
　　ISBN 1–85984–809–5
　　1. Brecht, Bertolt, 1898–1956 — Criticism and interpretation.
　I. Title.
　PT2603.R3997Z71265　1998　　　　　　　　　98–29362
　832'.912 — dc21　　　　　　　　　　　　　　　　CIP

Typeset by SetSystems Ltd, Saffron Walden
Printed by Biddles Ltd, Guildford and King's Lynn

For
Gert Weymann

Contents

Prologue

1 *Nützliches*

Brecht would have been delighted, I like to think, at an argument, not for his greatness, or his canonicity, nor even for some new and unexpected value of posterity (let alone for his 'postmodernity'), as rather for his *usefulness* – and that not only for some uncertain or merely possible future, but right now, in a post-Cold-War market-rhetorical situation even more anti-communist than the good old days. Brechtian slyness: so it was, for example, that instead of denouncing a 'cult of personality' that could not but nauseate him, he proposed that we should, rather, celebrate the essential 'usefulness' of Stalin (something not only Trotsky and Mao Zedong, but probably even Roosevelt, would have been willing to endorse).[1] Indeed, it was as just such a proposer of proposals that he himself wanted to be remembered:

> Er hat Vorschläge gemacht. Wir
> haben sie angenommen.
> (XIV, 191–2)

> He made proposals. We
> Carried them out.[2]

On the other hand, it is characteristic of the Brechtian dialectic that no such suggestions ever remain wholly unambiguous. So it is, for example, that precisely this argument, deployed by the 'modernist' architect of *Me-ti* (Book of the Turning Ways) to defend a Corbusian aesthetic of beauty and usefulness, draws upon itself the disgust and repudiation of his workers:

> Gerade so gut [they tell him] könntest du einem Kuli, der beim Kahnschleppen mit Lederpeitschen gepeitscht wird, Stühle anbieten, deren Sitze aus Lederriemen geflochten sind. Vielleicht ist wirklich schön, was nützlich ist. Aber dann sind unsere Maschinen nicht schön, denn sie sind für uns nicht nützlich. Aber,

rief Len-ti schmerzvoll, sie könnten doch nützlich sein. Ja, sagten die Arbeiter, deine Wohnungen könnten auch schön sein, aber sie sind es nicht.

(XVIII, 148)

You might just as well offer chairs with leather straps to coolies accustomed to being beaten by just such straps while hauling their keelboats. Maybe what's useful really is beautiful. But then in that case our machines aren't beautiful at all, since they are certainly of no use to us. But, Len-ti ruefully exclaimed, they could be useful. Of course, said the workers, and your buildings could also be beautiful, only they aren't.

'Useful' in this context would not only mean 'didactic', although, as I have suggested elsewhere, there are signs that the 'present age', with its new-found taste for impure aesthetics of all kinds, has also become more tolerant of didactic elements and attitudes than the more purist high modernities that preceded it. Yet if it means didactic, then we must add that Brecht never exactly had a doctrine to teach, not even 'Marxism' in the form of a system ('The ABC of . . . ,' to recall a once-fashionable way of doing it): rather, we will want to show in what follows that his 'proposals' and his lessons – the fables and the proverbs he delighted in offering – were more on the order of a method than a collection of facts, thoughts, convictions, first principles, and the like. Yet it was an equally sly 'method', which equally successfully eludes all the objections modern philosophy (as in Gadamer's *Truth and Method*) has persuasively made against the reifications of the methodological as such. Yet, as we will be attempting to elucidate these paradoxes later on, perhaps we may return for this introductory moment to that Brechtian usefulness, which, although it certainly involves teaching, is something a little more fundamental than mere didacticism (whether in art or anything else).

Remember, for one thing, that for Brecht, science – and in Germany *Wissenschaft* (knowledge) is also a little more than specialized 'science' in French and English – science and knowledge are not grim and dreary duties but first and foremost sources of pleasure: even the epistemological and theoretical dimensions of 'science' are to be thought in terms of *Popular Mechanics* and of the manual amusement of combining ingredients and learning to use new and unusual tools. But perhaps it is only the non-scientists who, in our time, think of science in the reified way: indeed, current science studies seem to have returned to a view of the history of scientific 'ideas' as something closer to the history of laboratory institutions and installations, of material operations and the social relations they presuppose, of transcribing physical modifications and juggling their shorthand to see if any new ones thereby become imaginable. Surely much of modern (or post-Kantian) philosophy has struggled in one way or another to de-epistemologize the concept of science-knowledge, to undermine it as a static representation and to set it in motion or translate it back into the practice it came from.

Brecht offers us a world in which that practice is entertaining, and includes its own pedagogy as a member of the class it subsumes – the teaching of practice also being a practice in its own right, and thereby 'participating' in the very satisfactions it holds out to its student practitioners. Under these circumstances, at least two terms of Cicero's famous triad (to move, to teach, to delight) slowly fold back into one another: 'to teach' again recovers its kinship with the injunction 'to delight', and the didactic again slowly reconquers the social respectability long since accorded that (only secondarily and marginally) approved social function for art as the embellishment of life. (As for the third term of the triad, Brecht notoriously problematized it: 'to move', to arouse emotion, to control, apply, express, inflect or purge strong feelings, is the object of a range of critical and qualifying formulations that have made problems for Brechtians and anti-Brechtians alike; we will deal with them in our own way in what follows.)

On the other hand, this popular-mechanics version of science and knowledge will necessarily be a modern one in Brecht: and this despite the immemorial peasantry that stands behind so much of his work and his language; and despite the 'postmodernity' into which we seek to welcome him and to rediscover his message. Leave aside the question of whether we have to do here with modernity, modernism, or modernization; for the moment the qualification of modern is crucial for us because the taboo on the didactic in art (which we moderns, we 'Western' moderns, take for granted) is in fact itself a feature of our own modernity. None of the great precapitalist classical civilizations ever doubted that their art harboured some fundamental didactic vocation; and to recover that vocation is very precisely the meaning of what may be called Brecht's Chinese dimension, as we shall see. But if this didacticism is a truth we need to recover from the precapitalist modes of production – a 'blasting open of the continuum of history' that can now reconnect us to ancient China, as Benjamin might have put it – we must vigilantly ward off all the antiquarianism that ceaselessly menaces it. This is no doubt the task of Brecht's 'modernism' in the narrower, technological or industrial sense: the delight in aeroplanes and in the radio, the dimension of 'workers' to be added to that of 'peasants' in any Gramscian aesthetic alliance.

So activity itself is also one of the features of knowledge and art as those flow back into the useful: the 'means' inherent in turning the useful slowly around into an end in its own right – yet not an empty formalist end, not the end-pretext, the 'any-old' purpose that we invoke in order to be able to keep ourselves busy: but, rather, a substantive and Hegelian coming together of means and ends in such a way that activity becomes worth doing in its own right; that immanence and transcendence become indistinguishable (or their opposition transcended, if you prefer); or, in other words, that 'the thing itself' appears. 'Die Sache selbst'[3]: such is the enfeebled memory, the word-on-the-tip-of-the-tongue, that Brecht reminds us about, and offers to help us reconstruct, if not re-create: the 'construction of socialism' is only one of the names for this concrete utopian process which, in what follows, we will try to block out – like the founding of an ancient city, the strips of rawhide laid out here and there, crowds trampling over the still empty site, which has been transformed from a space into a (still virtual) place, the beginning of the endless wranglings over law codes and rituals.

But it is important to remember that the Brechtian doctrine of activity – if it was once energizing because activity and praxis were very precisely on the agenda – is now urgent and topical precisely because they are not, and because so many people seem immobilized in the institutions and the professionalization which seem to admit of no revolutionary change, not even of the evolutionary or reform-oriented kind. Stasis today, all over the world – in the twin condition of market and globalization, commodification and financial speculation – does not even take on a baleful religious sense of an implacable Nature; but it certainly seems to have outstripped any place for human agency, and to have rendered the latter obsolete.

This is why a Brechtian conception of activity must today go hand in hand with a revival of the older precapitalist sense of time itself, of the change or flowing of all things: for it is the movement of this great river of time or the Tao that will slowly carry us downstream again to the moment of praxis. We have had to occult and repress it, because we have come to think of capitalism as natural and eternal, and also in order to conceal that related existential and generational thing, our own deaths. Brecht calls upon us to embrace the pain of that Becoming, that passing away, in order to reach our more satisfying human possibilities. It is no doubt a metaphysical proposition in the most august sense: and we may summon Heraclitus to testify to it in one tradition, and Mao Zedong in another:

One thing destroys another, things emerge, develop, and are destroyed, everywhere is like this. If things are not destroyed by others, then they destroy themselves. Why should people die? Does the aristocracy die too? This is a natural law. Forests live longer than human beings, yet even they last only a few thousand years. . . . Socialism, too, will be eliminated, it wouldn't do if it were not eliminated, for then there would be no communism. . . . The life of dialectics is the continuous movement toward opposites. Mankind will also finally meet its doom. . . . We should always be bringing forth new things. Otherwise what are we here for? What do we want descendants for? New things are to be found in reality, we must grasp reality.[4]

Yet such metaphysical perspectives have often been more narrowly called on to jettison the writer who professes them. Did not the rewriter of so many older texts recommend rewriting itself, a rewriting that must ultimately reach his own playbooks (as our classical *Berliner Ensemble* paradigm slowly turned before our own eyes into Heiner Müller and postmodernism); should we not indeed – as with the student-activist learners of Godard's *La Chinoise* – finally and reluctantly, with sadness but firmness and *en connaissance de cause*, draw one last chalk line through the subsisting name of Brecht that alone survives the gradual elimination of the once multiply named Western bourgeois tradition? Or – to put it the other way round, and in a form that more immediately and desperately threatens the current project – is there not something itself profoundly unBrechtian in the attempt to reinvent and revive some 'Brecht for our times', some 'what is living and what is dead in Brecht', some postmodern Brecht or Brecht for the future, a postsocialist or even post-Marxist Brecht, the Brecht of queer theory or of identity politics, the Deleuzian or Derridean Brecht, or perhaps the Brecht of the market and globalization, an American mass-culture Brecht, a finance-capital Brecht: why not? Ignoble slogans, which carry a repressed conception of posterity within themselves, and unconsciously fantasize the canon as a form of personal immortality, whose opposite must – naturally enough – be personal extinction.

2 Monadic Chronologies

I want to try to say why we do not have to be antiquarian or nostalgic to appreciate the ways in which Brecht is still alive for us: indeed, it is this very plurality of the actual and possible, virtual 'Brechts' that will begin to show us how. Nor is this a question of styles (which we will certainly deal with, but differently, and in another place) or of biographical epochs exactly, even though we will follow a somewhat biographical-chronological order. The canonical reading of Brecht founders on two reefs: first, that of the multiplicity of genres – was he first and foremost a man of the theatre, or was he really – as Western critics from Adorno on have tried to insinuate – (just) a poet? And what about the 'theory' – is it more than dramaturgy, and if so, what? There are fewer defenders of the prose fiction, although I might myself be willing, on a bet, to make a stand there:[5] certainly, the anecdotes and parables reveal a grand and subtle kind of storytelling. Yet one feels that it is equally undesirable to rank the parts of Brecht's production in this way, since whatever wins, we lose some of it in the process. And in any case, once you have solved this (perhaps false) problem, you have the job of distilling a canon, and of choosing the 'great' works: I certainly don't mind celebrating the great plays, but there are very different scenes I want to keep, and they are not always intelligible under the rubric 'play'. The same no doubt holds for the poetry and its various stages or epochs; but I am loath either to see in it a progression towards some final poetic quintessence (you could argue that for the *Bukow Elegies*), or to project a synchronic and phenomenological 'world' or coexistence of all the poems, early and late, in which some deeper poetic unity is identified.

For Brecht is modern first and foremost by way of his discontinuities and his deeper fragmentation: from that dispersal, we can proceed on into a certain unity, but only after having passed through it. This is a position Haug has defended,[6] seeing the entire Brechtian corpus as an immense unity-in-dispersal, across a host of generic discourses and speech practices, like Gramsci's *Prison Notebooks*, or Benjamin's *Arcades Project* (which are, to be sure, stylistically a good deal more limited than Brecht, and whose very 'unfinished' form imposes the dispersive method, whereas in Brecht there are also completed things from time to time).

As for the biographical, I think that now that we are long since out of the critical age of 'life and loves' (hunting for real-life originals), and of old-fashioned literary history as well, we can be less intimidated by that, but also more dialectical in our uses of it. In an age of great biography, it would be churlish to repress our pleasures in the anecdotes as well as in the turns of a life and its work (particularly in a helpless period like our own, where destiny seems once again disconnected from history, it is the world-historical contacts and evasions in the lives of the *Dichter* – in Blake and Yeats, in Eisenstein and Gide – that must fascinate us and give us sustenance).

In the case of Brecht, I will want to speak of layers of history, chronological monads, 'pyramids of worlds' (Leibniz) – this time over-lapping in time rather than space, and each with its own specific and distinct type of content: each imposing its own specific occasionality (for this kind of 'occasional poetry' it is History itself which is the occasion, or rather, the multiple sequence of occasions). Ortega wished that Goethe had had a different kind of life, one battered by history from all sides – a wandering, weather-beaten, 'shipwrecked' Goethe,[7] and so on. This is very precisely the kind of life Brecht had, and it coincided, as far as he lived, with the life of the century itself. Yet our point is not that this life is thereby interesting, however difficult it may have been for the one who had to live it, but rather that each of these layers crystallized a series of works and expressions, or organized a stream of fragments around itself. Just as in the Middle Ages, poets spoke of the *matière* of this and that – the 'matter' of Brittany, for example, in which the Arthurian cycle was central – so we can now speak of the various 'matières' of the Brechtian life, which then sang of that history, or that historical layer, as though it were autobiographical, because Brecht lived his own life outside in that history. To say that Brecht always thought politically, that he never had an idea or an experience which was not at once filtered through the political, is to say something like that: in other words, history was his private life, and we must now separate some of its moments and its tones.

But history also always impossibly confronts us with its prehistory; and biography with its juvenilia: in the case of Brecht, the problem of *Baal*. He himself was never quite so conventionally orthodox-Marxist as when in later life he tried to domesticate and interpret the beginnings of his work as the expression of the antisocial or, better still, the asocial [*der böse Baal der asoziale*]; which is, to be sure, a social way of saying it. Baal the monster, in other words, but the monster of appetite as such, which seems to me a more satisfactory word than the current 'desire'. Desire – even as a concept – emerges from a reflection on hysteria, on the absence of desire, the desire to desire, and the like. Sheer appetite does not need to pass through that narrow gap [*défilé*]: it is already there, knife in one hand and fork in the other, drumming on the table. Indeed, pushing things off the table is essential to it: the milk on the floor, the broken plates and glasses, the splattering of the pap – scandal is a necessary and constitutive part of what Freud called 'His Majesty the Ego';[8] and what we call 'egotism' (which ought not here necessarily to imply the formation of the ego or self) is its other element: something not quite present in the Id, which is rather impersonal, one would think, and no longer even has a self to pull everything towards, from out of which to grasp. The Id knows its strange and terrifying, but radically impersonal and even inhuman, manifestation in the Wild Man of the forest of the Middle Ages: a virtual yeti without speech, which steals its prey from human villages but is incapable of saying: Mine! Mine! This last is, rather, the language of Jarry's Père Ubu, or, at the other end of a historical spectrum, of Harpo Marx or of Crumb's Mr Natural. These are the slobs of literature rather than its zombies or living dead: creatures of physical and vestimentary neglect, satyrs, dirty old men, and the like, they are the archetypes of appetite, surging up from popular culture (rather than, as with supreme villains and manifestations of evil, from the lettered). Early Chaplin, the tramp in the first short films, was like that – revoltingly possessive, repeatedly kicking the gouty man (who, no doubt, represents society's warning against indulgence) down the stairs, lecherous, distracted impolitely by a variety of new objects, disrespectful and violent (not out of a violent nature or essence but, rather, in some immediate reaction to his surroundings). The first appearances of Mickey Mouse – in *Steamboat Willie*, for instance (1928) – were like that as well; both of them surging before the veneer of culture, the sentimentality of the tramp or of Mickey, came to spoil this arch-natural product: about whom stories cannot be told exactly. That is the next point, and it explains why *Baal* must be episodic: the figure of appetite must erupt and break the furniture; but it cannot evolve, it knows no interesting history but ultimate exhaustion and death. It is not even tragic-pathetic like the Id or Desire, which can be thwarted and pine away like unrequited love. For to deny an appetite is scarcely to unrequite; another will shortly take its place.

This is not yet Brechtian cynicism, nor is it yet even a historical layer: it takes the place of the layer of childhood so many writers have cherished, and in hindsight, had the latter been invented yet, it would no doubt correspond to that later thing called adolescence. Meanwhile, it is assuredly the source of a properly Brechtian materialism – perhaps, if it is historical at all, it is the place in between history, where the father figures, the Kaiser and the rest, have ignominiously disappeared, their place taken by obscure revolts of all kinds (from which one can take refuge at home in the upstairs flat in Augsburg), and before the new order of the modern world – Weimar – has taken its place. I think that the *gestus* of appropriation that it now sets in place – and which is perhaps also the very source of gestures in general and the dramatic, Flaubert's Garçon bellowing like his master – may know as its opposite number and principle of organization a moment of dissolution, as in the 'Drowned Girl's' body slowly dissolving into the element of water:

Geschah es (sehr langsam), dass Gott sie allmählich vergass
(XI, 109)

It came to pass (very slowly) that she faded from the mind of God

The opposition might well take many forms and bear many interpretations: the gender one, for instance, in which peremptory activity is opposed to a kind of absolute passivity; but it seems to me that the most useful one for the later poetry will be the identification of qualities and perceptions with this second pole – whence the washed-out skies of the later poems, the pallor that makes a variety of tones itself somehow more material: as though perception registered the fading sensations more surely than the emergent ones, and as though dissolution were more physical and materialistic than a view of sheer solids and resistant materials. This also plays a role in Weill's music: and it sets in place the great tonal and rhythmic oppositions of the Weimar years between the strident and the elegiac, between the rhythms of the men's 'basic appetites' [*saufen, essen, lieben, boxen*] and the 'song of the cranes' in *Mahagonny*.

The first genuine historical layer, then, is clearly enough Weimar itself and the tropes of cynicism: the emergence of the great demonstrandum of the Brechtian paradox and sarcastic reversal; of the cynicism, not of the writer, but of reality itself: the rawest, desecularized version of capitalism, without any of its French, English or Italian cultural veneer, beginning from the zero point of the war's end and the collapse of the state and of authority – a desperate and competitive situation lacking in all the exotic features of the much longer US experience in respect of the unvarnished (which we will meet again in a moment). This is no doubt the fundamental experience of a genuine 'peacetime' in Brecht – one that will never return, but one that necessarily marks his conception of reality itself. Yet Weimar is the most difficult to characterize in this respect, since it has long since (not least owing to Brecht himself) become an image and a cliché – a historicist poster, a 'jungle of cities' haunted by Mac the Knife and Lotte Lenya; add to this the romanticism of its doom, which we now know and it could not. What it seems at least fair to say is that Weimar gave Brecht an unalloyed experience of modernity as such – from Lindbergh to the great industrial city, from radio to nightclubs and cabarets, from unemployment to theatrical experiment, from an older Western bourgeoisie to the brand-new Soviet experiment next door. Strange that it is precisely this modernity which seems so old-fashioned to us today; and that its images of money and ferocious business competition, and of the mixture of sophistication and misery, should seem so exotic, and finally so 'uncultured', compared to the glossy styles of 1980s and 1990s US postmodernity. Is it fair only to salvage Brecht–Weill out of this general débâcle and to call it the Weimar moment, thereby at least marking the relationship to spectacle and the musical, to opera, along with a relationship to music which will be prolonged, via friend and collaborator Hanns Eisler, into the heart of contemporary musical experimentation?

But four or five other related layers or worlds need to be set in place alongside and even within this one. For one thing, Brecht is also 'Brecht': that is, the place of collective work as such, as though the individuality we ascribed to some period before history, with its unique qualities and obsessions, had been transcended almost at once into a collaborative subject – one which certainly seemed to have a distinctive style (the one we now called 'Brechtian') but was no longer personal in the bourgeois or individualistic sense. How Brecht pillaged the playbooks of the past and other cultures we know well, and are probably not unduly shocked: the more layers of human time, the more people of all ages who left their traces in the artifact, the richer and the better. But even today collaborative work arouses scandal: what about the private property of the signature, and did not Brecht exploit the people working with him (now called 'Brecht')? Worse than that, since so many of them were women, does not the pattern emerge of the office, with the male boss, even beyond that of the professor signing the research of his students? From there it is but a step to conclude (as Fuegi has[9]) that everything good in Brecht was written by somebody else, generally a woman: a proposition that can usefully be combined with Brecht's alleged traits of ruthlessness and authoritarianism. This is in reality a political issue (masked by moralisms of various kinds); it first seeks to play off identity-political themes against class ones, and then, on another level, to depreciate politics altogether – as the action of collectives – in the name of the personal and of individual ownership. In the 1960s many people came to realize that in a truly revolutionary collective experience what comes into being is not a faceless and anonymous crowd or 'mass' but, rather, a new level of being – what Deleuze, following Eisenstein, calls the Dividual[10] – in which individuality is not effaced but completed by collectivity. It is an experience that has now slowly been forgotten, its traces systematically effaced by the return of desperate individualisms of all kinds.

So it is that the properly utopian features of Brecht's collective work, and of collective or collaborative work of all kinds, are occulted and repudiated; yet this is one of the most exciting features of this work in general, and one of the unique sources of the excitement it has in store for us – the promise and the example of a utopian cooperation, down to the very details of those literary sentences which our tradition has attempted to reserve as the last refuges of true creation and the individual genius. It is a lesson whose Brechtian pleasures will surely return in future generations, however unfashionable it may feel to contemporaries in the current age of the market.

But this 'layer' of what Brecht can mean for us must be paralleled and doubled by another, larger one, namely that of the theatre itself, taken as the very figure for the collective and for a new kind of society: one in which the classic questions and dilemmas of political philosophy can be 'estranged' and rethought. Darko Suvin has written eloquently of the uses of the theatre as an institution microcosmic of society as a whole, and thereby of the symbolic and utopian allegories it offers as an experimental space and collective laboratory.[11] We will see later on how this dimension – whose practice is lacking, except figuratively, in the novel and in most poetry (but perhaps not in song as such) – modifies the nature of 'theory', and in particular of Brecht's theoretical writing, and allows it into the system of literary genres in a new way (rather different from the theory of prose in French structuralism and poststructuralism, whose very conception of theory, however, comes from Brecht himself, via Barthes).

For the moment we merely want to underscore this new experience of theatre as collective experiment (alongside the Soviets and Piscator, and leaping over from Weimar to the East German period) as something radically different from theatre as expression or as experience, even though many of the great modern theatrical experimenters – different from Brecht as they may be in their mysticism or their minimalist asceticism – also sacralize their work as the emergence of a new collectivity, and a reborn or utopian society. Brecht gives us all that without the religious overtones, and as an allegorical level within a practical exercise, in both of which we ourselves are involved.

Collaborative work, collective *praxis*: to these two feature or new levels of the Brechtian life-enterprise may be added two more, which are scarcely as specialized as they seem: the Chinese Brecht and the experimental Brecht – whatever one thinks of *Die Massnahme*, for example, it has inspired the effort at new forms ceaselessly since its inception; while the relationship between *gestus* and music is another more pervasive experimental area; and the very theory of estrangement itself – the V-effect – tends to transform even Brecht's more conventional plays (*Furcht und Elend des dritten Reiches*, for example) into so much Beckett- or Ionesco-like experimentality, to which we need to add the element of humour and buffoonery as the very space and realm of the experimental as such.

The well-made production is one from which the traces of its rehearsals have been removed (just as from the successfully reified commodity the traces of production itself have been made to disappear): Brecht opens up this surface, and allows us to see back down into the alternative gestures and postures of the actors trying out their roles: so it is that aesthetic experimentation generally – which has so often been understood as generating the new and the hitherto unexperienced, the radical innovation – might just as well be grasped as the 'experimental' attempt to ward off reification (something the other arts, from novels and films to poetry, painting, and musical performance, even aleatory performance, are structurally and materially less qualified to do).

I link this additional Brechtian space or dimension to the Chinese persona – not only because some of the experimental forms are East Asian (in particular the work with the Japanese Noh, which also stimulated Yeats and Pound), but mainly because this is both a characteristic and a distinctive space.[12] Characteristic in the way in which a kind of libidinal exoticism and historicism works as theatrical costume for Brecht's imagination: not flight but stylization, and the enlargement of the possible and its images – what Kenneth Burke would have described as the productivity of sheer scene as such, its unfolding into a variety of novel gestures and actions. But distinctive because the Chinese cultural space and world-view – sometimes associated here with a properly peasant and precapitalist history – is paradigmatic of the expansion of Brecht's work into that ultimate frame of the metaphysic or the world-view. It was a wise and subtle strategy: for throughout the modern elsewhere it has been the very notion of a world-view or a metaphysic which is the first casualty of modernity itself. The former then becomes a private obsession or personal hobby, inspiring a tug of war and an inner tension between our temptation momentarily to believe (they won't have confidence in me any more, worried Rimbaud on his deathbed,[13] just as our momentary belief in Lawrence or in Rilke in effect momentarily transforms both into prophets) and our suspicion that their 'systems' are little more than psychological and psychoanalytic rationalization, if not the sheerest social ideology. Hermeneutics of belief, hermeneutics of suspicion: the option is suspended when the Tao itself opens up around a secular and cynical Western writer like Brecht, who cannot be assumed to believe in this immemorial 'world-view' in that sense, but takes it as what Lacan would have called a 'tenant-lieu', a place-keeper for the metaphysics that have become impossible. Thus, not a 'philosophy' of Marxism exactly (for such a philosophy would immediately fall back into the category of degraded world-views we have characterized above) but, rather, what such a philosophy might turn out to be in a utopian future (as perhaps also with Heidegger's pre-Socratic not-yet-thought of the *Ereignis*[14]). Yet Brecht's theatricality saves his *sinité* even from this provisionality: it is enough to imagine a real return to Confucianism in present-day China (or a real opposition to that Confucianism in the name of Mo-Tze, even closer to Brecht himself) for us to grasp the difference. Antony Tatlow has shown us how we can use Brecht's China – neither a kitsch stereotype nor any concretely historical one – as a way into the radical otherness of Chinese culture which makes this last 'useful' for us, and not only on the historicist level.[15]

Yet there is another parallel universe coexisting with this one, an overlapping Leibnizian monad which should not too quickly be connected up with either experimentation or China either: and this I will call the Balzacian Brecht, a stage conventionally referred to as the one in which Brecht is, from 1928 on, 'learning Marxism' from his 'teacher' Karl Korsch; in which he is reading *Kapital* and the like, studying and appropriating.[16] But I prefer the allusion to Balzac, because it shifts the issue from one of doctrine (What did he think Marxism was? When did he 'become' a Marxist? When does he try to embody Marxist ideas in his works, etc., etc.) to the rather different one of the representation of capitalism itself: how to express the economic – or, even better, the peculiar realities and dynamics of money as such – in and through literary narrative. Politics have been with us since the dawn of time, along with power and its vicissitudes: money in the form of riches – gold, adornment, monumental piles – is also an old, if decorative, reality. But economics in our modern sense – the perpetual transformation of money into capital, as well as the discovery of the ways in which this economic dynamism circulates through modern politics – is a phenomenon as new as Adam Smith, its fundamental theory rapidly evolving over the three-quarters of a century between the Scottish Enlightenment and the work of Marx himself. So Lukács was right to privilege the immense predecessor, but for all the wrong reasons: not because Balzac was a realist (whatever that may mean), or progressive (in fact he a was horrible Tory), but because he tried to include 'economics' (in the same sense as in Pound's definition of the epic as a 'poem that includes History', it being understood, for those who know, that Pound's idea of 'History' also very much included 'economics' in some modern, if idiosyncratic, sense). Thus Brecht's Marx-study – notoriously associated with Korsch, but also with American materials, as in Ida Tarbell and Gustavus Meyers's *History of the Great American Fortunes*, that treasure-trove of economic anecdotes – very much turned on problems of narrative representation, as can be gathered from its twin monuments, *Saint Joan of the Stockyards* and *The Three-Penny Novel*. By this I do not mean to suggest, as the 'revisionists' so often do, that the later Brecht, preoccupied with other themes than this particular representational one, is thereby no longer Marxist; but only that this is a specific layer or monad in its own right, in communication with all the others, yet knowing its own semi-autonomy and even its own specific time-frame.

Now we again approach layers or monadic worlds which are historical in some chronological sense: the preceding ones overlapped many stages of Brecht's life, but exile and Hitler came all together at once and catastrophically. Yet they are to be separated: for there is a Brechtian life with Hitler and within a Hitlerian Germany he was never himself to experience which is significant and unique in its turn, and which we must pause to appreciate. Nazi memorabilia and the fascination with the Third Reich were no passing stage in the West, as the postwar turnover in films and biographies testified: its current form, however, at the moment when the Holocaust generation is virtually extinct, has involved a return to that moment and an intensified effort to reimagine it; and this at a time when, even among the grandchildren – the politicized youth of the 1970s – the memory in Germany itself of the Hitler years has died out (now replaced by an obsession with the DDR). Brecht cannot help us with either of those things: his East Germany was not that of current *Stasi* obsessions, nor did he deal with the Holocaust as such. Indeed, the principal critique of a play like *Rundköpfe und Spitzköpfe* – to me one of his finest – is that it omits the Jews and seems to fail to grasp what was historically unique in the Nazi politics directed towards them. But perhaps this is precisely what Brecht's Nazi layer has to offer us: a Nazi Germany of daily life and of precisely that banality of evil that made it so hard to think Eichmann.[17] Brecht's Germany is, rather, the Germany in which Nazism is akin to all conservative regimes everywhere, and to the very spirit of repression as it slumbers in a petty-bourgeois population: not yet even the non-Holocaust fact of sheer ethnic massacre (as we see it everywhere from Yugoslavia to Central Africa and India), but simply the 'mentality' of a people who welcome radical Nazi conservatism and its spectacle pleasures (Nuremberg) and modernist developments (VWs, television, the Autobahn): that deeper truth, not of hatred, but of *ressentiment*, from which violence can surge just as surely as from the more dramatic or 'noble' emotions. This 'deutsche Misère' is not, then, to be factored back into some culturalist picture of Germany as a unique and enigmatic historical tradition but, rather, to be generalized, and made a part of our own national self-analysis, our own criticism-self-criticism, were we ever really prepared to confront such a thing.

And so on to the Hitler period's other face: that of exile, where we must separate out, as two distinct 'layers', the generalized figure of a Brecht-in-movement, Brecht-in-exile, as he passes across Denmark and

Sweden, Finland, and the immensity of Stalin's Russia, and boards at Vladivostok the SS *Annie Johnson*, off which he will stroll some months later with his family into the sunny port of San Pedro; from a more distinctive figure of Brecht in his American exile, a Brecht-in-America,[18] which, oddly enough, reaches back to include all the American iconography and exoticism that his work registered from the Weimar 1920s onwards (at a time when the real America could not have been imagined as existing, any more than the real war).

We have to invent a (perhaps Lacanian) position for ourselves in which we are willing to understand that this imaginary USA is also Brecht's American reality: from hurricanes, gangsters and the electric chair all the way, most famously, to Hollywood:

> Hierorts
> Hat man ausgerechnet, daß Gott
> Himmel und Hölle benötigend, nicht zwei
> Etablissements zu entwerfen brauchte, sondern
> Nur ein einziges, nämlich den Himmel. Dieser
> Dient für die Unbemittelten, Erfolgenlosen
> Als Hölle.

> (XII, 115)

> Hereabouts
> People have concluded that God,
> Requiring both a Heaven and a Hell, didn't need to
> Plan two establishments but
> just the one: Heaven. It
> Serves the unprosperous, the unsuccessful
> as Hell.

> (Poems, 380)

This layer, in its transition from unionization and the Depression to the McCarthyite postwar retains a strange temporality for Americans, as though the 1930s lasted essentially until the failure of the Wallace campaign, the end of the American Old Left, the beginnings of the Cold War, the blacklist, and the new postwar boom as such (when all the spare part orders built up during the war are exhausted, and all the great new household machinery hits the market, along with the new suburbs and the immense new federal highway system that makes them possible). Then begin, not the 1940s (which are omitted), but the 1950s and the Eisenhower era: or perhaps it would be better to say that the 1940s take place in a wholly different space, an alternate world from this real one of 1930s/1950s, and concurrent or simultaneous with it: this is the America of the war, a truly utopian America in which it is World War II itself which becomes the 'moral equivalent' of revolution and socialist construction: a productionist and anti-consumptionist space of some populist levelling and consensus – genuine democracy, genuine equality for a time – where the immensity of the superstate, just coming into its true geographical form in the American Imaginary, for one long moment enters and lives in History. It is important to understand that Brecht never knew, never lived in, this moment, like some fitful visionary realm which it was not vouchsafed to him to glimpse, so that he had to be content with the more dreary materiality of the 1930s/1950s continuum, with its more doubtful 'angels' (see the *Hollywood Elegies*). We do not know exactly how Brecht will find his place in his properly American (literary) history, for the good reason that we have not yet fully recovered our 1930s, and its history has not yet taken its own rightful place in our Imaginary.[19] We cannot, therefore, invite Brecht into it; but we will some day – nor will it be a purely honorific position, in so far as his American texts also belong to us.

And so on to the end, to East Germany and the DDR, to Berlin and its new/old theatre, to socialist construction as such (B.B. was imposed on the returning German Communist Party veterans, it seems, by his Soviet admirers among the occupation forces). A close friend of Brecht, and an architect of some very well-known East Berlin monuments, told me that Brecht arrived back in Germany, and in what would soon enough become the capital of the new socialist state, 'not only with new ideas for the theatre, but with new ideas for everything': traffic regulations, for example, and city planning, taxation and garbage collection, the utopian ideal of the urban and the agricultural, the condition of the socialist citizen, and the role of culture itself in the politics of the new socialist state, which, in the very heartland of Marxism, the country Lenin considered to be the most advanced towards socialism, and despite the inadequacies of a hidebound party leadership, could be expected to set the pace for the future. This is why Brecht's last years must be considered under the light of socialist construction itself and as such, despite the propaganda campaigns in which he was called upon to participate (most notably the peace and anti-disarmament ones, presided over by Picasso's dove, and juxtaposing Galileo and Oppenheimer), yet perhaps including more centrally what we may now call the 'plebeian uprising' of 1953, which Brecht himself had somehow 'rewritten' in advance in his *Coriolanus*.

Meanwhile, as far as socialism itself is concerned, we must accustom ourselves to reading an underlying Maoism into what is more standardly termed Brecht's 'Stalinism' (simply on the grounds that he, like Althusser, remained committed – for good reason – to the idea of a party apparatus:

leaving aside the fact that unlike Althusser – and probably for equally good reasons – he was never officially a party member himself). But here it is with China in the late twentieth century as with Russia in the early: and just as Lukács, along with the other bemused and uninformed members of the Weber circle in Heidelberg, ascribed their enthusiasm for Lenin's unique historical breakthrough to the traditions of the 'Slavic soul' and a well-nigh Dostoevskian Russian mysticism, so also here, with far more historical justification, the historical immensity of Mao Zedong's revolution becomes immediately linked with the Chinese fact, with the various forms of cyclical and peasant wisdom associated for Brecht with classical Chinese philosophy and poetry alike.

All of which – and with this we conclude our semi-biographical enumeration of the worlds or monads, the historical layering of 'Brecht' as such – now folds back into the sheerest celebration of change, change as always revolutionary, as the very inner truth of revolution itself. This is what the dialecticians have always understood and clasped to their hearts: I think of Lukács in Moscow, patiently enduring the prospect of an imminent German victory and a Nazi hegemony over all of Europe, with the conviction that even within Hitler's victorious Cabinet, class struggle will slowly but surely begin again; or the incorrigible optimism with which, in New York, the aged Mike Gold kept the faith up to the very eve of May '68 itself. History puts its worst foot forward, Henri Lefebvre taught us; it proceeds by catastrophe rather than by triumph. So the true dialectician – of whom Brecht, and behind him the tutelary scroll of the ancient Chinese sage, is emblematic here – will always wish patiently to wait for the stirrings of historical evolution even within defeat:

> daß das weiche Wasser in Bewegung
> Mit der Zeit, den mächtigen Stein besiegt.
> Du verstehst, das Harte unterliegt.

>   (XII, 33)

> [he taught] that over time the movement of the yielding water
> Will overcome the strongest stone.
> What's hard – can you understand? – must always give way.
>   (Poems, 315)

One is tempted, it is true, to add a not insignificant anticlimax on Brecht's posthumous fortunes, which already began in his lifetime with the legendary visit to the *Théâtre des nations* in 1954 (*Mother Courage*), followed by triumphant tours around the world by a theatre company already enhanced (as are Cuban groups today) by the nimbus of blockade

and diplomatic sanction. In this 'Brecht' of the 1960s and 1970s, three
conditions met to ensure a uniquely 'Brechtian' reputation. For bourgeois
publics, fasting on a diet of theatrical minimalism, there had to be
something Shakespearian about the lavish costumes and settings, and
the texts which ranged across the entire world repertory (from Noh to
Molière, from Shakespeare himself to Beckett, if not the epics of Chinese
romance and the Chicago gangster saga), it was not hard for him to
become, for a time, 'the greatest playwright in the world'. For the Left,
a whole theory and strategy and political writing was set in place which
could be transferred to other media and situations (to the confection of
'Brechtian' films, for example, by a Godard; not to speak of the
'Brechtian' stories by Kluge, or even Brechtian painting and art in a
Beuys or a Haacke), and had the signal advantage of allowing one to
return to the older pre-Stalinist combination of avant-garde art and
politics; while at the same time reassuring the more orthodox about the
propriety of its political positions. For the Third World, finally, the
peasant aspects of Brecht's theatre, which made plenty of room for
Chaplinesque buffoonery, mime, dance, and all kinds of pre-realistic
and pre-bourgeois stagecraft and performance, secured for Brecht the
historical position of a catalyst and an enabling model in the emergence
of many 'non-Western' theatres from Brazil to Turkey, from the Philip-
pines to Africa. Three kinds of need were thus fulfilled here: that of
theatrical and theoretical innovation in a period particularly avid for
such new theories and modes of staging, after the war (as witness all
the other great theatrical experiments, from Peter Brook to Grotowski,
from the revival of Artaud to the emergence of national theatre ensem-
bles all over the world, particularly where the renewal of a 'New Wave'
cinema did not yet offer worthy competition of either an economic or an
artistic nature); that of a new kind of agitprop and political literature
after the bleak enforcement of Zhadanovite forms in one bloc of
countries and a renewal with the rich and multiple traditions of avant-
garde art that preceded the consolidation of Stalin's power; and finally
the possibilities to be explored by decolonized peoples trying out new
voices, for whom the exile and wanderer Brecht was himself non-
Eurocentric to the degree to which he treated his own country like a
Third World one. These situations no longer being present, and Brecht,
in whatever form, having known a moment of world literary success
given to only a few, it seems to be customary today to complain of
'Brecht fatigue', and to wonder how to go about continuing to be a
Brechtian today, as others wonder that one could continue to be a
Marxist, or even a socialist, after 1989. But probably this fatigue has
mainly to do with the last in this series of Brechts, the stereotype

developed during the 1960s and 1970s. I suspect that we will find enough in the other ones, and in some of their more unusual intersections, to keep us not only busy, but even interested.

3   Triangulating Brecht

What is distinctive, and unmistakable, about Brecht's work seems to be describable only in misleading categories, principally those of style, thought and plot, which we will consider in succession. Thus, in some first place there is an obvious Brechtian style, for which the expression 'turn of phrase' (the very sense of tropes, as what are *détourné*, hijacked and misdirected away from ordinary speech) is apt indeed. Yet 'just as Language is on this side of literature', Barthes tells us,

> so what we call style is almost beyond it: images, a certain manner, a lexicon, all surge up out of the body and past of the writer little by little to become the very reflexes of his art. ... Style ... has a merely vertical dimension, plunging into the subject's sealed memory, constructing its own opacity from a unique experience of matters ... its secret is a remembrance shut away inside the writer's body.[20]

But if this is what style is – the mark of a unique subjectivity, like a fingerprint or the sound of a familiar voice – then Brecht's work can be observed slowly, over the years, to remove all of this, to file it down or absorb it with as few leftover traces as possible: the washed-out colours of the early poetry, pallor, the faded hue of the style, the predilection for words like 'fahl' (pale), and those related thematics of drowned bodies and underwater slow motion to which we have already referred. ... These things form thematic and stylistic constellations that wane against the morning sky; what remains of them stands:

> Am See, tief zwischen Tann und Silberpappel
> Beschirmt von Mauer und Gesträuch ein Garten. ...
> >   (XII, 307)

> By the lake, deep amid fir and silver poplar
> Sheltered by wall and hedge, a garden. ...
> >   (Poems, 439)

leaving a house with smoke rising from its chimney:

> Felte er
> Wie trostlos dann wären
> Haus, Bäume und See.
>   (XII, 308)

> Were this smoke missing
> How dreary then
> House, trees and lake.
>   (Poems, 442)

The objects that hitherto expressed the body's *Weltanschauung* have become the content of the later verse; the earlier 'style' has ceased to be a medium and is now something the language itself interrogates and produces like an object, as Althusser says of artistically embodied ideology.[21] It is a very different trajectory from that of the great modernist writers and poets Barthes had in mind, whose very vocation was given in the deepening of just such instinctive verbal mannerisms, their faithful stubborn pursuit into ultimate blocks of words, unnatural and far distant from ordinary language.

If style, then, is a category that threatens to lead us back into subjectivity for its ultimate explanation, then perhaps rhetoric will suit us better; for rhetoric, quite the opposite of style, aims outwards and seeks to influence its possible publics, as any political and public, antisubjective literature presumably ought to do. Perhaps, then, in the largest sense of the word, there is a Brechtian rhetoric whose ambitions are cast as widely as Aristotle's, which seeks the Good in its most august classical city-state form, and about which it has been said that it should be 'grasped as the first systematic hermeneutics of social daily life'.[22] In that case, it will be something a little more comprehensive than the scoring of a point over the adversary, and will imply strategies of thought and action that exceed our concepts of the verbal.

Still, there are a few rhetorical concepts in the narrower sense that seem appropriate: that of irony, for example, as a comprehensive category for the varieties of invective, sarcasm, cynical paradox, sly reversal, which we find so often throughout Brecht's sentences. The concept of irony brings with it a double bonus: it is one of the few rhetorical strategies which is considered a trope in the narrower sense (or in the more post-contemporary one, as in Paul de Man), while as a more general attitude it has been more generally ascribed to the world-view of all the great moderns, or was at the least a fundamental part of the ideology of modernism until the latter came under attack and historical obsolescence in the postmodern period. So the 'ironic German' (Erich Heller's characterization of Thomas Mann, who did indeed make a fetish of irony as such) spread the influence of this category across all of modern literature for a time; and the ironic attitude was famous for doing everything from preserving the freshness of language, like salt (as in T. S. Eliot), to the distancing of unwanted and overly political positions, which irony allows one now to endorse and repudiate all at once. This is certainly not what Brecht had in view, and indeed, his is, rather, that more limited 'stable irony' which Wayne Booth seeks to differentiate from the general modern ironic *Weltanschauung* we have just alluded to.[23] Yet the more we draw Brecht's irony in the direction of old-fashioned rhetoric in this way, the less is the concept capable of doing the descriptive work which the concept of style made available to us, and the more 'irony' in this rhetorical sense becomes a property of Brecht's own *Weltanschauung* (if he has one), or at the very least a feature of theatrical demonstrations as such.

In either case, we rescue Brecht from a now conventional notion of modernism (the uniquely subjective style, the characteristically ironic attitude), but by the same token we find ourselves unable to characterize a distinctiveness in the language which everyone recognizes, including foreigners: the dry, witty, ironic qualities of this language use tempt one to add Brecht to Nietzsche's list (proposed in a relatively anti-German spirit) of the three best German books (Luther's *Bible*, Goethe's *Conversations with Eckermann*, and his own). This would, however, heighten stylistic analysis to an allegorical and 'geopolitical' reading in which the very attributes of the language constitute a pointed rebuke to the author's countrymen – who have chosen fascism, but whose heavy-handedness is also the sign, from the eighteenth century onwards, of a certain 'Third-World-type' backwardness ('Keep it quick, light and strong', he warned his company, on their way to England shortly before his death; remember that foreigners consider our art 'terribly heavy, slow, laborious and pedestrian'[24].) Thus at the term of this or that approach to the language as such, whether stylistic or rhetorical, an interpretation emerges which shifts gears and at once repositions us on a different level, that of *Haltung* (stance), of collective interrelationship or symbolic act, of 'rhetoric' in the social and relational sense, or of 'meaning' and 'interpretation' in some code which transcends the merely linguistic or verbal.

So that dimension of Brecht's work which is the inner or symbolic meaning of his language or style would seem to retain a distinctiveness in its own right, yet to be susceptible of formulation in at least two other different areas: we may well feel that what gives the language its uniquely Brechtian flavour is some uniquely Brechtian mode of thinking; if not the shape of the gesture – not to say the *gestus* – of this language may ultimately be considered as a symbolic act in its own right. This third possibility leads us in the direction of plot-formation in Brecht, and of the 'distinctive' and 'unique' features (to continue to use our leitmotiven) which mark the construction of a characteristically Brechtian scene or narrative, or a Brechtian appropriation and transformation of somebody else's narrative.

Shifting to our second area, then, the alternative of a distinctive doctrine, we may well pause to remember T. S. Eliot's revealing remarks, at the very dawn of the modern movement, on the relationship between 'ideas' and literary texts. They are remarks which conjure up an atmosphere of philosophical pragmatism hostile to system and to speculative philosophy (the American School in which Eliot was himself trained comes to mind, but also, from a very different standpoint, that Vienna Circle from which Brecht derived a certain number of philosophical attitudes through the intermediation of Karl Korsch[25]); but also of a general Imagism in literature, which (far more widely than the rather narrow Hulmean movement to which this school designation generally applies) marked a feeling of modern writers generally that the idea in the text was a kind of foreign body; that such 'literary' ideas demanded special precautions, and at the outside limit, in the extremist cases, demanded to be tracked down and eliminated altogether ('say it, not in ideas but in things'). This literary-ideological attitude, which makes the question of the relationship between conceptuality and literariness over into a crucial and topical form-problem (and, by implication, tends to preclude didacticism altogether), is perhaps most memorably formulated in Eliot's grand celebration of Henry James: 'he had a mind so fine no idea could violate it'.[26] Yet the form-solution in Brecht evidently involves a combination avoided in the case of the other moderns: a choice of immanence over transcendence, but in his case a didactic or pedagogical stance which is either absent altogether from – shunned by – the other moderns, or has taken forms we have insufficiently examined: thus, Pound's inveterate schoolmasterish *Haltung* is dismissed as secondary and insignificant (on the grounds of the outlandishness of his economics, his Confucianism, or whatever). But Eliot himself is an interesting case here, for while a kind of standard Catholicism and monarchist conservatism neutralizes the ideational content and renders it conventional, respectable and thereby invisible, there is in Eliot very much a didactic posture not without its analogies to that of Brecht himself. Thus it is that Eliot has a second curious remark, a second lesson, equally instructive for us in the present context; it is to be found in his suggestive essay on William Blake, in which he comes to terms with the latter's 'philosophy', by observing drily:

> We have the same respect for Blake's philosophy ... that we have for an ingenious piece of home-made furniture: we admire the man who has put it together out of the odds and ends about the house.... But we are really not so remote from the Continent, or even from our own past, as to be deprived of the advantages of culture if we wish them.[27]

'Culture' here signifies for Eliot an already systematic body of doctrine which is widely accepted in society, even institutionalized, and whose signal 'advantage' for the writer is that it obviates the need to divert a considerable portion of creative energy in the direction of personal 'philosophizing' and (we may say) 'bricolating' a private philosophy for himself and for his 'distinctive' modernist work. Leave aside the fact that so many moderns have felt obliged to concoct just such a private philosophy for themselves, alongside their evidently equally private language: as witness Lawrence or Proust, Rilke or Wallace Stevens, Musil or Khlebnikov. The warning also concerns the readers themselves: though it is difficult enough to imagine a gauge to measure the mental energy required to figure out the system itself or the private mythology in question, it is surely plausible that such a necessary effort on the part of the reader will inevitably drain or divert mental and perceptual resources better reserved for the sheer exposure to and evaluation of poeticity or, in other words, the language itself. It is this, of course, that has led some to characterize the experience of modernism, or of the various modernisms, as one of a quasi-religious conversion, in which we are called upon – as our entry ticket to the unique phenomenological 'world' in question – to convert to its dominant ideology, and to learn its codes, to absorb its structure of concepts of values, in some relatively exclusive way which, in our literary enthusiasm, tends to block off an approach to other rival literary codes and languages, until at length we are deprogrammed in disabusement, and reluctantly deconverted; and pass on to a similar commitment to this or that other modern writer, at which point the whole (quintessentially modernist) process repeats itself all over again. Whatever the value of this particular description, it is worth noting that Eliot himself proposes to short-circuit it and to recommend a very different framework for the poet's or the artist's work: 'a framework of accepted and traditional ideas which would have prevented him from indulging in a philosophy of his own'[28] – which is to say, in his own case, the Roman Catholic tradition as preserved in the rituals of the established Church of England.

But it is precisely this proposal for neutralizing the incompatibility between ideational content and poetic language which allows us to see the question of thought and meaning in Brecht's work in a new light. For the equivalent of Christian doctrine in the latter's context is, obviously enough, Marxism itself, perhaps the only fully codified philosophy, sanctioned by whole collectivities and by state authority itself, which is comparable to Christianity and its scriptural traditions and archives of commentary (neither Islam nor Judaism has the same kinds of doctrinal codification, while the other 'major' religions or even secular philosophies have never had the same relationship with state power).

No doubt Brecht's Marxism might well be read in this way: as a framework which obviated the need to cobble together a 'private philosophy' of his own, and thus provided a framework for a non-problematized aesthetic production. But a serious (yet productive) question may precisely be raised here by the very nature of Brecht's Marxism as such: for on one view, what he learned from Korsch was not a set of doctrines and principles, which could serve as just such a framework, but, rather, an attitude hostile to system in general, the so-called 'logical empiricism' of the Vienna circle, which was equally hostile to the dialectic (and to Hegelian versions of Marxism) and, while committed to a radical and Marxian politics, felt able to denounce abstract doctrine and belief in fully as thoroughgoing a way as the modernist littérateurs evoked above. Where, then, is Brecht's Marxism as a doctrine to be found in the first place? Where are his ideas? And even if, as Lukács so scandalously suggested in 'What is Orthodox Marxism?' (as decisive an essay on 'ideas' in the Marxian tradition as the above-cited Eliot one for non-secular bourgeois philosophies), 'Orthodox Marxism ... refers exclusively to *method*'[29] – a hint we will try to follow up below – there remains the matter of the ideational content Brecht's work is supposed to teach, since it is precisely didacticism that offered our other stumbling block.

Yet we might also want to think of the kind of didacticism inherent in teaching a particular mental *Haltung*, a characteristically Brechtian type of pragmatism (rather than 'Marxism'), of which I offer three examples here. It may initially be described as follows (at first leaving out its philosophical consequences and presuppositions): you turn a problem into its solution, thereby coming at the matter askew and sending the projectile off into a new and more productive direction than the dead end in which it was immobilized. Thus, for example, evoking the classical Platonic contempt for the actor (would you trust him more or even as much as your doctor, asks Socrates; more than your politicians? more than your judges?), Brecht recommends building on this contempt and using it, rather than attempting to do away with it by disappearing into the role:

> Die Ansicht des Zuschauers über den Beruf des Schauspielers als einen absurden, auffälligen und gerade durch ihre Auffälligkeit bemerkenswerten gehört, auch wo sie ins Verächtliche abgleitet, zu den Produktionsmitteln des Schauspielers. Er muß etwas aus ihr machen. Des Schauspieler soll sich also die Ansicht des Zuschauers über sich selbst zu eigen machen.

(XXI, 388)

The public's opinion of the profession of actor – as an absurd and outrageous, and by that very outrageousness a noteworthy one – belongs to the means of production of the actor himself. He must do something with this opinion. The actor has then to adopt this opinion of the public about himself.

I think he means that instead of concealing the act of acting (and the profession that results from it), the spectacle as a whole should try to demonstrate to the audience that we are all actors, and that acting is an inescapable dimension of social and everyday life.

The most thoroughgoing demonstration of this procedure, however, lies in the form of the notorious 'Dreigroschen Prozess', or 'Three-Penny Trial', in which he converts his discontent into a real lawsuit, the latter into a written lawsuit, that written and imaginary suit into a sociological experiment, finally 'subsuming' the latter itself [*Aufhebung*] into a critique of sociology on its way to something else.

A final illustration may serve to refute the idea that Brecht's self-avowed 'vulgar Marxism' (so-called *plumpes Denken* or 'crude thought') is functionalist, and reduces ideologies and even literary works to the service of material 'interests': but what Brecht said, rather, was something like the inversion of all this, since it was precisely what was 'folgenlos'[30] – what had no particular material consequences, and fostered no particular changes – that he accused of being ideological. Indeed, it is tempting to suggest that it is precisely Brecht's well-known slyness that is his method, and even his dialectic: the inversion of the hierarchies of a problem, major premiss passing to minor, absolute to relative, form to content, and vice versa – these are all operations whereby the dilemma in question is turned inside out, and an unexpected unforeseeable line of attack opens up that leads neither into the dead end of the unresolvable nor into the banality of stereotypical doxa on logical non-contradiction.

To recapitulate: we have sought a certain specificity of Brecht's work in his linguistic practices, both stylistic and rhetorical, both of which seem to posit some extra-linguistic field of inquiry – the one in his ideas or attitudes (Brecht himself will call these, throughout his life and work, *Meinungen* or *Absichten*, opinions or even ideologies); the other in quasi-dramatic and quasi-narrative postures, *Haltungen*, stances, characteristic gestures, which presumably constitute the germs and anecdotal sources of his narratives themselves and as such. But the question about his thought seems to have led us back to a formalism in which the main 'ideas' vehiculated by this aesthetic discourse are simply so many empty recommendations as to method itself: so many thoughts, without a content of their own, but fundamentally consisting in a projection as to what thinking ought to be in the first place, and how it ought to be conducted.

Even within Marxism, this looks dangerously like a purely methodological 'system' of the type found everywhere in bourgeois philosophy, particularly those mesmerized by the truth promises of the sciences, in which metaphysics of some older systematic type have been shouldered aside in the name of this or that 'method' (whether it be so estimable a prescription as that of American pragmatism or Deleuzian 'problem-solving', or the baser forms of empiricism and logical rules or the positivisms in general). The truth content of this emphasis on 'method' – which one finds everywhere in modern philosophy – evidently lies in its negative effects, in the repudiation of the metaphysical principles or content the consequences of whose repudiation it now seeks to overcome, with whatever intellectual or philosophical ingenuity. But surely the fetishization of 'method' not only deserves all the opprobrium summoned down on it, it is also part and parcel of, and an inevitable accompaniment to, that institutional self-justification into which philosophy has seemed to be called again and again (perhaps since the very beginnings of a secular philosophy in the Renaissance), and which might well merit a rather different, and this time Bourdieu-inspired, denunciation.

How, then, can the notion of *Brecht and Method* be justified, let alone some more general argument for the originality of a specifically Brechtian thinking or doctrine? This originality, however, takes on a somewhat different form – or rather, as I am tempted to say, finds itself productively *estranged* – when we consider 'method' to be a kind of *gestus* and, above and beyond the 'dramatistic' and interpersonal framework always implicit in rhetoric as such, restore to such acts the immanent or virtual narrative situation implied by them.

So it is that what we were tempted to call 'method' when we approached it as an abstract idea now, in some third dimension, unfolds itself, dramatically, into the very situation of pedagogy itself as it is variously staged, mocked, analyzed, prophesied and utopianly projected, throughout a work single-mindedly obsessed with this concrete ideal, which – extending, to be sure, to that 'educating of the educators' of which the third *Thesis on Feuerbach* speaks – can eventually be grasped as the very correlative and other face or *verso* of the theme of change itself. Running abreast of change, catching up with it, espousing its tendencies in such a way as to begin to inflect its vectors in your own direction – such is Brechtian pedagogy: which now, unexpectedly, lifts the curtain on a whole dimension of this work which is neither that, micrological, of the language and the style, of the sentences; nor that of the immanent or the concept, that of Brecht's thinking and philosophizing, that of his 'way' with philosophizing, the slyness with which he navigates the concept and its official appearances and façades; but now, rather, the distinct realities of embodiment and storytelling – or, if you prefer other words (those of Marx himself), of the 'concrete individuals', who, 'developing their material production and their material intercourse, alter, along with this their real existence, their thinking, and the products of their thinking'.[31] The thought to which Marx here invites us is not only that of factory production (as so many tropes in *Capital* suggest), but that of daily life in general ('their material intercourse'). I hope it does not neutralize the materialistic reversal and shock-producing impulse in Marx's text to co-opt it for the narratological, and to suggest that storytelling – or, better still, embodied storytelling, the acting out – thereby becomes the realm of some deeper truth about its abstract after-images in language games and in conceptual figures or the 'shapes of thought'.

The shapes of acts, then: long before the official terminologies of the so-called semiotics of narrative (or narratology), it was no doubt dimly or unconsciously understood that writers tend to organize the events they represent according to their own deeper schemas of what Action and Event seem to them to be; or that they project their own 'subjective' fantasies of interaction on to the screen of the Real, even where such projections are taken in tow by a whole cultural and collective episteme, and shown to be social and thereby 'objective' beyond and even through their very subjectivity. So there are no doubt specific movements characteristic of the great medieval poems – *gestus* and *Haltung* alike – which define the very processing of reality and daily life in this predominantly agricultural and feudal mode of production; while the conventions of Greek tragedy or the Noh play themselves offer some kind of unique 'primal scene' to be socially analyzed in ways analogous to the reading of dreams or deliria.

Yet for the most part, the reading of such privileged storytelling structures has been the object of a classic tug of war between the objective and the subjective: the latter, following style study, wishing to carry off the scenes in question into a uniquely private storehouse of personal fantasies (marked, however, by the dominant value of the unique or the particular, the unmistakable products of genius or madness), while on the other side the narrative idiosyncrasies are apt to harden over into conventions, which themselves tend ever more towards immutable human forms, psychologically eternal, and somehow detectable in all historical societies, however simple or complex. In what follows, we will draw on André Jolles's still too little known 1929 work *Einfache Formen*,[32] which has at least the advantage of being ambiguous enough to accommodate the subjective and the objective versions alike without choosing between them; and to invite historical analysis without prejudicing the outcome. Here, however, we must for the moment be briefer; for even Brecht's own dramaturgical categories – from *gestus* itself to the estrangement-effect and the judgements it calls for – along with many of the most famous scenes in his works: the courtroom episodes of *The Chalk Circle*, for example, but also the *mise en abyme* of *The Chalk Circle*, itself an exhibit in a larger 'courtroom drama' – all confirm Darko Suvin's wonderfully fruitful suggestion that it is André Jolles's category of the *casus* – the exemplary 'case' calling for judgement – which is the dominant one in Brecht's practice of narrative, and not only in the theatre as such. At any rate, we will find ourselves embroiled in the attempt to show that Brechtian storytelling, looked at in this way, is indeed informed by something like a 'method', but one which is rigorously non-formalistic, and thereby evades the philosophical objections to sheer method as such which have been outlined above. *Casus*, in other words, must be shown to be a form with genuine content, not merely an abstract frame into which narrative content of all kinds can be neatly arranged and subsumed.

Yet now we must triangulate these propositions, for it has been the assumption that none of the areas or dimensions of Brecht's work already touched on – his language, his mode of thinking, and finally his storytelling – has any special priority over the others; but, rather, that they can be seen as so many projections of each other into different media, just as a crystalline phenomenon might take on a wholly different configurative appearance in the domain of light waves, while remaining 'the same'. The object of study and characterization, then – something which can be identified as vaguely as the 'Brechtian' – takes on its various precisions as it is observed and measured through the three fundamental dimensions in question; but this triangulated and invisible object has no analytic language of its own or in its own right: we must therefore continue to translate each dimension into the languages of the two others, verifying and correcting each by way of the next. The order of discussion need not be as cyclical as this programme suggests; and it necessarily arouses expectations which a brief essay of this kind will never fulfil satisfactorily (that every verbal feature find its equivalent in the realms of doctrine and fabulation, and vice versa); but it seems to me a working hypothesis which at least has the advantage of forestalling unwanted determinisms and hierarchies (the temptation to turn everything back into language, for example, if not into *Weltanschauungen* or even the *fantasme*).

But what becomes of 'method' in all this: has it been successfully erased from the programme? I hope not altogether, as I want to retain the connection between Brecht's 'usefulness' for us today and a whole range of possible activities into which it might be expected to energize us. Indeed, I will want to suggest that, interesting and important – indeed, significant – as are any number of Brecht's texts for literary history itself, what distinguishes these achievements from the literary work of any number of other 'great writers' is some more general lesson or spirit they disengage. This amounts to saying that 'the idea of Brecht' is as important as his individual texts; or perhaps – to be somewhat more measured – that it is distinct from them (all the while including them). I believe that we can still live and move in this idea; and that it is preeminently one which helps us to dissolve the multiple paralyses in which we are all now historically seized, which derive as much from a keen sense of the impossibility of *praxis* on all these levels as from the facts themselves and from any iron-clad 'conditions of existence'. I wish to avoid the bourgeois pieties of the 'life-enhancing' fully as much as the infantile-leftist dangers of voluntarism; but think the notion of enablement is still not a bad one for the release of new energies we have in mind here; nor is the characteristically Deleuzian word 'joyous' (which means, I think, much the same thing) out of place.

So, should we decide to keep the word 'method', let us then fabulate it a bit, and absorb it into a language, thought and narrative practice that can lend it a specifically Brechtian resonance and distinctiveness. We will therefore now unmask it, not as method in general, but as the 'Great Method', that doctrine taught by the legendary Me-ti in some alternate prehistory to our own. Indeed, Brecht's untranslated *Book of Changes* clearly imposes itself on our discussions here; and just as Gramsci's euphemism for it – the 'philosophy of praxis' – modifies that Marxian 'dialectic' he wished to smuggle past his fascist censors, so also the Brechtian Great Method stages that same traditional dialectic in a rather different way, disclosing its metaphysical or pre-Socratic dimensions ('in der Grossen Methode ist die Ruhe nur ein Grenzfall des Streits'

– 'in the Great Method, rest is only a special case of strife' – XVIII, 184)
very differently from Stalin's dialectical materialism, and offering Marxism its own uniquely non-Western – or at least, non-bourgeois –
philosophy in the form of a kind of Marxian Tao:

> Me-ti sagte: Es ist vorteilhaft, nicht nur vermittels der großen Methode zu
> denken, sondern auch vermittels der großen Methode zu leben. Nicht eins mit
> sich zu sein, sich in Krisen drängen, kleine Änderungen in große verwandeln
> und so weiter, das alles kann man nicht nur beobachten, sondern auch
> machen. Man kann mit mehr oder weniger Vermittlungen, in mehr oder
> weniger Zusammenhängen leben. Man kann eine dauerndere Veränderung
> seines Bewußtseins erzielen oder anstreben, indem man sein gesellschaftliches
> Sein ändert. Man kann helfen, die staatlichen Einrichtungen widerspruchsvoll
> und entwicklungsfähig zu machen.
>
> (XVIII, 192–3)

> Me-ti said: it is advantageous, not merely to think according to the great
> Method but to live according to the great Method as well. Not to be identical
> with oneself, to embrace and intensify crises, to turn small changes into great
> ones and so forth – one need not only observe such phenomena, one can also
> act them out. One can live with greater or fewer mediations, in more
> numerous or less numerous relationships. One can aim at or strive for a more
> durable transformation of one's consciousness by modifying one's social
> being. One can help to make the institutions of the state more contradictory
> and thereby more capable of development.

Notes

1. Brecht's originals are referenced within the text by volume and page according to
   the *Grosse kommentierte Berliner und Frankfurter Ausgabe* (Aufbau/Suhrkamp,
   1989–98), ed. Werner Hecht, Jan Kopf, Werner Mittenzwei and Klaus-Detlef Müller.
   Thus the allusion to Stalin is to be found at XVIII, 66.
2. Whenever available, English translations are cited, even though I frequently use my
   own: most commonly, and thus referenced within the text, are *Poems 1913–1956*, ed.
   John Willett and Ralph Manheim (London: Methuen, 1976), indicated simply as
   'Poems'. Thus, 'I need no gravestone' is to be found on p. 218. Other references:
   Brecht on Theater, ed. and transl. John Willett (New York: Hill & Wang, 1957),
   indicated simply as 'Willett'.
3. The term appears in Chapter V.c of the *Phenomenologie des Geistes*, and is historically
   limited to a transitional stage from traditional to modern society in which the activities
   produced by the social division of labour still seem to be immediately meaningful, and
   to carry their own 'reason for being' within themselves, immanently.
4. *Chairman Mao Talks to the People*, ed. Stuart Schram (New York: Pantheon, 1974),
   pp. 227–9.
5. One might, for novelistic narration, rest one's case with *Die Geschäfte des Herrn
   Julius Caesar* (XVII), or in the short story, with 'Die unwürdige Greisin' (XVIII); there
   is also an extraordinary concision, reminiscent of Kleist or Hebbel, in the production
   of anecdotes, as witness 'Der Arbeitsplatz' (XIX) or many of the 'parables' in *Me-ti*
   (XVIII, and see below). The *Three-Penny Novel* (XVI) seems to me to try to combine
   both these impulses, to the detriment of the first.

6. Wolfgang Fritz Haug, *Philosophieren mit Brecht und Gramsci* (Berlin: Argument, 1996).

7. Jose Ortega y Gassett, 'In Search of Goethe from Within', in *The Dehumanization of Art and Other Essays* (Princeton, NJ: Princeton University Press, 1968), pp. 136–7. 170–71.

8. 'His Majesty the Ego, the hero alike of every daydream and every story': 'Creative Writers and Daydreaming', in Sigmund Freud, *Standard Edition of the Complete Psychological Works* (London: Hogarth, 1959), vol. IX, p. 150. The original is to be found in volume VIII of the *Gesammelte Werke* of 1941, pp. 213–23.

9. John Fuegi, *Brecht & Co.* (New York: Grove, 1994). Mr Fuegi thinks that as Brecht consorted with so many sexually doubtful intellectuals in his youth, he must have been one himself. His subsequent involvement with so many women can thus be explained by his innate perversity and also his lifelong delight in scandal; in any case, he exploited them shamelessly, besides being wildly unfaithful. This does make for a problem for Mr Fuegi, whose preferred heroic stance (although he took the trouble to explain to Helene Weigel that he was really a genuine proletarian) is the compassionate indignation of the male feminist, something his rather unfashionable homophobia renders a little suspect. At any rate, Brecht was a monster, whose ordinary human vices (egotism, ruthlessness, authoritarianism, lust, possessiveness, and a few others I cannot remember right now) are usefully magnified by the world-historical situation itself, which makes it possible to compare him favourably (if that is the word) with Hitler and Stalin. His return to and 'espousal of' the East German regime is surely quite enough to justify the second of these comparisons; as for the first, it is a well-documented fact that his tirades against his actors resembled nothing quite so much as the Führer's more unbuttoned rages. Yet here one hesitates: for surely it was, rather, his training in Hollywood, where all the German exiles were called upon to fill a variety of Nazi roles in war movies, with their various accents, which must be credited. In any case, one does have to admit that Mr Fuegi's Hitler stories (the Führer-to-be peddling his watercolours in the Englisher Garten, and being rescued from the right-wing massacres of the Freikorps putsch in Munich at the end of World War I) are among the enjoyable bonuses of this delightfully scurrilous, if a bit obsessive, 'biography'. Clearly its author knows how to spin a yarn; and one is not disappointed with the satisfying climax, in which it is more than suggested that at the end, among fears of B's impending defection to the West (under the guise of a Munich clinic), Helene Weigel had the great man murdered, on Ulbricht's orders. Werner Mittenzwei (*Das Leben des Bertolt Brecht* [Berlin: Aufbau, 1986, 2 vols]) is not nearly so amusing, even though he is willing to tell us something about what these people actually thought, and talked and corresponded about – something you must not expect to find in Mr Fuegi, whose recent conversion to anti-communism is certainly politically correct (although perhaps a bit belated for *Zeitgeist* which gives some signs of increasing anxiety about neo-liberalism). At any rate, his book will remain a fundamental document for future students of the ideological confusions of Western intellectuals during the immediate post-Cold War years.

10. See his extraordinary pages on Eisenstein as dialectician: they are the only ones anywhere to give Eisenstein his due as a serious philosopher: Gilles Deleuze, *Cinéma*, vol. I (Paris: Minuit, 1983), chs 3 and 11; *Cinéma*, vol. II (Paris: Minuit, 1985), ch. 7.

11. Darko Suvin, *To Brecht and Beyond* (New York: Barnes & Noble, 1984), ch. 3: 'Politics, Performances and Organizational Mediation', pp. 83–111. Suvin's innumerable works on Brecht and on world theatre have been invaluable for me; as has his exemplary combination of passions: Brecht, Science Fiction and Utopia.

12. See on this Darko Suvin, *To Brecht and Beyond*, and *Lessons of Japan* (Montreal: CIADEST, 1996); also Tatlow (Note 15 below).

13. Enid Starkie, *Arthur Rimbaud* (New York: New Directions, 1961), p. 429.

14. See, for a Marxian view of Heidegger's 'pragmatism', my 'Heidegger and Nazism', in the forthcoming *Valences of the Dialectic* (London: Verso, 1999). The notion of *Ereignis* is, however, the centre of the posthumous *Beiträge zur Philosophie* (*Vom Ereignis*), which constitutes volume 65 of the Heidegger *Gesamtausgabe* (Frankfurt: Klosterman, 1989).

15. Here I must particularly express my debt to Tatlow's work in general, but especially to his masterwork *The Mask of Evil* (Bern: Peter Lang, 1977), which discusses Brecht's debt to Chinese and Japanese poetry and drama, and to Chinese philosophy, in a leisurely and wide-ranging, rich and suggestive, scholarly and subtle way. I should also draw attention to his little book *Brechts chinesische Gedichte* (Frankfurt: Suhrkamp, 1973), whose startling yet ultimately plausible thesis runs as follows: we know that Brecht translated from Waley, a *fin-de-siècle* poet who refashioned the Chinese originals, in particular Po chü-yi, in his own image. It turns out that without any knowledge of Chinese, Brecht's versions are more faithful to their originals than Waley's, since he instinctively restored to them the social dimensions and details that (equally instinctively, no doubt) Waley omitted.

16. The relevant surviving materials can now be found in Karl Korsch, *Gesamtausgabe*, vol. 5: *Krise des Marxismus: Schriften 1928–1935*, ed. Michael Buckmiller (Amsterdam: Stichting beheer IISG, 1996). See also, for an interesting discussion of Brecht's possible relations with the Vienna Circle and 'logical empiricism', Ulrich Sautter, ' "Ich selber nehme kaum noch an einer Diskussion teil" ', *Deutsche Zeitschrift für Philosophie* 43, 4 (1995), pp. 687–709; and Steve Giles, *Bertolt Brecht and Critical Theory* (Bern: Peter Lange, 1997), chs 4, 5. Finally, for this and other biographical details, we must now all be grateful for Werner Hecht's superb *Brecht Chronik* (Frankfurt: Suhrkamp, 1997).

17. The reference is to Hannah Arendt, *Eichmann in Jerusalem* (New York: Viking, 1964).

18. The title of James K. Lyons's definitive work (Princeton, NJ: Princeton University Press, 1980).

19. But now see, for an exciting first step, Michael Denning, *The Cultural Front* (London: Verso, 1996). The ill-fated visit of 1935–36 to the USA on the occasion of the equally ill-fated Theater Union production of *The Mother* is the obvious first taste of America, but in a left-wing New York, rather than on the Right in a commercial Hollywood.

20. Roland Barthes, *Œuvres complètes* (Paris: Seuil, 1993), vol. I, pp. 145, 146.

21. See Louis Althusser, 'Letter on Art', in *Lenin and Philosophy* (New York: Monthly Review Press, 1971).

22. Martin Heidegger, *Sein und Zeit* (Tübingen: Niemeyer, 1957), p. 138.

23. Wayne Booth, *The Rhetoric of Irony* (Chicago: University of Chicago Press, 1974).

24. Werner Hecht, *Brecht Chronik*, p. 1249: 'schnell, leicht und kräftig' . . . 'die deutsche Kunst . . . ist schrecklich gewichtig, langsam, umständlich, und "fussgängerisch" '; Willett, p. 283.

25. See Note 16 above.

26. T. S. Eliot, *Selected Prose*, ed. Frank Kermode (New York: Harcourt Brace Jovanovich, 1975), p. 151.

27. T. S. Eliot, *Selected Essays* (New York: Harcourt Brace, 1950), p. 279.

28. Ibid., p. 279.

29. Georg Lukács, *History and Class Consciousness*, trans. Rodney Livingstone (Cambridge, MA: MIT Press, 1971), p. 1.

30. For example:

Alle unsere ideologiebildende Institutionen sehen ihre Hauptaufgabe darin, die Rolle der Ideologie *folgenlos* zu halten, entsprechend einen Kulturbegriff, nach dem die Bildung der Kultur bereits abgeschlossen ist und Kultur keiner fortgesetzen schöpferischen Bemühung bedarf.

(XXI, 554)

All of our institutions for the development of ideology ['Ideological State Apparatuses', in other words?] see as their fundamental role the duty to prevent ideology from having any consequences in the first place; in keeping with the conception of culture which holds that the formation by and of culture has already taken place and needs no further creative attention.

It is clearly a doctrine which makes a place for pedagogy fully as much as it stakes out a political art, and also defines the nature of the *Tui*-intellectual (to have no consequences).

31. Karl Marx and Friedrich Engels, *The German Ideology* (Moscow: Progress, 1974), p. 42. 'Die Moral, Religion, Metaphysik und sonstige Ideologie ... haben keine Geschichte, sie haben keine Entwicklung, sondern die ihre materielle Produktion und ihren materiellen Verkehr entwickelnden Menschen ändern mit dieser ihrer Wirklichkeit auch ihr Denken und die Produkte ihres Denkens' – Karl Marx, *Die Frühschriften*, ed. S. Landshut (Stuttgart: Kroner, 1953), p. 549.
32. Tübingen: Niemeyer, 1982.

Part I

Doctrine/*Lehre*

4 Estrangements of the Estrangement-Effect

That Brecht somehow includes a doctrine will have been felt by many who also find it difficult to identify, in either its form or its content. If it is simply 'Marxism', and even if the question of tendency is resolved (the Korsch line? Luxemburg? An emergent sympathy for Maoism?), the works seem to stage a good deal more than that; or perhaps, as the critics have so often jubilantly maintained, the lack of orthodox doctrinal content in the late works simply proves that Marxism is not really a philosophy or a world-view after all. Indeed, did not Brecht himself say as much:

> Me-ti fand in den Schriften des Klassiker nur wenig Fingerzeige für das Verhalten der Einzelnen. Meist wurde von den Klassen gesprochen oder anderen großen Gruppen von Menschen.
>
> (XVIII, 188)

> Me-ti found few enough indications in the writings of the classics about the behaviour of individuals. Most often they spoke of classes or of other large groups of people.

Marxism is thus a doctrine of the aggregates, a statistical doctrine from which any equivalent for ethics is excluded – leaving aside the implicit and explicit critiques to which it has subjected the traditions of ethical philosophy, and indeed leaving aside Brecht's own reservations about philosophy as a form. Perhaps, on the other hand, something like classical Chinese 'wisdom' is there to compensate for this lack (if not this incapacity) in Marxism, and to close the gap. Indeed, Tatlow usefully reminds us how different the emphasis of the classical Chinese thinkers was from Western philosophy in general:

> We cannot say that there were no 'metaphysics' or epistemology in Chinese philosophy, but these two areas – so crucial for Western philosophy – were

very differently conceived. The early Chinese philosophers were practical
humanists, concerned with the social order.... Apart from the human
standard and a constant awareness of the social context, perhaps the most
striking quality of Chinese thought is the insistence on the closest possible
connection between knowledge and action.[1]

This distribution of emphases tends to draw philosophizing away from
the realm of individual ethics, and in the direction of that strategic and
tactical lore we often call 'political theory' and associate primarily with
Machiavelli and Lenin. But it is also thrown into a new light by the role
of personal example – what Brecht will call *Haltung*,[2] or stance – in the
philosophical discourse which transmits their teachings.

But this now suggests a very different way of reorganizing our question
about Brecht's doctrine, for it suddenly raises the possibility of a
philosophical dramaturgy, or even of philosophy as dramaturgy, after
which the idea of dramaturgy as philosophy will itself already seem less
paradoxical. Indeed, Brecht's thought has for the most part (particularly
outside the German language) been associated with his specifically
dramatic or theatrical ideas (epic theatre, the estrangement-effect, anti-
Aristotelianism, *gestus*, various other acting techniques). At best these
ideas might be said to come together into an aesthetic of some kind, and
while an aesthetic is generally philosophical in its implications, for the
most part the various philosophical systems have transcended the
aesthetic components or subsystems they may or may not have included.
On the other hand, aesthetics have also tended to project symbolic or
disguised meditations on social or political dilemmas or ideals. Thus,
Aristotle's *Poetics* can be seen as a meditation on the clan system;[3] while
much in the later aesthetic tradition reflects the opacity of the body and
its social capacities for repression or sublimation.[4] Most often, the
aesthetic experience is itself called upon to function as a utopian
suspension; while in modernism, aesthetic value has most often been
conceived as a call to radical innovation – whether as a substitute for
modernization or revolution or, on the contrary, as a reinforcement of
either or both of those things, it is never very clear; and sometimes as a
compensation for them.

Brecht has generally been characterized as the champion of an
intellectualistic theatre – a didactic one, no doubt, if it were a little
clearer what he wanted to teach – and as an adversary of entertainment
(and of what he called the culinary, in theatre or music;[5] however, he
himself was a great reader of detective stories). It is then said that he
tried to soften this rather austere and puritanical image in the *Short
Organon* or *Kleines Organon* (completed 1948),[6] in order to facilitate

his return to the postwar European stages: since, as I have suggested above, he always thought that science and the acquisition of scientific 'knowledge' [*Wissenschaft*] was entertaining, this modification can be thought to be relatively rhetorical (although the philological study of the emergence and replacement of Brechtian terminology and formulations is clearly a significant and useful activity indeed).

Yet he seems to have posed questions of pleasure, entertainment and the 'culinary', in a non-moralizing and more functional or situational way: thus, speaking about the theatrical classics[7] and the progressive and intellectual content they once had, but have lost today, he observes:

> Das Bürgertum mußte seine rein geistigen Bemühungen so ziemlich liquidieren in einer Zeit, wo die Lust am Denken eine direkte Gefährdung seiner wirtschaftlichen Interessen bedeuten konnte. Wo das Denken nicht ganz eingestellt wurde, wurde es immer kulinarischer. Man machte zwar Gebrauch von den Klassikern, aber nur mehr kulinarischen Gebrauch.

(XXI, 310)

The bourgeoisie was obliged to liquidate its purely intellectual exertions in a period when the pleasures of thinking were likely to involve immediate risks for its economic interests. Where thought was not completely turned off, it became ever more culinary. Use was still made of the classics, but an ever more culinary use.

It is a thought that would offer a strange and defamiliarizing juxtaposition with Lukács's diagnosis of bourgeois philosophy in *History and Class Consciousness*; and might suggest a somewhat different reading of the ills of mass culture from that notoriously proposed by the Frankfurt School (in 'The Culture Industry' chapter of Adorno and Horkheimer's *Dialectic of Enlightenment*). There is here the suggestion, not of outright censorship, but of an instinctive self-repression of real thought, of an all-too-knowing turning away from anything that might lead you to unpleasant truths and to ideas of action which either promise guilt or ask you to change your life. This is not, I think a 'vulgar Marxist' analysis (although it has implications for Brecht's conception of ideology, which we will have to explore later on). On the contrary, it would seem to have its affinities with Freud's view of the patient he called the Rat Man, who had to make himself stupid, to stop himself from thinking, in order not to confront the unwanted and thereby unconscious realities of his own existence.[8] Consumer society today, in the United States and increasingly elsewhere, faces a similar dilemma and a similar block when it comes to thinking about the end results of its socioeconomic system; and has certainly sacrificed its classics to far more elaborate culinary distractions. But it should be clear that Brecht's position on such mass-cultural pleasures cuts across the old opposition between populism and elitism in an unexpected way; not pleasure, but its function, is the issue in thinking historically about aesthetics and culture.

This also places Brecht aslant the traditions of artistic modernism as such, which might otherwise have offered a transition from the specialized exposition of Brechtian dramaturgy to its deeper philosophical implications. Brecht could be as crude a philistine as Lukács himself when it came to modernism's more hermetic currents;[9] but he refused the latter's condemnation of then 'experimental' techniques in the name of a supposedly decadent 'formalism', proposing to discuss the matter in terms of 'reality' rather than 'realism':[10] Robbe-Grillet defended his own new novel in much the same way against the ideal image of a canonized Balzac.[11] But today we are beyond all the technical scandals of a now classical modernism, so that this outmoded debate seems to have been replaced by a very different one which opposes literature in general (realism along with modernism) to mass culture or, in other versions, to the visual or the spatial, to the televisual or the electronic. Brecht's thinking on modernism thus demands to be *umfunkioniert* (rebuilt and readapted, one of his favourite terms) along the late modernist or Robbe-Grillet lines, in which the philosophical content of the aesthetically modern is to be found in the critique of representation as such.

In fact, Brecht himself played a central role in the development of that theme and that critique, owing to the work of his most important disciples, whose prestigious fortunes have in fact tended to obscure Brecht's own share in the matter. But no satisfactory study of the career of Roland Barthes can afford to omit his Brechtian (as well as his Sartrean) origins: his classic *Mythologies* paved the way for the triumphant entry of the estrangement-effect into French theory. As for Walter Benjamin, his posthumous influence (rising as inexorably as Barthes's has fallen, and seemingly impervious to the Brecht-fatigue in which it has launched a whole new career since 'unification') now appears to be inflected in two distinct directions all at once: in the postmodern, drawing on the untarnished prestige of his technology essays; and in that of language mysticism, as a result of greater familiarity with his early writings. The first of these, at least, is bound to look rather different when it is replaced in its original Brechtian context; while the lineaments of a later, profoundly Brechtian Benjamin have not yet clearly emerged, owing to general unfamiliarity with his indefatigable production as a literary critic and book reviewer. What we need to retain provisionally from Benjamin is his remark that what Brecht taught him was the intellectual and the socioeconomic situation of the writer under capitalism:[12] it is a reflexivity which gives its distinctive quality to all his subsequent work, and uniquely characterizes Benjamin as Marxist and modernist simultaneously.

The V-effect, then,[13] is not the only feature of Brecht's modernism, nor even the central one (in particular, we will have occasion to examine a specifically *autoreferential* feature of his work in Part II). But it does seem advisable to 'estrange' or 'defamiliarize' the so-called estrangement-effect in its turn, in order to convey something of its original and historic function, as well as to surprise the variety of forms it is capable of taking. Brecht offered many 'definitions' of this term, which seems to have migrated from the 'ostranenie' or 'making-strange' of the Russian Formalists via any number of visits to Berlin by Soviet modernists like Eisenstein or Tretiakov.[14] Like Eisenstein's concept of 'montage', it permitted him to organize and coordinate a great many distinct features of his theatrical practice and aesthetic.

Sometimes it is evoked in terms of the effect itself that names it. To make something look strange, to make us look at it with new eyes, implies the antecedence of a general familiarity, of a habit which prevents us from really looking at things, a kind of perceptual numbness: this is the emphasis most often given by the Russian Formalists, which offers a kind of psychologizing of the *Novum*, and a defence of innovation in terms of the freshness of experience and the recovery of perception.

But Brecht also, and more often, inventoried the techniques whereby things could in fact be 'estranged'; and while he did not limit himself to the theatre (there are wonderful pages on Breughel, for example[15]), for the most part such techniques are the stagecraft in which a specific form of acting and distanciation is recommended – quotation of the lines, for example, or showing the character you are playing and its traits without trying to 'become' the role. These techniques extend on into the physical issues of set design and 'intertitles', and of the use of music. But it would be important also to understand all this in the fashion of Loyola's meditations or Grotowski's spiritual discipline as a symbolic way or method of processing reality: the 'techniques' themselves have a symbolic meaning in their own right; they are not simply means to an end.

Yet that end also affords yet a third way of approaching the V-effect – or rather, perhaps a third and a fourth; since the first of these two ends or aims is also a kind of effect, and itself a means to something else. This is, of course, the turning off or shutting down of *Einfühlung*, of empathy or even sympathy: the object of polemics against Aristotle ('pity and fear') and Stanislavski, and the most notorious slogan in the Brechtian arsenal, which allows one (with a side glance at *Die Massnahme*) to accuse this theatre of being cold and intellectualistic on the one hand,

and propagandistic and didactic on the other. Its ambiguity stems from the negative formulation, which enables a whole range of polemics of the type just mentioned, but leaves the nature of the effect – that is to say, its purpose or function – unclarified.[16]

Whence the fourth and final, ultimately political, formulation of the V-effect, which is meant to subsume all the preceding descriptions, and place them in a new light as well. Here, the familiar or habitual is reidentified as the 'natural', and its estrangement unveils that appearance, which suggests the changeless and the eternal as well, and shows the object to be instead 'historical', to which may be added, as a political corollary, made or constructed by human beings, and thus able to be changed by them as well, or replaced altogether. This final form, and the very categories in which it is framed, will be the version Barthes popularizes in France and the starting point for some properly Brechtian poststructuralism, as we shall see in conclusion.

For the moment, however, it is worthwhile not merely to historicize the V-effect itself, but also to grasp its political function in the bourgeois Enlightenment. Brecht himself collected any number of examples from the 'classics' while taking, as the occasion for his first full-dress exposition, the conventions of Chinese theatre.[17] There are also modern versions: 'A man drinks wine in front of kneeling women.'[18] What Sartre's sentence alerts us to is the constitutive relationship, in its first or eighteenth-century deployment, of the V-effect to the critique of religion as such, along with its institutions. In this period of the bourgeois revolution, and of the political work of revolutionary writers in undermining the *ancien régime* as such, it is above all religion which is 'unnatural' and demands to be defamiliarized and shown up in all its strangeness. Religion, Voltaire's 'l'infâme', is the ideological foundation of the aristocratic or caste system; and the assault on the latter demands a ceaseless critique of those conceptions of blood and rank, of natural differentiation, which hold the old regime in place, and of which the increasingly frequent images of villainous priests and their influence in a whole range of historical despotisms is only the most melodramatic expression. From Montesquieu to Voltaire, then, the estrangement-effect is called upon to underscore the artificiality of the old regime and to promote new bourgeois conceptions of simplicity and universal human nature.

One should add that Brecht's representation of religion and gods always shows them as a floating superstructure: the gods are there, as in *The Good Person of Szechuan*, to uphold purely ethical standards; but they cannot intervene, above all because 'in das Wirtschaftliche können wir uns nicht mischen' (VI, 184: 'we can't get involved with economics').

God explains himself more extensively in the following fragment, a very early scrap from the *St Joan* drafts:

> Ich habe da ein Buch über die Konjunkturforschungen. Die Krisen sollen da auf Naturgesetzen beruhen. Da frage ich Sie aber doch, davon müßte schließlich ich auch etwas wissen. Und ich sage Ihnen, kein Wort davon ist wahr! Ich habe mit Wirtschaft nie das Geringste zu tun gehabt. Für mich ist Wirtschaft überhaupt nicht vorhanden. Ich habe mich nie in sie eingemischt, und ich werde mich nicht einmischen.

(III, 453).

> I have a book here about research on conjunctures. Crises are supposed to be governed by natural law. But now I ask you, wouldn't I know something about it in that case? I tell you there is no truth in it whatsoever. I have never had the slightest thing to do with economics. I have never got involved in it and I never will get involved in it.

Thus God testifies against himself and against the superstructures generally (which is to say: liberalism, ethics and philanthropy, but not art and culture[19]), thereby opening in the process a space and pretext for judgement, and for a juridical ritual which can sometimes (as in *Mahagonny* or the *Three-Penny Novel*) turn against himself.

But this tail end of the great Enlightenment political strategy – its polemic against religion, in which the fundamental weapon of the V-effect is developed in the first place – raises questions about the timeliness of estrangement in the secular world of the twentieth century. Do we still believe that our institutions, and their consequences for our subjectivities and our behaviour, are somehow timeless and eternal? Barthes thought so, and his patient yet decisive demonstration of the deeply felt naturality of our social world (in *Mythologies*) validates the estrangement-effect as a political weapon.

Yet the argument could also be made that religion – even secularized religion – has ceased to play a fundamental ideological role in modern capitalism. In Auguste Comte's influential concept of the three stages of history, it is, rather, metaphysics which supersedes religion in the bourgeois era, philosophical abstractions taking the place of what were hypostasized as forces in the theological period. In that case, it is precisely the critique of metaphysics – and within it the critique of representation – which stands in continuity with the older Enlightenment critique of religion; the implication being that the third stage – positivism, the gradual withering away of metaphysics in favour of the empirical – would demand a rather different strategy. In the event, it was a masterstroke for Habermas to locate the parting of the ways of modern critical thought at the moment of the Hegelian succession,[20] and

to stage his diagnosis of contemporary philosophical currents in the light
of that three-way split between Marx himself, the conservative Right
Hegelians and Bruno Bauer's Young Hegelians, in many ways the
predecessors of all contemporary critiques of metaphysics. For the latter
not only continue and perpetuate the tradition for which it is the
undermining of metaphysical concepts which replaces the critique of
religion as the most fundamental radical act; they also offer the richest
arsenal of methods for the critique of ideology and, indeed, for theories
of ideology itself (however that phenomenon be named in its various
contemporary versions).

In the present context, therefore, we will want to interrogate the
Brechtian estrangement-effect further for its philosophical implications;
and in particular we will wish to juxtapose two paths which seem to lie
open to a contemporary radicalism. If we decide to identify the V-effect,
for example, with a nominalism that some have positioned at the very
emergence of modernity itself,[21] then this strategy confronts a situation
in which the artificial categories of the various universals – so many
words or names – serve to classify a host of radically distinct existents,
and to obscure or occult their differentiation. To remove the names thus
becomes a form of philosophical therapy which promises to lead us back
to the freshness of raw experience itself (in a kind of philosophical
equivalent of the aesthetics of the Russian Formalists). We may indeed
remember that Schopenhauer accused Kant of forgetting to include the
category of the 'thing' within his list of the mental forms with which we
organize the outside world;[22] at that point, stripping away this final
name, the category of thingness, or objecthood, would indeed seem to
confront us with some ultimate and primal form of the Bergsonian or
Deleuzian flux. Yet it is somehow paradoxical to juxtapose this version
of reality with the Sino-Brechtian one, seemingly so affiliated in spirit, of
a well-nigh Heraclitean stream of the Tao into which one never steps
twice.

Meanwhile, Brechtian nominalism, if we wish to call it that, works on
a rather different system of names: not only our traditional nomenclature
for human institutions and social behaviour, but also the historical
system of 'psychology' as such, the inherited words and concepts for the
various feelings and emotions. Here, the V-effect would seem to generate
social satire, rather than the critique of metaphysics; so we will at least
want to ask ourselves how incompatible these two targets really are.

5 Autonomization

It seems possible to redefine the estrangement-effect in terms of a rather different linguistic substitution, particularly if we trace its spirit back to those theories of 'epic' drama or theatre which preceded it in the late 1920s. For it is always necessary to remind the English-language reader, and perhaps the German one as well, that the crucial term – epic – by no means involves the lofty and classical associations of the Homeric tradition but, rather, something as humdrum and everyday as narrative or 'storytelling'. In that case: a storytelling theatre versus a theatrical one, anecdotes versus speeches, one event leading to another, rather than posture and poses in sculptural conflict.

And when we remember the traditions of modern research on oral or 'epic' storytelling, we also understand that one of the features of narrative in general, particularly in the practice of master-storyteller, is that it can expand or contract, be spun out in great or savoury detail over hours, or concentrated into the most pithy anecdote. It is this particular property of narrative that yields a first approach to estrangement, along the lines of that remark of Döblin that Brecht often quoted: 'Epik könne man im Gegensatz zur Dramatik sozusagen mit der Schere in einzelne Stücke schneiden' (XXII, 107–8): 'Unlike the dramatic, the narrative you can cut up into so many separate pieces as though with scissors' (Willett, 70). It is a process that operates indifferently on the real and on the pre-given cultural text; yet it is also a literary tendency, developing and intensifying throughout modernism, which we will call 'autonomization', from the way in which the episodes of a narrative thus cut up into smaller segments tend to take on an independence and an autonomy of their own (the 'separate pieces' remain 'lebensfähig', to continue Döblin). Joyce's *Ulysses* clearly offers the most striking exemplification of such narrative production, in which the separate chapters end up going their own ways, developing different styles and structures from each other, and finally looking as distinct from one another as the various organs in the body (Joyce's own analogy). What needs to be added, however, is that autonomization is not a process that can be set in motion with impunity: on the contrary (as the example of Joyce equally testifies), once in force, it tends to descend into the smallest units of the narrative, potentially making the individual sentences autonomous as well, as both Sartre and Nathalie Sarraute have noted about the sentences of Flaubert himself, at the very emergence of modernism as such.

Autonomization in the Brechtian theatre will, to be sure, look rather different from this, since it takes place within a different medium in which action must first be translated into narrative form (as we shall see in the next essay), before that narrative form can itself be subjected to segmentary analysis and disjunction. But the emblem of the process is there for all to read in what must be the most famous of Brecht's theatrical *Merkmale* – namely, the titles that drop down out of the catwalk to frame a given scene or to name a song and are reminiscent of the chapter headings of eighteenth-century novels which announce their contents to the curious – or, perhaps, the reluctant – reader: 'in which' could then be transferred immediately to the Brechtian sequence of scenes:

> ... der Marketenderin Anna Fierling, bekannt unter dem Namen Mutter Courage, kommt ein Sohn abhanden. (VI, 9)

> ... der Feldprediger beklagt, daß seine Talente brachliegen, und die stumme Katrin bekommt die roten Schuhe. (VI, 53)

> [In which] Anna Fierling, known as Mother Courage, loses a son.

> [In which] the chaplain complains about the neglect of his talents, and Katrin the mute receives the red shoes.

These narrative titles, to be sure, also mark and record the chronology of the greater history – the Thirty Years War – through which the smaller destinies of Mother Courage and her family are doomed to pass: indeed, they mediate between the two, thereby approaching Brecht's other characteristic recommendation, to tell the story of individual experience like the history in the history books. But the scenes – and in this particular play, deliberately projected in chronicle form, the scenes are episodes, and the episodes are temporally separated from each other – also constitute the stages of a great lesson, which Mother Courage fails to learn; and it is the components of that lesson which are here broken down for us and laid end to end like a negative learning process.

What a positive one would look like we can then see in another maternal drama, his version of Gorki's *Mother*, in which the lesson can be more confidently broken down and segmented, beyond the obvious title:

> Die Mutter sieht mit Kummer ihren Sohn in der Gesellschaft revolutionärer Arbeiter.
>
> (III, 265)

> The mother is pained at the sight of her son consorting with revolutionary workers.

The 'pain', however, can itself be broken down into its component parts and thereby, productively, used to transform itself. Thus, in the first moment, Pelagea Wlassova, disapproving of radical activity, is displeased and worried by her son's bad associations. In a second moment, however, she learns something about danger, and in particular about police repression. In a third, she develops a curiosity about the contents of the flyers the police had searched for, and which her son and his friends had planned to distribute. These flyers themselves hold a lesson. And in a final segment of this scene, she decides to distribute the flyers herself, in order to spare her son danger, possible arrest and imprisonment. It is not yet a complete conversion to revolutionary activity: that will take up the rest of the play. Yet it is an autonomized sequence, in which the separation of the moments from each other in time is crucial to the way in which the form of the play articulates its 'message'. It would clearly be tedious for each of these segments to be formally separated from the others by the system of titles, but it is enough to think of silent film, and its far more thoroughgoing interpolation of 'subtitles', for the spirit of Brechtian autonomization to be clear. Here, however, it is not the words of the dialogue but, rather, the meaning and functions of the gesture – the *gestus*, including spoken dialogue as such – that is segmented and paid out moment by moment.

Modernist autonomization includes within itself the twin contradictory (yet dialectically identical) tendencies of the work towards minimalism on the one hand, and the mega-structure on the other. For if the logic of the work's production lies in analysis – in the literal sense of the Greek term, *ana-luein*, to break up – it is all one whether the ultimate ideal consists in that least common denominator of a kind of silence which stands in a Beckett play for aesthetic purity, or on the other an addictive and well-nigh infinite expansion of the work which, as in Musil, needs no particular closure, even though 'incomplete' may not be the word for it. Both tendencies are present in Brecht, along with a good deal of genuine incompleteness as well.

The process needs an identification that transcends the aesthetic as such; nor are the different versions of 'analysis' – medical, logical, mathematical, critical: to dissolve the links and interrelationships, release the 'object' back into its constituent parts – ultimately so relevant as its most powerful and succinct historical formulation in Descartes's second methodological precept: 'de diviser chacune des difficultés que j'examinerais en autant de parcelles qu'il se pourrait et qu'il serait requis pour les mieux résoudre'.[23] The slippage between dividing problems up into their smallest parts and performing the same process of analysis on things or on other substantive phenomena is itself an index of reification:

we do not need Bergson to observe that if an entity – whether thing or problem – is divisible in this way, it was in any case already *en route* for spatialization and reification generally. This is why, at the other end of the history of capitalism, the supreme triumph of Descartes's method arrives with Taylor and 'scientific management': here again it is in reality time rather than space which is 'analyzed' and broken down into its smallest units (the spatial analogue – Ford's assembly line – then follows on the new temporal reorganization), and Weberian 'rationalization' finds its primary exemplar and privileged manifestation in the way in which for traditional practices, work procedures handed down from generation to generation in the form of relatively completed gestures and meaningful 'wholes', are substituted new and artificial segments and series of meaningless isolated movements whose regulated succession has .the result of enhanced efficiency and greater, more rapid productivity. Lenin's and Gramsci's admiration for the new methods should be noted here, even though the function of Taylorism – and Harry Braverman's great book on the subject shows that it was a deliberate intention of the process[24] – was to strip the workers of all decision-making power and control over the labour process, relinquishing them to the relatively new caste of the managers.

But reification – in this specifically Weberian and Bergsonian sense of the divisibility of a process which has been made over into a thing-like entity – is a tendency not at all limited to science and technology on the one hand, and the labour process on the other: rather, it is a tendential social law which has ultimate effects on and implications for aesthetics and the work of art as well. Adorno is only the foremost among those who have tried to define aesthetic modernism itself in terms of reification, and that in a twofold way: for reification defines the situation and the element which the work wishes to resist, but it also defines the logic of that resistance, as a kind of homeopathic remedy which fights a general logic of objectification by way of the objectification of its own forms.

Clearly enough, Brecht's adoption of reification as a dramatic and representational 'method' will be even more ambivalent than this, for it incorporates the spirit of the Leninist admiration for Fordism, while at the same time it seeks more immediately to restore what is truly comprehensible in human action and behaviour by making that behaviour incomprehensible: a realism achieved by means of Cubism might be a more apt description. Yet the doubt raised by critics like Lukács – does the reified modernist work distance and subvert the more general social reifications of modernity, or does it simply replicate and perpetuate them? – is evidently less relevant here, where it is clear that Brecht himself wishes to eliminate the peculiar forms of behaviour he is in the process of estranging on stage, and displaying in the form of their atomic or constituent units or parts.

For the moment, however, we want to return to the philosophical implications of this logic of autonomization, and its implication for human action generally. (We will see that it is accompanied by a kind of autonomization in the realm of subjectivity as well, whose significance is not inconsiderable.) Indeed, it is already a dereification of action to posit its analytic malleability – or, in other words, to release it from the unity of its form. There was always – to return to our previous discussion – the positive side of Weberian rationalization: the new freedom consequent on the destruction of tradition. In Brecht, however, this kind of liberation issues not into a rhetoric of freedom but, rather, into something more productive: the whole political message and content of the V-effect itself – namely, to reveal what has been taken to be eternal or natural – the reified act, with its unifying name and concept – as merely historical, as a kind of institution which has come into being owing to the historical and collective actions of people and their societies, and which therefore now stands revealed as changeable. What history has solidified into an illusion of stability and substantiality can now be dissolved again, and reconstructed, replaced, improved, 'umfunktion-iert'. The process of aesthetic autonomization, breaking the action up into its smallest parts, thus has symbolic as well as epistemological meaning: it shows what the act 'really' is, no doubt, but the very activity of breaking it up and 'analyzing' it is itself a joyous process, a kind of creative play, in which new acts are formed together out of pieces of the old, in which the whole reified surface of a period seemingly beyond history and beyond change now submits to a first ludic un-building, before arriving at a real social and revolutionary collective reconstruction. One hesitates to call this individual symbolic meaning either an ethical or a psychological or psychoanalytic reenactment, although the idea of a kind of ethics of production is an attractive one, which might serve to rescue this much-maligned term (in a historical situation seemingly dominated by consumption and distribution/communication) and to reconnect it with an emergent constructivism which can also be read as an attempt to overcome both paralysis and impotence, the failure of individual action and the sense of a global situation that cannot be changed. Such, at any rate, is the supplementary allegorical energy of Brechtian autonomization: its capacity to act out our own possible and virtual actions, its use of a one-time (and thus apparently unchangeable, but only apparently unchangeable) spectacle to energize a public into a sense of multiple possibilities.

It is a philosophical dimension of one feature of Brechtian dramaturgy which his disciples took further in the direction of metaphysics than he seems to have been willing to go himself. Thus Benjamin, embodying and objectifying Brechtian method in a new apparatus, the camera, celebrates the latter's capacity to uncover spatial dimensions of our existence which had been, as it were, concealed by the conventionalities of human stature: it is a passage worth quoting in some detail, and not only for the characteristically Benjaminian juxtaposition of cinema with Freud's 'psychopathology' of slips of the tongue (which themselves 'revealed dimensions of depth in a conversation which had seemed to be taking its course on the surface'[25]) but also, and above all, for its revelation of the Brechtian nature of the camera, so to speak:

> By close-ups of the things around us, by focusing on hidden details of familiar objects, by exploring commonplace milieus under the ingenious guidance of the camera, the film, on the one hand, extends our comprehension of the necessities which rule our lives; on the other hand, it manages to assure us of an immense and unexpected field of action. Our taverns and our metropolitan streets, our offices and furnished rooms, our railroad stations and our factories appeared to have us locked up hopelessly. Then came the film and burst this prison-world asunder by the dynamite of the tenth of a second, so that now, in the midst of its far-flung ruins and debris, we calmly and adventurously go travelling. With the close-up, space expands; with slow motion, movement is extended. The enlargement of a snapshot does not simply render more precise what in any case was visible, though unclear: it reveals entirely new structural formations of the subject. So, too, slow motion not only presents familiar qualities of movement but reveals in them entirely unknown ones 'which, far from looking like retarded rapid movements, give the effect of singularly gliding, floating, supernatural motions' [Rudolf Arnheim]. Evidently a different nature opens itself to the camera than opens to the naked eye. . . .[26]

Benjamin's version, however, seems a relatively hermeneutic one: even when he is insisting on the technological processes concealed from us in montage, he underscores the ways in which 'the mechanical equipment has penetrated deeply into reality';[27] so that the climactic comparison with the surgeon is already implicit:

> Here the question is: how does the cameraman compare with the painter? To answer this we take recourse to an analogy with a surgical operation. The surgeon represents the polar opposite of the magician. The magician heals a sick person by the laying on of hands; the surgeon cuts into the patient's body. The magician maintains the natural distance between the patient and himself; though he reduces it very slightly by the laying on of hands, he greatly increases it by virtue of his authority. The surgeon does exactly the reverse; he greatly diminishes the distance between himself and the patient by

penetrating into the patient's body, and increases it but little by the caution with which his hand moves among the organs. In short, in contrast to the magician – who is still hidden in the medical practitioner – the surgeon at the decisive moment abstains from facing the patient man to man; rather, it is through the operation that he penetrates into him. Magician and surgeon compare to painter and cameraman. The painter maintains in his work a natural distance from reality, the cameraman penetrates deeply into its web.[28]

Not only is the hermeneutic perspective a more contemplative and epistemological one than what we have found in Brecht's own work; we may also observe that however welcome the emphasis on diagnosis, illness and cure, the image of the purely surgical intervention does not incite to activity or arouse praxis in the same way as the theatrical texts; even though it may in some sense produce them: 'the more frequently we interrupt someone in the act of acting, the more gestures result.'[29]

We have here, in a sense, analysis without any subsequent reconstruction. But it also seems possible that this is a result of the medium in question: splendid achievement as *Kuhle Wampe* may be, Brecht's Hollywood thoughts and projects do not particularly suggest an imagination receptive to the possibilities of film in quite the same way as with his later cinematographic would-be disciples (like Godard, for example). He had a keener sense of the montage possibilities of photography as such; while Benjamin himself, perhaps, took the Brechtian 'ethics of production' much further and as far as it would go for the film of his own period, transforming it, in his other great technological essay, 'The Author as Producer', into a classic form of modernist autoreferentiality, in which the productivity of the art form stands as an allegory for the productivity of the socioeconomic system itself. But this comes closer to Brecht's ideas about modernity than it does to his ideas about art.

As for the written or literary, printed text, it is perhaps Roland Barthes who goes farthest in developing a form of autonomization specific to it, and now only very distantly related to its Brechtian origins. Borrowing the term 'prohairesis' (rational choice) from Aristotle, he theorizes a so-called 'proairetic code', a prescription for estrangement which takes us deep into the structures of the act itself, even deeper than Benjamin's camera, in the process abandoning a Benjaminian hermeneutic model for what he clearly thought of as a semiotic one, which we may also compare with translation:

What is a series of actions? The unfolding of a name. To *enter*? I can unfold it into 'to appear' and 'to penetrate'. To *leave*? I can unfold it into 'to want to', 'to stop', 'to leave again'. . . . Two systems of folding (two 'logics') seem to be required alternatively. The first breaks down the title (noun or verb) according to its constituent moments (the articulation can be orderly: *begin/continue* or confused: *begin/stop/leave*). The second system attaches contingent actions to a guide word (*to say farewell/to confide/to embrace*). These systems, one analytical, the other catalytical, one definitional, the other metonymical, have no logic other than that of the *already-seen, already-read, already-done*: that of empires and culture. . . .[30]

Here the emphasis is shifted from the divisible nature of the reality itself to the system of words and names according to which it is unified: a rather structuralist and period comparison with money and exchange is none the less pursued less in the direction of synonymy than in that of closure (or, on the other hand, a fan-like opening up which has little enough to do with Deleuze's Leibnizian and baroque 'folds'):

> Thus, to read (to perceive the *readerly* aspect of the text) is to proceed from name to name, from fold to fold; it is to fold the text according to one name and then to unfold it along the new folds of this name. This is proairetism: an artifice (of art) of reading that seeks out names, that tends toward them: an act of lexical transcendence, a labor of classification carried out on the basis of the classification of language – a *maya* activity, as the Buddhists would say, an account of appearances, but as discontinuous forms, as names.[31]

Barthes's flight here towards the nameless, towards some ultimate uncoded Deleuzian flux that might underlie all things, is evidently rather different in spirit either from the materialism of Benjamin's organs and macro- or micro-spatial dimensions or from that very different flow of the Tao in Brecht's more Chinese moments. Indeed, the Barthesian passage beyond the surface seems more Germanic in the stereotypical sense – more of a kin with Schopenhauer or Wagner – than does the staccato clarity proposed by the Germans themselves, with this qualification: that Barthes – himself also a satirist very much in the Brecht tradition, particularly in those *Mythologies* so indebted to Brecht – also usefully insists on the necessary dialectical counterpart to this stream of nameless being: namely, on the stereotypical terms, on the preexisting empiricality of the words and names that code or organize it. This preexisting social raw material – what the work, in its analytic operations and processes, needs to work over, to cut up, satirically to anatomize – this is the vital link between Brecht's modernism and the realities to which his realism wishes to remain faithful. Just as his texts are aggressively intertexts, notoriously plagiarizing or working over their preexisting 'originals' (much as a thousand years of classical Chinese poetry built on allusions to previous verses), so also the dramaturgical operations bear on the preexisting subtext, which is itself an intertext, of the named social material – the substance, as Hjelmslev might have put it – itself already organized into stereotypical expression, society already fully verbal through and through, and carrying its names and interpretations, its folds, within even the most seemingly non-linguisitic and material of its components. Barthes's insistence thus brings out everything which is already profoundly poststructural and 'textual' in Brecht.

But it also secretly names the dramaturgy it carries within itself: for indeed, the curious Aristotelian term which Barthes borrows for his Greek neologism – prohairesis[32] – means originally choice or decision, an odd word for the stereotypical name for an action. The stereotypicality of the 'fold' suggests that we have nothing to do with the matter: there is a whole dictionary of such act-entities – to enter, to leave, to begin, to stop – about whose structure we have little enough to say. The 'I' always accompanies our actions, Kant said: we have only to add our appropriate personal pronoun to the act already formed and waiting for us. Yet we do finally have the alternative of yes or no: we can enter or not enter; the ultimate choice of the being or the not-being of the act remains. This is thus dramatistic, and restores the theatrical element which Benjamin's cinematic apparatus dispelled. Here, at the very heart of the Aristotelian concept, we can see the actor hesitate before this act, and foreground his possibilities and his alternatives.

Yet Barthes's development none the less leaves us before an alternative of a rather different kind: between being and not-being on the one hand, and becoming on the other. Thus, the proairetic moment may be the theatrical space in which an already existing, stereotypically pre-formed event may or may not take place; or it may be a rather different stage on which, by the multiple processes of analysis and defamiliarization, the division into parts, their reconstruction in wholly new and unsuspected ways, a transformation may result – something new and as yet unnamed may emerge from the lexicon of the already classified. Nor is it enough to remember that both kinds of event happen in Brecht's plays: Grusha takes the baby instead of leaving it; but Galy Gay is dismantled and put back together in a new and frightening way, a very *Novum* of ferocity. We will come back to such reconstruction later on.

6 *Episch*, or, the Third Person

But the insistence on the primacy of the 'narrative' over the 'dramatic' can take other forms as well, and have other consequences – can 'estrange' in different ways. We have observed the way in which, following Döblin, a narrative can be stretched out and sliced up like a sausage, its parts and incidents slowly becoming fully fledged scenes and episodes in their own right. The overlap of the words 'epic' and 'narrative' in German, in fact, also reminds us that something like this theory was already developed by Goethe and Schiller in their April 1797 correspondence about Greek epic, and later elaborated by Auerbach in *Mimesis*: namely, what the latter calls the 'hypotactic',[33] the tendency of the various scenes to be not only additive and segmentary, but also 'immediate to God', to use Ranke's expression – each one bathed in a full light which excludes perspectivism and displays what should be only a secondary or subsidiary episode in the unfolding of a larger plot or intrigue, as though it were interesting in itself and a complete object of contemplation and delectation in its own right, like a series of independent tableaux side by side. The replacement of Brechtian theatre in such a classical tradition also offers a useful estrangement, and lends an interesting ambiguity to his own modernities.

But the effect of narrative is rather different when it is the subject or the character, the protagonist, who is its object. Now the result is not so much to make the objective action, with all its episodes and incidents, susceptible of a divisibility and an analysis that casts a different light on them, so much as to bring an uncanny strangeness to the subjective moment of decision and action itself, the 'proairesis' of the protagonist, with its wavering motives and intentions, its psychological impulses as well, and even its unconscious drives. After all, Freud's 'talking cure' was itself just such a narrative, in which the patient's story gradually returned upon its protagonist to throw all the latter's notions of self into a new light: can I really have been the one who . . . it certainly begins to sound as though I really wanted. . . . The analyst himself then does the prompting and provides the hints; your feelings for Herr K. . . . for Frau K. . . . Habermas has argued that Freudian psychoanalysis fundamentally proposes a rewriting, a retelling, a new way, of the subject's implicit life narrative:[34] so that finally what emerges is less some new conception of the Unconscious as such than, rather, the capacity of narrative to restructure our 'imaginary' representation of that *actant* which is self, ego, first person, or whatever; to modify our inner distance from this 'identity'; to reshape and construct in new ways that 'I think which must accompany all my representations'.

But it is important to think of what is thereby modified in a relational rather than a substantive way: not a self-entity so much as very precisely the 'function' designated by narrative semiotics or narratology. Remembering that for Kant the 'self' was also a noumenon, a thing-in-itself inaccessible to conscious thought and its categories, one can no doubt here also imagine the metaphysical flights we discovered when the names were stripped from things and events, allowing some primal nameless flux to be glimpsed underneath. But perhaps the play of social masks in Brecht is no less fascinating and mysterious, particularly when it is registered in the narrative prose of, say, the *Three-Penny Novel*, in which a multiplicity of Macheath-protagonists passes bewilderingly across the stage.

These narrative conversions or displacements are closely related to another familiar Brechtian technique, that of quotation: thus it is recommended that the actor quote his speeches and transmit his lines and his character's utterances to us as though in italics or between quotation marks – a rather peculiar recommendation which is generally understood as part of Brecht's onslaught on 'empathy' and Stanislav-skian emotion. So presumably there is a first-person and also a third-person emotion which can be represented on stage: in the first, the actor 'would drown the stage with tears/and cleave the general ear with horrid speech . . .' thereby eliciting a sympathetic fellow-feeling in the public thus called upon to 'identify' with him and with his 'dream of passion' and finally, in the last instance, to feel 'pity and fear' at the prospect of a fate the spectator might also have confronted.

Yet this notion of 'identification' is one of the most problematic and unexamined concepts in the arsenal of sociological cliché; nor are the sociologists the only ones to construct elaborate theoretical models of 'sociability' and 'society', of 'intersubjectivity' and 'interpersonal relations'. There exists, no doubt, some impersonal instinct, a life-anxiety or what is improperly personalized and anthropomorphized by the term 'self' in the expression self-preservation, which is manifested in the mute terror of birds, for example, in the face of the spread-eagled remains of one of their species nailed upon a barn door; and embodied even more ambiguously by the crowding of humans, full of visceral fascination and pleasurable horror, in front of a human corpse. But this has little enough to do with the pseudo-psychological concept of 'identification', which can at best be imagined in the form of some Lacanian mirror-stage. And in that case, would the 'lack of identification' between such selves mean that the 'other' was somehow excluded from the category of the human altogether?

In fact, I think that Brecht's positions are better read not as a refusal of identification but, rather, as the consequences to be drawn from the fact that such a thing never existed in the first place. In that case, 'third-person acting', the quoting of a character's expressions of feeling and emotion, is the result of a radical absence of the self, or at least the coming to terms with a realization that what we call our 'self' is itself an object for consciousness, not our consciousness itself: it is a foreign body within an impersonal consciousness, which we try to manipulate in such a way as to lend some warmth and personalization to the matter. The simplest models of identification are therefore rendered meaningless by this situation, in which at best, in a Lacanian complexity, two self-objects would entertain a complex and mediated relationship with each other across the gaps of isolated consciousness as such.

Quotation, then, or third-person acting, is a way of outflanking this situation, with its evident impossibilities, and ratifying the 'imaginary' nature of the self by holding it at a distance on stage and allowing its ventriloquism to designate itself. Yet something must be quoted, some 'already existing' and recognizable (or at least nameable) gesture must make up the substance of the quote, just as the gesture of the actor quoting his lines should also be identifiable as a type of conduct (if only the historically recognizable and legitimated conduct of acting itself). Thus, I must feel that the now classic Straub/Huillet film *Nicht Versöhnt* (1965), which has long been admired as some first Brechtian form of cinema, is not always consonant with the spirit of Brechtian narrative. This shorthand or Xeroxed film version of Heinrich Böll's complex novel *Billiard um halb-zehn* (1958), in which, either as a voice-over or in long deadpan monologues, the original text is somehow attached to a series of filmic images, can certainly offer any number of examples of 'quotation'; yet our temptation is always to remotivate what is given to us as utterly toneless and unmotivated in the first place. Thus the mother's hallucinatory stream-of-consciousness about the inhumanity of the Nazi period is cleverly transferred on to a long rambling speech to her son during his weekly visit to her in the asylum; but the non-professional to whom the role (or, better still, only the speech itself, the words of the monologue) have been confided only too successfully fulfils what must have been the Straubs' direction of her – namely, simply to read through the sentences as fast as possible without any expression whatsoever: at best, then, the spectator is tempted to reinterpret this very tonelessness as a symptom of that mental disorder the novel wishes emphatically to deny she has.

On the other hand, it seems possible that the medium is itself at fault and at stake: the 'acting' has already been done and is now irremediable, forever registered on a film that can be played again and again without the slightest changes or modifications being possible. On stage, however, we are at the very present of time of the performance: it is no longer available when it goes into the past (however irremediable its already acted gestures, they can never be witnessed again, only remembered) – but for this one long moment of its present the actor's gesture can still be modified; any number of possibilities throng the present of the stage, which is surely invested by what Deleuze called 'virtuality' – something

far richer than mere possibility, and a kind of thronging within a present
in much the same spirit in which Heidegger reinterpreted Nietzsche's
will to power as an Aristotelian *energeia*. Whatever film can do, it
cannot give that sense of emergence and *praxis*.

Yet all these arguments no doubt also give aid and comfort to Brecht's
critics, who always maintained that Brechtian distanciation was impossible in the first place, and that we inevitably identify with Mother
Courage and her 'tragedy' in spite of ourselves. Yet this is perhaps still
to reify the self and 'personality' of the spectator rather than to grasp
the nature of the 'third-person' narrative distanciation proposed by
sentences like:

> 'der Marketenderin Anna Fierling ... kommt ein Sohn abhanden ...' 'the
> travelling camp merchant Anna Fierling ... loses a son ...'.

Brecht's own technical recommendations are perhaps initially more
useful than any merely interpretive analysis. So it is that he proposes
three 'techniques' for his actors:

> drei Hilfsmittel, [die] bei einer Spielweise mit nicht restloser Verwandlung zu
> einer Verfremdung der Äusserungen und Handlungen der darzustellenden
> Person dienen:
> 1. Die Überführung in die dritte Person.
> 2. Die Überführung in die Vergangenheit.
> 3. Das Mitsprechen von Spielanweisungen und Kommentaren.
>
> (XXII, 644)

> three aids which may help estrange the actions and remarks of the characters
> being portrayed:
> 1. Transposition into the third person.
> 2. Transposition into the past.
> 3. Speaking the stage directions out loud.
>
> (Willett, 138)

But I imagine that the critics' objections would then bear on the difficulty
of identifying these techniques during an actual performance. During
rehearsals we can always stop to compare the alternatives, but how can
we tell during the play itself whether Olivier is quoting Shylock, acting
the role out with genuine feeling, or simply hamming it up?

Perhaps in this instance, however, the actor is more important than
the spectator, and we ought to begin by thinking of this Brechtian
'method' as a kind of ethos; or at least a moral training of a specific
type. Loyola's use of narratives is well known, and has been the object
of renewed attention precisely at the moment in which the whole

question of performance is itself under renewed scrutiny.[35] Meanwhile, I have already mentioned some of the other charismatic or cult-founding directors for whom acting itself becomes a symbolic ethical practice – of impoverishment, for example, as in Grotowski.

Brechtian quotation is, I believe, that as well, although it is an ethic directed towards very different flaws and weaknesses in the human constitution. But how this is meant to work can better be observed in another place: thus, in a famous essay, Sartre conveys the effect of John Dos Passos's style in a way that is remarkably consistent with these Brechtian hints and recommendations. It is a style as simple and neutral as Camus's in *L'Étranger*, but as peculiar at the same time: betraying the internal operation of a strange kind of mechanism which shuts off the empathy (or 'identification') that might otherwise be expected, and thereby manages to seem mannered and artificial through the very transparency of its plainness and its everyday colloquial ordinariness. In Camus's French, the operation of a tense we do not use in the same way (and which the French do not use in written narration) – the *passé composé* – allows the trick to be identified. This is not so easy to do with Dos Passos's English. Sartre manages, however, to tease out Dos Passos's mechanism: he is writing first-person narrative in the third person – that is to say, he is doing in his prose what Brecht recommended to his actors. One is tempted (following Bakhtin and Deleuze) to think of a kind of foreign language within the familiar one (yet a foreign language which has, in some Borgesian way, exactly the same words as ours, the same syntax and grammar, etc., etc.). But that – which is true of all modernism (following Bakhtin) or all minoritarian speech (following Deleuze) – is rather different and specific here. Here Sartre's critical machinery rewrites one of the principal interwar narratological oppositions (deriving from Gide and Ramon Fernandez): that between the novel (with its open present and future) and the *récit* (as a closed and henceforth immutable past): Dos Passos thus translates a novelistic present into the terms of that past, that immutability, which he conveys by way of the language of journalism, like a news report: 'From our special envoy: "Charlie Chaplin declares that he has just killed off the Tramp." Now I get it: Dos Passos reports all the utterances of his characters in the style of the press conference. . . . How simple and efficacious this technique: all he has to do is narrate a life in the style of American news coverage and life crystallizes into the social. . . .'[36] It is clear that Sartre here goes one step further than Brecht in identifying the language of the third-person narrative rewriting of a given act in terms of what is alienated and socially or collectively inauthentic (the Heideggerian 'man' or 'anybody' is mentioned, and a kind of Flaubertian vision of the omnipresence of the cliché and the stereotype under capitalism is also evoked).

But more to the point in our present context is the way in which this enthusiastic Sartrean endorsement includes its own specific type of ethic, an ethic in which the old opposition between individual morality and collective norms is transcended: At this point let Simone de Beauvoir, in her memoirs, have the floor:

> We were immediately bowled over by the deliberately shocking effects that Dos Passos had contrived. Cruelly, he observed mankind both in terms of the comedy labeled 'freedom' which they play out inside themselves, and also as the mere helpless projections of their situation. Sartre and I frequently attempted to observe some third person, or more often ourselves, in this stereoscopic fashion. Though we might walk through life in cheerful self-assurance, we were not guilty of self-complacency; Dos Passos had furnished us with a new critical weapon, and we took full advantage of it. For instance, we sketched out our conversation at the Café Victor as Dos Passos might have handled it: 'The manager smiled in a satisfied way, and they both felt furious. Sartre drew at his pipe, and said that perhaps it was not enough merely to sympathize with the revolution. The Beaver pointed out that he had his own work to do. They ordered two large beers, and said how hard it was to sort out what you owed other people from what you owed yourself. Finally they declared that if they had been dock workers they would undoubtedly have joined the Communist Party, but in their present position all they could be expected to do was always to side with the proletariat.' Two *petits bourgeois* invoking their unwritten work as an excuse for avoiding political commitment: that was the truth, and indeed we had no intention of forgetting it.[37]

It is less clear to what degree Sartre and Beauvoir practised this 'method' in their own novels; at any rate, their emphasis on social class and on the development of a critical self-consciousness of class among bourgeois intellectuals contrasts usefully as a technique with the Brechtian emphasis on history. For in Brecht it is less a matter of consigning a given individual to a preexisting social class, with its specific ideological values and outlook, than of transcending the double standard of individual and collective events. It is as though retelling individual events as though they were historical ones were not merely a satiric technique but also a new mode of self-knowledge. Thus, the quotation from *Me-ti* with which we began this Part, and in which Me-ti remarked on the absence of ethical precepts in the 'classics' (in other words, in Marx, Engels and Lenin), concludes as follows:

;s fand er also sehr nützlich gepriesen den historischen Stand-
ifahl er dem Einzelnen nach vielem Nachdenken, sich selber
Klassen und großen Menschengruppen historisch zu betrachten
isch zu benehmen. Das Leben, gelebt als Stoff einer Lebensbe-
vinnt eine gewisse Wichtigkeit und kann Geschichte machen.
r Ju Seser seine Erinnerungen schrieb, schrieb er in der dritten
h selber. Me-ti sagte: Man kann auch in der dritten Person

leben.

(XVIII, 188)

He also thought in this context that the historical viewpoint had been most usefully recommended. So it was that after much reflection he advised the individual to consider himself historically just like classes and large groups of people and to behave historically. Life, when lived as the material for a biography, takes on a certain gravity and can make history in its turn. When the warlord Ju Seser [Julius Caesar] wrote his memoirs, he wrote about himself in the third person. One can also live in the third person, Me-ti said.

7 Dualities of the Subject

But even on the basis of rewriting old stories into new ones, the issue of preexisting empirical content (as Barthes puts it) must necessarily come up; the third-person narrative may not look much like the first-person one, but it does not dissolve into some nameless flow of sheer perceptual or even sensory experience either. Yet my feeling is that this philosophical tension between the social and the metaphysical, between the named and the nameless, does not, for all that, disappear. It is simply displaced into a somewhat different yet related philosophical context which can be described as the tension, if not the opposition, between dualism and multiplicity – a tension which, in that sense, is something like a member of its own class: is this a dualism in itself, or, as Deleuze argues,[38] some kind of new multiplicity we have not yet identified? I want to avoid any truly addictive or life-threatening indulgence in these philosophical debates, but merely wish to point out that they are central to certain influential 'postmodern' ones.

To return to the concrete and to the texts: it would seem clear that the very first and simplest form of what we are calling 'dualism' in Brechtian theatrical practice is that of simple affirmation or denial. This is the most obvious space of Brechtian freedom, since in it a single gesture aims to project not only what will shortly have been done – that is to say, what is being done in front of us – but what might just as well not have been done, what might have been something else altogether, or simply have been omitted. This may be thought of as the most rudimentary representational form of Barthes's proairesis: the unfolding positively or negatively. And it would seem to offer a somewhat different style of play-acting from the one in which I segment my gestures or act myself out in the third person:

> Geht [der Schauspieler] auf die Bühne, so wird er bei allen wesentlichen Stellen zu dem, was er macht, noch etwas ausfindig, namhaft und ahnbar machen, was er noch nicht macht: das heißt, er spielt so, daß man die Alternative möglichst deutlich sieht, so, dass sein Spiel noch die andern Möglichkeiten ahnen läßt, nur eine der möglichen Varianten darstellt. Er sagt zum Beispiel: 'Das wirst du mir bezahlen' und er sagt *nicht*: 'Ich verzeihe dir das'. Er haßt seine Kinder und es steht *nicht* so, daß er sie liebt. Er geht nach links vorn und *nicht* nacht rechts hinten. Das was er *nicht* macht, muß in dem enthalten und aufgehoben sein, was er macht. So bedeuten alle Gesten und Sätze Entscheidungen, bleibt die Person unter Kontrolle und wird getestet. Der technische Ausdruck für dieses Verfahren heißt: Fixieren des *Nicht-Sondern*.

> (XXII, 643)

> When he appears on the stage, besides what he actually is doing he will at all essential points discover, specify, imply what he is not doing; that is to say he will act in such a way that the alternative emerges as clearly as possible, that his acting allows the other possibilities to be inferred and only represents one out of the possible variants. He will say for instance 'You'll pay for that', and not say 'I forgive you'. He detests his children; it is not the case that he loves them. He moves down stage left and not up stage right. Whatever he doesn't do must be contained and conserved in what he does. In this way every sentence and every gesture signifies a decision; the character remains under observation and is tested. The technical term for this procedure is 'fixing the "not . . . but"'.

> (Willett, 137)

But even in this fundamental text on the matter, it is clear that it is a good deal more comprehensive than the duality it seems at first to suggest. To be sure, Grusha's pity and mother-love, her decision to take up the abandoned baby and rescue it, is at first staged against the stark background of the other possibility: to get out of the besieged and burning palace as fast as she can, to save herself, to leave the royal baby behind for others to worry about or to be slaughtered by the rebels, as the case may be. But this does not exactly imply a range of other 'possible variants'; it is the decision, yes or no: just as Galy Gay's 'Umfunkionierung' into an imperialist soldier does not exactly convey, despite what Brecht himself says, the message that you can turn a man into *anything*: for the randomness of the anything is somehow lacking here, and the pedagogical demonstration does not really convince us that with the proper equipment and procedures, we could turn the 'mild-mannered fishmonger' into a statesman, for example, or an intellectual, or a great courtier, or a Mafia chief or pimp. Maybe one could do all those things, but it is not in the logic of this theatrical demonstration to prove this particular point: all we are shown is the binary transformation from 'mild' to 'ferocious', from 'civilian' to 'soldier', from 'married man' to 'bachelor', from 'colonized' to 'colonizer' and, no doubt, from Indian to British. It is an interesting meditation on what will in only a few years become fascism; yet from a literary point of view, it none the less seems locked into a Molière-type social satire, or drama of humours, in which we are given a standard or 'typical' starting point (the miser, the melancholia, the hypochondriac, etc.) on which we then ring the changes.

Yet I think it is important to argue against the notion that Brecht is simply a satirist, something that would lock him unduly back into his own era and his own specific society and milieu. History, in any case, opened that up for him explosively, and in the 1930s scattered his social experiences to the four corners; but it is not particularly a biographical point one wants to make either. Rather, the philosophical Brecht, the 'modernist' Brecht we want to project here, is something a little more than a social commentator or a critic of 'mœurs': even the Weimar dramas stand in a rather different relationship to Weimar itself than, say, Ibsen to the Norwegian society of his time, or almost any contemporary American playwright to the USA today. At the same time, as I have argued above, it is very important to rescue Brecht from 'irony' as the dominant value of a now traditional high modernist ideology: Northrop Frye has argued powerfully for a separation of satire from irony, which Wayne Booth, with equal plausibility, wishes to dispel (in order to reoccupy the terrain of satire with his normative idea of 'stable irony' against which he wishes to play off the modernist or unstable version).[39] But Brecht, as I want to show, is neither of these things, nor is he somewhere in between.

As a matter of fact, however, this kind of binary projection of opposite alternatives, of simply affirmation or denial, does not lead us back into the empirically rich, yet contingent content of social types and social satire but, rather, on into the stark abstractions of the so-called learning plays [*Lehrstücke*], about which we therefore need to say a word here.

This is the most experimental space of Brecht, at least taken in the modernist sense: and it is also the space of a kind of Brechtian minimalism, derived more, one would think, from the conventionalism of East Asian, but especially Japanese, theatre (and also of the Chinese performances of Mei lan-fan) than from European experimentalism from expressionism to Beckett. Here demands are made on both audience and actors for a radical simplification of experience, a reduction of action and gesture alike to the very minimum of decision as such, within a situation itself reduced to the most minimal machine for choosing. Here, then, the shreds and traces of content – the historical setting in ancient Rome or in revolutionary China, the representatives of opposing forces, the few sparse character traits of the virtually unnamed protagonists – remind us somewhat of those 'Merkmale' of the physical theatrical setting about which Brecht also theorized at some length, raising again the question of the difference between knowledge and appearance ('konstruktive Elemente der Dinge oder ihr spezifisches aussehen?': 'their constitutive elements or their specific perceptual appearance?'). But by this he did not mean the distinction between two kinds of static knowledge, between phenomenological contemplation as opposed to the abstract and the structural; rather, he had in mind very specifically the difference between production – construction as activity – and reception – or, in other words, contemplation as consumption: the confusion results from the state of things today, 'daß wir uns, Kinder des Zeitalters der Ware, den Dingen entweder produzierend *oder* konsumierend nähern und im allgemeinen überwältigend mehr konsumierend' (XXII, 247): 'we children of the commodity age approach things either in the stance of the producer or that of the consumer, and are generally overwhelmingly more given over to the process of consumption'. But in order to be staged or represented in its turn, this particular dualism must itself be given a rather different form or twist.

I also think we have every interest in disentangling the evolution of the *Lehrstück* from the related yet independent destiny of music in the Brechtian theatre. We know that in the earliest experimental period, in the late 1920s and early 1930s, music was integrated into a form of the cantata pioneered for radio as such, as in the *Lindbergh Flight*: this cantata is sometimes also described as a *Lehrstück* or 'learning play' (Brecht's own English invention, apparently); but so is the adaptation of Gorki's *Die Mutter*, which, however pedagogical it may be, does not quite seem of the same species as *Der Ja-sager* or *Die Massnahme*. Despite Hanns Eisler's intimate theoretical collaboration with Brecht, both during this period, in the American exile, and after the war in East Berlin, it seems to me important on the one hand to grasp how much more active and productive the connotations of music were in a Germany in which the performance of scores in the home, along with improvisation, was a far more natural matter than in many other countries, and also the degree in which, in the radio cantata, music also bears the sign of the technological and is associated with everything that constitutes a Brechtian conception of modernity (as opposed to purely aesthetic 'modernism', but by way of a relationship of form to content not fundamentally disjoined from Eisler's past as a disciple of Schoenberg and a proponent of the most 'modern' musical techniques). Whatever the destination of the cantatas and their interrelationship with radio technology, the more classical *Lehrstücke* (if I may put it that way) are, rather, associated with the classroom and with student pedagogy, whether in acting or in activism, and the discussion of them needs to be oriented in that direction first and foremost.

The sparseness of these plays, which return to an East Asian aesthetic of the void and the isolated object or item, is to be associated with precapitalist culture, I believe, rather than to that post-Auschwitz desolation so often identified in the plays of Samuel Beckett.[40] The radical dénouement of the Brechtian *Lehrstücke* is thus not to be grasped as symbolic training in some Grotowskian spiritual and mystical impoverishment, but it clearly does have an allegorical meaning, which the structuralist and poststructuralist thematics of the end of humanism and the death of the subject also convey, perhaps themselves even descending from it. For in Brecht's period, what is later called anti-humanism is essentially a polemic against an individualism which was necessarily part and parcel of bourgeois culture on the one hand, and was also clearly enough 'centred' from another, phenomenological or psychoanalytic, perspective.

Yet that very askesis of the post-humanist or post-individualist subject is subject to historical misunderstanding, particularly when the principal exhibit for the *Lehrstücke* in general is the notorious *Die Massnahme*, which has so often been taken as an apologia for Stalin's purge trials (to come), and as a call for literal self-sacrifice to the impersonal demands of revolution as such. The young comrade does indeed call for his own execution as a result of his own failures, thereby dramatizing his selfless commitment to the Party: and such lessons are peculiarly unsuitable to a time like our own, in which all repression or sacrifice tends to be interpreted as a mystification, and attributed to this or that ideological conspiracy. But we do not need either to be defensive about the unpleasantness and ruthlessness of *Die Massnahme*, or more deviously to defend Stalinism in order to avoid condemning it in the first place.

We need, rather, to understand that it is incomplete (despite the centrality Brecht supremely assigned it in his theatre work): for it is enough to examine the earlier related works, the pair of mirror-plays called *Der Ja-sager* and *Der Nein-sager*, to see what was missing here. For these plays, modelled on a traditional Noh play,[41] offer the alternating gestures already implied and recommended in the performance theories quoted above. In the first, the injured boy agrees to his own

death in order to follow ritual custom and avoid the failure of the
expedition. In the second, as its title suggests, the boy refuses to be
sacrificed, and the expedition turns back. This is spelling out the yes and
the no with a vengeance, the for and the against; and opens wide the fan
of choices and possibilities. It would have been enough to add a
counterpart to *Die Massnahme* itself for the misconceptions outlined
above to be discredited: the young comrade might refuse, and be
executed anyway; he might refuse and be carried on by his comrades,
who might in their turn fail on account of him, or unexpectedly succeed.
The political lesson in all these cases would be the same: the lesson about
the situation itself and its primacy; at the same time as the other
misconception of the *Massnahme*, surely even more galling for Brecht
than the imputation of Stalinism – namely the identification of this
drama as a genuine tragedy, which arouses our pity and fear – would
also have been preempted. But it is not a tragedy, it is a dramatization
of the dialectic, the primacy of the collective situation over individual
ethics. Yet if this is what the play means, and what the dialectic itself
means, then the central yet enigmatic status of *Die Massnahme* in
Brecht's work as a whole is secured.

We must now, however, draw another lesson, of a different kind,
from the peculiarities of the *Lehrstücke*: and this is no doubt the moment
to say that Reiner Steinweg's radical thesis on the *Lehrstücke*[42] still
seems to me to offer productive and not yet fully explored insights. To
be sure, a 'revolutionary' intervention of 1972 which has hardened into
orthodoxy, albeit not even classical status, lends its flank to every kind
of revisionism; nor is it to be unexpected that philological investigation
should leave it behind in this or that detail.[43] Yet Steinweg's proposition
unexpectedly completes the demonstration we have undertaken here: to
show how a specific kind of difference or opposition – the alternative
yes or no, the decision that foregrounds the 'Nicht/sondern', the 'not
this, rather that' – forms at least one of the levels of this dramaturgy –
or, shall we say, translates at least one philosophical implication of that
theatrical theory and practice.

Steinweg, as it will be recalled, argued that what was specific to the
Lehrstücke – and, indeed, unique in those experiments in stage dynamics
– was their exclusion of the public and, at the same time, a rotation of
the actors throughout the various roles. In other words, it is what in the
theatre is called a master class, but one which does not necessarily have
a master director present either: even though we must imagine *Schiff-
bauerdamm* as one continuous master class, to which a paying public is
invited only on selected occasions: Brecht's significance to the state was
such, indeed, that he was given the money and the resources, including

the personnel, not so much merely to create yet another theatre, as to
indulge the supreme wish of any true theatre person: infinite rehearsals,
in which, in true Brechtian fashion, all the alternatives can be tried out
in turn and endlessly debated. Meanwhile, the passage of the various
actors through all the roles necessarily creates a multidimensionality
which is the very essence of repertory theatre – that is to say, of theatre
as such – but can scarcely ever be realized programmatically and itself
theorized. This implies that as the text and its performance slowly blur
and disappear into enlarged discussions, into fights about interpretation
and the proposing of all kinds of alternative gestures and stage business,
we must begin to invent a new conception for the kind of art and
aesthetics that the *Lehrstück* seems to rehearse. It will have to avoid the
reification of the usual language of art works and objects, this new term,
but will have to include the discussions and the revisions, the proposed
alternatives, in some more substantial way than is generally done when
we think of the discussions with the audience that the Berliner Ensemble
and other dramatic companies have often advocated in the years since
the 1960s. Indeed, if something like the idea of a 'master class' is adopted
for such a strange new process-entity, one feature it makes clear is the
inseparable presence of so-called *theory* within the larger 'text' itself. It
is not that the theory becomes a work of art in its own right, nor does
the artistic text simply reincorporate the theory and become a new kind
of collage or experiment in 'mixed media'. Rather, theorizing, as we
have some of these processes noted down for us in Brecht's own
dramaturgical writings, is part of the process itself, and you could just
as easily claim that the original play or text exists in order to provoke
the theory and give it content, occasion and raw material as, more
conventionally, that the theory is simply there to guide a more fitting
production of the text. We will come back later to this point, whose
implications have not been exhausted.

What must now be shown, however, is that the Steinweg thesis – or,
if you prefer, the Steinweg aspect of Brecht's dramaturgical 'unity of
theory and practice' – also involves a negation or philosophical reversal
of the category of difference that has been proposed above. For the
operation can also be formulated as the supersession of just such an
opposition, and in particular the transcendence and *Aufhebung* very
precisely of the distinction between actor and public:

Die große Pädagogik verändert die Rolle des Spielens vollständig. Sie hebt das
System Spieler und Zuschauer auf. Sie kennt nur mehr Spieler, die zugleich
Studierende sind.

(XXI, 396)

The Great Learning completely transforms the role of acting itself. It sublates the system in which player and spectator are correlative. It henceforth knows only players who are learners [students, studiers] at one and the same time.

The differentiation on one level – the decision to act out this particular gesture; or not to act it out, or to act out its opposite – now proves to be the annulment of difference on another, and perhaps even more basic, one: namely, that between actors and public. Perhaps one should even go as far as to say that the achievement of identity on this second level requires the exercise of various forms of differentiation on the first: yet it is not clear which level is philosophically the more fundamental one. For is not the alternation of the 'not/but' a crucial one in the training of its performers in a specifically Brechtian freedom, in the conviction that *praxis* is possible in various forms, and that nothing is really necessary or inevitable in that sense?

On the other hand, the abolition of the difference between player and observer is philosophically no less fundamental, as the following fragment (from much the same period as the first, 1930–31) makes clear:

Die bürgerlichen Philosophen machen einen großen Unterschied zwischen den Tätigen und den Betrachtenden. Diesen Unterschied macht der Denkende nicht. Wenn man diesen Unterschied macht, dann überläßt man die Politik dem Tätigen und die Philosophie dem Betrachtenden, während doch in Wirklichkeit die Politiker Philosophen und die Philosophen Politiker sein müssen.

(XXI, 398)

Bourgeois philosophers insist on a fundamental distinction between action and contemplation. But the true thinker [the dialectician] does not make this distinction. If you do so, you leave politics to those who act and philosophy to those who contemplate; whereas in reality the politician must be a philosopher and the philosopher a politician.

That any number of other fundamental 'Western' or, at least, 'bourgeois' oppositions are also subsumed here – that between mental and manual labour, for example,[44] or that between art and life, that between ruler and ruled, and so on – is evident from the thematic range of Brecht's other notes and writings. Yet this particular 'sublation' or 'transcendence' is meant not to abolish both sides of the opposition but, rather, to complete both, to intensify what may be called the 'usefulness' of each, as the continuation of the previous quotation emphasizes (where the term 'state' means the socialist or revolutionary state):

Die Lust am Betrachten allein ist für den Staat schädlich; ebenso aber die Lust an der Tat allein. Indem die jungen Leute im Spiel Taten vollbringen, die ihrer eigenen Betrachtung unterworfen sind, werden sie für den Staat erzogen.

The pleasure in contemplation alone is harmful for the state; but so is the pleasure for the deed alone. To the degree to which young people play through symbolically complete deeds which are at one and the same time subjected to their own judgement, they can be said to be educated in view of the ideal state.

8   From Multiplicity to Contradiction

Yet there is an alternative to mere alternatives: instead of the movement that leads us simply *not* to be angry rather than to be angry, we can incongruously feel something else altogether – relief, for instance, or a distracted thankfulness, or euphoria or depression. Alongside the *Nicht/ sondern*, in other words, there is available a whole multiplicity of named feelings and emotions which are rarely opposites of one another, and can indeed sometimes seem to be mingled, surcharged, chemically combined.[45] What these psychological affects are exactly, how to tell feelings from emotions, how to rationalize the Mendeleev table of elements they constitute in the first place – these are the shifting sands on which 'sciences' such as psychology have been built. What is certain is that every culture has its own particular enumeration and configuration of such phenomena, which in our own run from the *Nichomachean Ethics* to Descartes's *Passions of the Soul*, before breaking apart, in the bourgeois era, to make a place for hitherto unnamed species: such as Rousseau's 'sympathy' – somewhere between the ancient 'pity' and the Brechtian 'empathy', a primordial discovery of the existence of the Other – along with Kierkegaard's 'anxiety' or *Angst*, Baudelaire's *ennui*, and perhaps even various modern forms of the feeling of the 'sublime'.

But this very enumeration reminds us that the opposition between simple presence or absence and sheer articulated multiplicity is then intersected by that very different matter of the named and the unnamed, or the unnameable: a new opposition between what Barthes called the empirical, the already existing and stereotypically familiar, and that fresh and new kind of intensity which, for good or ill, is like nothing we have ever known or will be likely to know again. Modernism has been professionally interested in these last, adding a few new names in the process (Dostoevskyan? Jamesian?) in a race and a patenting process Brecht does not seem to have been particularly interested in, even though his own V-effect is certainly a way of doing something to the familiar, satiric, preexisting entities which does not simply leave them stamped with moral disapproval yet preserves them as still known social quantities. Peachum's psychic turmoil, for example, already familiar to us from the *Three-Penny Opera* as a frugal concern over the waste involved in Polly's secret marriage to Macheath, but immensely darkened and intensified by his financial anxieties in the *Three-Penny Novel*, is only one aspect of the psychological novelty of this particular character, whose representation can be juxtaposed in complexity with Nietzsche's critique of religion and altruism. In the episode that interests us here, however, the scheme to profit from government contracts during the Boer War, and to sell off three unseaworthy ships at top prices, affords a unique context in which to record and register some of Peachum's more naive reactions to this scam of which he himself is a victim:

> Er war in das Geschäft eingestiegen, weil die Regierung betrogen werden sollte. Das hatte ihm ein blindes Vertrauen eingeflößt.
>
> (XVI, 46)

> He got into the scheme in the first place because it was a question of cheating the government, a prospect which had inspired him with blind gullibility.

It would be a mistake to think of this, as it is no doubt easier to do for the *Three-Penny Opera* as such (on which we will in any case also touch later), as the simple techniques of inversion of Brechtian cynicism. What is proposed is a whole new psychological system, in which the basic building blocks remain the same — there is trust, for example, conduct based on honesty, a moral sense of outrage and judgement of good and evil: all these are as traditional as one likes, and certainly to be found at least as far back as Weberian Protestant capitalism and the forms of thrift and upright activity developed there. Only the relations between all these things have been utterly modified. In particular Peachum's view of human nature ('die Welt ist arm, der Mensch ist schlecht', as we know already from the *Three-Penny Opera*), while certainly infused with a religious sense of sin and guilt, has been deepened and expanded, to the point where its resonance is scarcely the same:

> Andere Leute zu betrügen, das konnte wirklich die ehrliche Absicht eines Geschäftsmanns sein. Nun war die Welt eben immer noch schlechter, als man sich denken konnte. In der Schlechtigkeit gab es ja überhaupt keine Grenze. Das war Peachums tiefste Überzeugung, eigentlich seine einzige.
>
> (XVI, 46)

> After all, the intention of any businessman to deceive other people is an honourable one. Yet the world was even more rotten than one could imagine.

There were no limits to its rottenness. This was Peachum's deepest conviction, indeed his only genuine conviction.

As in the greatest moments of a delirious satiric transcendence (as in Pope's *Dunciad*, for example), a well-nigh metaphysical dimension comes into view that inspires the dizziness and the nausea of the very greatest things: save that, unlike Pope or Juvenal, or Wyndham Lewis, here the author can scarcely be said to express his own *Weltanschauung*: at best he opportunistically takes advantage of one of his own characters to test his voice in the metaphysical resonance. But it is only one voice among many others, even though in a later situation, *The Good Person of Szechuan*, we may imagine Mr Shui ta (the 'bad cousin') to espouse something of a Peachumesque view of human nature, and thus to turn the multiplicity of the *Three-Penny Novel* into precisely one of those dualities of the previous section, the alternating gesture which chooses now generosity and now harsh debt-collection and a conviction of the general worthlessness of human beings.

Yet all this can be treated in different combinations yet again: so it is that Mac himself, a good deal more permissive than Peachum in his immediate reactions (albeit a very good deal more enigmatic as an identity in general, in that very different from the flamboyant Mac of the *Opera*), ruminates upon related matters as follows, wondering if friendliness may not be the best policy after all:

Der Kunde trete dem Ladeninhaber gewöhnlich gegenüber als ein bedürfnisloser, am Geld hängender, übelwollender und mißtrauischer Bursche. Er sei ganz eindeutig feindlich eingestellt. Im Verkäufer erblicke er nicht seinen Freund und Ratgeber, der alles für ihn zu tun bereit ist, sondern einen bösen Menschen mit Hintergedanken, der ihn verführen und betrügen will. Demgegenüber verzweifle der Verkäufer zumeist, von vornherein eingeschüchtert, und gebe jede Bemühung auf, den Kunden wirklich für sich zu gewinnen, ihn zu bessern, menschlich aufzuschließen, kurz, ihn zum Käufer von Format zu machen. Er lege gottergeben seine Waren auf den Tisch und setze seine einzige Hoffnung auf den Mangel und das nackte Elend, das den Kunden hin und wieder einfach zwingt, einen Kauf zu tätigen.

   In Wirklichkeit werde der Kunde dadurch aber zutiefst mißverstanden und verkannt. Er sei im Grunde seines Wesens nämlich besser, als er aussehe. Nur gewisse tragische Erlebnisse im Schoße seiner Familie oder im Erwerbsleben hätten ihn mißtrauisch und verschlossen gemacht. Im Grunde seines Wesens lebe eine stille Hoffnung, als das erkannt zu werden, was er sei: ein ganz großer Käufer! Er wolle nämlich kaufen! Denn ihm fehle ja so unendlich viel!

Und wenn ihm nichts fehle, fühle er sich unglücklich! Dann wolle er, daß man ihn überzeuge, daß ihm etwas fehle! Er wisse so wenig.

(XVI, 135)

The client normally materializes before the shopkeeper as a skin-flinted, ill-intentioned, mistrustful individual without any needs at all. His attitude is unequivocally hostile. He perceives the seller, not as a friend and counsellor, prepared to help him in every way, but rather as a two-faced and evil person who is out to seduce and deceive him. In this situation the seller, chastened, most often becomes discouraged, and abandons any attempt to win the client over, to improve him, to open genuinely human relations with him – in short, to transform him into a first-class buyer. Trusting in God alone, the shopkeeper simply lays his goods out on the table and sets a last hope on improvidence and sheer misery, which now and then simply force a customer to bestir himself. But this perspective truly misconceives and truly misrepresents the client. For at the very core of his being the latter is better than he looks. It is only tragic experiences in the bosom of his family or in business life that have made him closed and mistrustful. At the very core of his being there persists a quiet hope ultimately to be recognized for what he really is, namely, a buyer of grand proportions! He actually wants to buy! He needs so very very much! And when he has no wants, he is miserable! So he really wants to be persuaded that he needs something. He requires instruction!

Here it is not the ethical recommendation that is unfamiliar but, rather, the background of values, the *Weltanschauung*, against which it is staged: we are also used to the Darwinian struggle for survival among the social classes as in the jungle itself: capitalists against other capitalists fully as much as against labour (it is a story we will encounter again in *St Joan*). But it is less customary, even though plausible enough in hindsight, to grasp business itself and the market as a ferocious struggle between two eternally hostile groups.

Estrangement can finally also be inscribed within the narrative itself, as when, whether in jest or not, Macheath is offered a rather wooden satirical caricature, an anecdote in which a black sheep of the Rothschild family decides to try an utterly novel and hitherto unheard-of strategy: honesty itself. He is examined by psychiatrists, kept away from the family business for many years, and so on. It is Mac's reaction which displays the genius of Brechtian narrative, the sudden emergence of the unexpected and the new, the ruthless tearing apart of a familiar character to reconstruct him afresh, in the form of a plodding and dim-witted Mac who seems utterly unrelated characterologically to other more daring Macs, those 'captains of industry' filled with an initiative comparable only to that of the great military leaders; this one, however, strikes us as the representative of another species altogether:

Macheath hörte angestrengt zu. Er konnte den Inhalt der Erzählung des alten
Miller nur schwer verstehen; er kam ihm sozusagen nicht auf den Grund.
   Man sieht daraus, sagte er schließlich unsicher, daß man im Geschäftsleben
alles ausprobieren muß. Meinen Sie das? Wenn man vorwärts kommen und
am Schluß des Jahres ein anständiges Plus haben will, muß man es mit allem
versuchen, sogar mit den ausgefallensten Sachen.

                                                                    (XVI, 134)

Macheath listened with furrowed brow; he could scarcely follow old Miller's
story, let alone understand it. He did not get the point, so to speak. 'So it
follows,' he hesitantly observed, 'that you have to try everything in business
life. Is that what you mean? If you want to get ahead and have a respectable
balance sheet at the end of the year, you have to try everything, even the most
ludicrous ideas?'

   But this is precisely the point at which the flux of inner stages intersects
with questions of identity: who is this new Mac, for example? Is 'he'
simply the result of the cobbling of named emotions and reactions
together in new ways (a proposition that might also be expressed in the
Russian Formalist notion of the representation of character as sheer
opportunism dictated by the nature of the effects you wish to combine)?
But even this – which might be based on a conception of aesthetic
illusionism, of making the audience believe in this or that more 'realistic',
which is to say, in Brechtian terms, more stereotypical and familiar,
character or psychology – does begin to presuppose a very postmodern
metaphysic indeed: that of the construction of the psychological and the
personality, if not that of the 'death of the subject' itself, its void and
nullity, its minimal existence as a kind of *béance*.
   At any rate, two related conceptions or categories need to be introduced here, which begin their lives as elements in Brecht's dramaturgy,
in his theatrical texts, but seem to me gradually to take on a heightened
philosophical significance in their own right: these are *Trennung* (or
separation) and *distance* – inner distance being, if you like, simply a
special form of *Trennung*, while the latter necessarily implies and
imposes the production of distance as such (where none may have
existed or been visible before). On the other hand, for *Trennung* to be
visible as itself, the two separated items or dimensions need to be
somehow superimposed, held together within a perception that registers
their distance from each other as 'a radical separation of the elements'
('eine radikale Trennung der Elemente': XXIV, 79; Willett, 37): 'Musik,
Wort und Bild mussten mehr Sebständigkeit erhalten': 'words, music
and setting must become more independent of one another' – XXIV, 79;
Willett, 38). Yet this is not yet a positive or substantive formulation, let
alone an aesthetic in its own right, in so far as Brecht's programme is

still, at this point (1930), directed against *Verschmelzung* or, in other words, *fusion* of the various elements (what has in recent times rather loosely been called the 'organic' as opposed to the 'mechanical' or the 'heterogeneous'):

> Solange 'Gesamtkunstwerk' bedeutet, daß das Gesamte ein Aufwaschen ist, solange also Künste 'verschmelzt' werden sollen, müssen die einzelnen Elemente alle gleichermaßen degradiert werden, indem jedes nur Stichwortbringer für das andere sein kann. Der Schmelzprozeß erfaß den Zuschauer, der ebenfalls eingeschmolzen wird und einen passiven (leidenden) Teil des Gesamtkunstwerkes darstellt.
>
> (XXIV, 79)

> As long as the expression 'Gesamtkunstwerk' (or 'integrated work of art') means that the integration is a 'soup', as long as the arts are supposed to be fused together, the various elements will equally be degraded, and each will act as a mere 'cue' to the rest. The process of fusion extends to the spectator, who also gets thrown into the melting pot and becomes a passive (suffering) part of the total work of art.
>
> (Willett, 37–8)

Yet the clarity with which clashing elements stand out over against each other – as opposed to a formless loss of specificity which extends to the very precision or intoxication of the spectator's feelings – is not necessarily the primary aesthetic function of *Trennung*: although it may be that as well, and the decentred structure of Brecht's theatrical writings allows one to wheel them around in various directions, and to foreground a specific theme or rhetorical emphasis, to mould them into what looks like an unambiguous polemic situation. Here, however, it would be equally pertinent to rewrite the call for dissonant clarity, in the work and within the spectator alike, as a formal category that can apply to the audience and therefore, by extension and implication, to the collectivity itself. Thus, Aristotelian catharsis is meant to unite an audience, symbolically to unify a disparate public:

> Die herrschende Ästhetik verlangt vom Kunstwerk, indem sie eine unmittelbare Wirkung verlangt, auch eine alle sozialen und sonstigen Unterschiede der Individuen überbrückende Wirkung. . . . An die Herstellung dieses [auf der Basis des allen Zuhörern gemeinsamen 'allgemein Menschlichen' entstehenden] Kollektivum ist die nichtaristotelische Dramatik vom Typus der *Mutter* nicht interessiert. Sie spaltet ihr Publikum.
>
> (XXIV, 128)

In calling for an unmediated impact, the aesthetics of the day call for an effect that flattens out all social and other distinctions between individuals. . . . Non-Aristotelian drama of *The Mother*'s sort is not interested in the establishment [on the basis of the 'common humanity' shared by all spectators alike] of such a collective entity. It divides its audience.

(Willett, 60)

This is not to say only that theatre is political in its formal effects, but also that it is itself a figure for the social more generally, which it seeks to divide and set against itself. The theatre must thus even symbolically reenact class struggle; and the theory of the theatre will become allegorical of the process itself, generating on the one hand an abstract aesthetic or formal doctrine – that of *Trennung* and dissonance, inner distance and the like – and on the other the shape of a whole politics (involving class division and polemic struggle), while on yet another level a specific figure for subjectivity is produced.

These levels are themselves distinct from the individual performance which is a part of the theory and entertains an inner distance with it: this is not, then, a conventional work-of-art situation in which it is the work which is allegorical and generates the specific levels of meaning out of itself. Brecht's dramaturgy, I believe, turns this inside out: the theory envelops the individual work, rather than the other way around. It is this which guards the Brechtian work against a wholesale aesthetization, against a complete foundering into the sensory and the aesthesis of spectacle and performance, as in postmodern heterogeneity. For the latter is also allegorical; its surcharged and swarming perceptual spectacles also mean 'the subjective', in the *éloge* of inner schizophrenic flux, or the multiplication and flow of identities and subject-positions; and also political or collective, in the commitment to identity politics and hybridization, the combinations of micro-groups and the slippage between them on a social level in which the political is itself inherent (rather than, as in liberal democracy, standing outside the social in the form of institutions). But this complex postmodern allegory is immanent; it does not express itself in a theoretical level which can surround and articulate it. Alongside all the specific features and values Brecht shares with the postmodern, then – in the present case, the aesthetic of *Trennung* – stands out the glaring absence of the dramaturgical writings, of the very idea of the (Brechtian) theatre itself: or rather, a specifically Brechtian theatre is one for whom the idea of the theatre is a pulsating allegorical process, including, but greater than, the individual work or performance.

Yet the theory is not an idea, exactly: that is to say, it is not a meaning, which might be embodied in the work, and to which everything else would be hierarchically subsumed: as witness his dismissal of standard play form and the well-made aesthetic:

Aber diese Manier, alles einer Idee unterzuordnen, die Sucht, den Zuschauer in eine einlinige Dynamik hineinzuhetzen, wo er nicht nach rechts und links, nach unten und oben schauen kann, ist vom Standpunkt der neueren Dramatik abzulehnen. Auch in die Dramatik ist die Fußnote und das vergleichende Blättern einzuführen.

(XXIV, 58–9)

this way of subordinating everything to a single idea, this passion for propelling the spectator along a single track where he can look neither right nor left, up nor down, is something that the new school of playwriting must reject. Footnotes, and the habit of turning back in order to compare notes, need to be introduced into playwriting too.

(Willett, 44)

The specific impurity recommended here concerns the titles, about which we have already spoken; yet a larger conception of internal multiplicities speaks through these lines. One would be tempted to cite Flaubert's remark: 'il faut qu'il y ait à boire et à manger sur chaque page', if these multiple dishes, tastes, textures and liquids, did not smack so aggressively of the culinary and consumption. Eisenstein's 'montage of attractions' also comes to mind for the joyous mixed chaos of the aesthetic in question, yet is at the same time too linear and insufficiently allegorical.[46]

For here, once again, the dramaturgical recommendation is precisely allegorical, and the taste for the intervention of foreign bodies like footnotes is also a statement about acting and the virtuality of the act as such:

Der Schauspieler spielt so, daß man die Alternative möglichst deutlich sieht, so, daß sein Spiel noch die anderen Möglichkeiten ahnen läßt, nur eine der möglichen Varianten darstellt.

(XXII, 643)

the actor will act in such a way that the alternative emerges as clearly as possible, that his acting allows the other possibilities to be inferred and only represents one out of the possible variants.

(Willett, 137)

But it is also a symbolic reenactment of multiple hesitations and alternative possibilities within interpretation itself (which, of course, is not merely a spectator sport and a form of commentary but determines the actor's choices, and the way in which he shows the meaning of his own gesture). This is not exactly undecideability, this interpretive hesitation: it does not spill out into the formless; on the other hand, it incites the spectator to form further thoughts and test them against each other and against the initial event or happening which is their pretext.

Thus, with reference to the opening scenes of the *Galileo*, in which the
scientist teaches Andreas about the solar system, Brecht tells us:

> Was die Lektion anlangt, magst du übrigens entscheiden, ob bloß dem das
> Herz voll ist, das Maul überläuft, so daß er zu jedem davon reden würde,
> selbst zu einem Kinde, oder ob das Kind ihm das Wissen erst entlocken muß,
> indem es, ihn kennend, Interesse zeigt.
>
> (XXIII, 90)

> you will have to decide whether this means that [Galileo] is so obsessed with
> his idea that he can't help talking about it, even to a child, or whether the
> child, knowing how he is, has had to draw it out of him by showing his own
> interest.
>
> (Willett, 199)

Perhaps these are indeed inseparable and perfectly consistent 'interpretations'; yet they offer distinct faces, or *Abschattungen*, of the situation
under inspection: the second harking back to the end of the Lao-tse
poem –

> Aber rühmen wir nicht nur den Weisen
> Dessen Name auf dem Buche prangt:
> Denn man muß dem Weisen seine Weisheit erst entreißen.
> Darum sei der Zöllner auch bedankt.
>
> (XII, 34)

> But the honour should not be restricted
> To the sage whose name is clearly writ.
> For the wise man's wisdom needs to be extracted
> So the customs man deserves his bit –
>
> (Poems, 316)

– while the first directs our attention to Galileo's possible weaknesses: is
he obsessed by speculation, as one might be obsessed with physical
pleasures? Is it good to be so obsessed by truth and ideas; are they not
somehow perhaps eclipsed by this rather different passion? Meanwhile,
can Galileo then be so obviously manipulated by others? Allegorically,
is possession by an idea not precisely that univocality, that 'restlos' (utter
and complete, Stanislavskian) transformation into a single thing, which
the Brechtian aesthetic resists? Should one not have a certain distance
from one's idea? And so forth: the questions are not the meanings of the
play, exactly; rather, they indicate how it must be used; nor are they
some doctrine which it teaches like a *Lehrstück* in the literal sense of
thesis drama. Yet as questions and lines of reflection they must be
separated from each other, each one kept at a certain minimal distance,

even though the scene on stage is their concrete embodiment unification.

So from *Trennung* we come back again to the question of distance itself, and even to that of the distance which distance maintains from itself, so to speak. Whatever Brechtian acting may be in reality (a question always answered by designating what it is not – Stanislavskian or Aristotelian, for example), I must think of the way in which the greatest actors – an Olivier, for example, both star or protagonist and character actor all at once, irrespective of his age and the roles he chose at various moments of his career – maintains just that slight distance from Heathcliff or Othello, as from the fictional version of Dr Mengele (in *Marathon Man*): this, which in the actor's earliest career might have been thought of as a certain coldness and haughtiness – which might, in other words, have been interpreted as an acted character trait in its own right – in fact deploys just that slight barely perceptible silence around the lines themselves, and also very much that process of watching one's self act that Brecht so admired in the Chinese theatre:

Der Artist sieht sich selber zu . . . und sieht . . . mitunter nach dem Zuschauer, als wolle er sagen: Ist es nicht genau so? Aber er sieht auch auf seine eigenen Arme und Beine, sie anführend, überprüfend, am Ende vielleicht lobend.

(XXII, 201)

the artist observes himself . . . as though also looking at the spectator and saying, is it not like this? But he also looks at his own arms and legs, presenting them, examining them, perhaps ultimately praising them. . . .

(Willett, 92)

This slight distance across which he also examines his own role (Olivier catching his breath at the diamonds, showing his astonishment manneristically with quivering hands) might then, of course, be reinterpreted as narcissism, being drawn back into the ordinary aesthetic situation as content and read as a specific trait, not as a form; or it might – using the word we have just written – be thought mannered, and thereby attributed to Olivier as a real person, a psychology with certain kinds of character traits, rather than to the impersonal gesture itself. Perhaps distance thus needs to be exemplified in a more purely temporal way, in that strange rubato, that slight hesitation, of Rubinstein as he separates out the individual notes of a theme of Chopin, and seems to designate each note on the keyboard an instant before he presses the key and plays it. Yet the notes do not come too late; each is struck with a decisiveness that none the less surrounds them with silence and offers them to us like a kind of demonstration. For at this point distance has become that minimal space around each stroke, and in the theoretical object, as it turns, the grand and central Brechtian gesture of *showing* (to which we will return) has slowly come to displace that of surcharge and bristling heterogeneity; the silence around each element (like the empty places in those Chinese paintings he so admired) has taken the place of the piercing overlay of notes and cries, the acidic savour of differentiation.

Now we must say why such distances and separations do not simply fold back into the general taste of the *Zeitgeist* for the discontinuous rather than the organic, the break rather than continuity, the conflictual rather than unification. And of course they do exemplify that as well, and this general disengagement of forms and categories which we feel to be actual – and which thereby constitute a symbolic repudiation of the formal values of the past, and the emergence of a *Novum* whose ugliness, as Gertrude Stein put it, is 'part of this very struggle to be born'[47] – this is surely one of the great historical meanings of Brecht's work in general, to have theorized and thereby foregrounded a process at work all around him in various aesthetic and ideological forms and spaces, and to have made it possible for us to perceive it abstractly, and to give it a name and an expression.

But it is also crucial to understand that for Brecht, these qualities which we have been enumerating – dissonance, *Trennung*, distance, separation, surcharge, multiplicity, and so on – also have a meaning. And it is a meaning rather distinct from that of non-identity or heterogeneity, which are the current terms of ideological celebration, even though it includes those and draws them into its own allegorical centrality. For that meaning is *contradiction*, and a Brechtian method is not fully realized if we have not begun to understand how the merely distinct and differentiated is gradually to be drawn into contradiction itself, or rewritten as contradiction, unveiled and disclosed as contradiction; or finally, like a role one studies, acted and acted out in the form of sheer contradiction as such. (We might also have identified contradiction as sheer change, and reinterpreted it in that new light of the passing and emergence of all things; but this new gesture of turning the theoretical object around and showing or revealing, demonstrating, yet another of its faces, will be reserved for later on.)

The issue of contradiction as such then becomes the central difference between Brecht (and his whole era) and our own *Zeitgeist* (by which I mean a progressive *Zeitgeist*, not the dominant market-rhetorical one): the question about adjustment or consistency between the two positions can be framed in different ways depending on whether the aesthetic or the philosophical level is at stake. As for subjectivity itself – which, I believe for most contemporaries is the really crucial issue, and which allegorically masquerades itself through the other arguments – I think I can show that this is not particularly a problem, and that Brecht, rather, prepares current notions of subjectivity and is a forerunner in this regard, rather than an old-fashioned personality – a centred or individualist subjectivity – which would always stand in conflict with current values.

But even before the emergence of a political allegory within the level of a discourse of psychic fragmentation, we must note the identification of the two levels, and in particular the association of external with internal multiplicities, which alone authorizes an analogical association between the collective as aggregate or multiple and the fragmentation of the psyche into so many distinct subject-positions. Here once again *Mann ist Mann* is instructive as a prototype; and an insistence on Galy Gay's psychic de- and re-construction [*Umbildung*] needs to be completed by a reminder of his 'external' and social relationship, as a loner, to the male collective of the army. It is a theme which perhaps reflects some still pre-Marxian ambivalence about collective values on the part of the playwright; or perhaps we should simply register a kind of withdrawal of judgement and investment from these stereotypes – the imperialist army is certainly a bad collective, but Galy Gay's 'individualistic' hesitations and plans for happiness – 'I have decided to buy a fish for dinner' – are not unequivocally and ideologically endorsed either. Brecht rewrote the 1926 play several times later on; and for a radio version, paradoxically, began to argue that 'this Galy Gay is no weakling, on the contrary he is the strongest. But to be sure he is the strongest only after he stops being a private person, he becomes strong in the group': 'dieser Galy Gay ist kein Schwächling, im Gegenteil, er ist der Stärkste. Er ist allerdings erst der Stärkste, nachdem er aufgehört hat, eine Privatperson zu sein, wird erst in der Masse stark' (II, 409). Meanwhile, a few years later still, a variant of the central poem (something like the 'moral of the play') will read like this:

Denn der Mensch is gerne zu dritt und am liebsten zu viert
So dass er gern aus einem einer von vieren wird.

(XXI, 333)

For man loves the company of fours and threes
And is only too happy to stop being one and start being one-fourth.

Thus the dramatic situation makes it virtually impossible to distinguish between the external or social – the emplacement among a number of people or characters – and whatever readjustment on *Trennung* may be taking place inside the head, within the psychic functions or the old-fashioned organic unity of the individual. Some remarkable prose fragments, however, make up for this formal incapacity:

> 'Ich' bin keine Person. Ich entstehe jeden Moment, bleibe keinen. Ich entstehe in der Form einer Antwort. In mir ist permanent, was auf solches antwortet, was permanent bleibt.
>
> (XXI, 404)

> 'I' am no person. I come into being in every moment and scarcely last. I emerge in the form of an answer. The only permanence in me is what answers that call for an answer, what thereby remains permanent.

It is a Beckett-like drift scarcely held in place by the afterthought of a situation-and-response framework: if the former self is nothing but a series of reflexes, then at least what is responded to can be thought to lend it some greater, but very different, stability. But this dawning of a proto-Marxian conception of the situation (and even of the *ground* or of History itself) can equally well, from a post-contemporary position, seem a mode of containment, and a way of managing the otherwise frightening chaos of psychic flux that threatens individuality's dissolution.

Such an objection will probably be even more appropriate for another, even more written and literary, fragment from the same period (1930):

> Sie [die Person] fällt in Teile, sie verliert ihren Atem. Sie geht über in anderes, sie ist namenlos, sie hort keinen Vorwurf mehr, sie flieht aus ihrer Ausdehnung in ihre kleinste Grösse, aus ihrer Entbehrlichkeit in das Nichts – aber in ihrer kleinsten Grösse erkennt sie tiefatmend übergegangen ihre neue und eigentliche Unentbehrlichkeit im Ganzen.
>
> (XXI, 320)

> The person falls to pieces, loses its breath. It passes over into something else, is nameless, no longer hears reproaches, fleeing its extension into its smallest dimension, fleeing its dispensability into nothingness – yet on reaching that smallest dimensionality, with a deep breath at having passed across, it recognizes its indispensability in the whole.

The language (Cartesian 'Ausdehnung' or extension, for example) betrays Brecht's extensive readings in classical philosophy during this period; and we will see later on how his *Me-ti, or, the Book of Twists and Turns* refashions this inherited terminology into a whole new doctrine of aggregates. Just as the spark of existence is identified in the earlier quoted fragment with its capacity to answer some external sense of situation, so here too the process of divisibility (never quite infinite) comes to rest in a swarm of atoms or molecules which it does not seem quite right to reidentify with older organic totalities.

In any case, what I have wanted to show here is something rather different: that contemporary theoretical struggles, ostensibly waged around aesthetics (political versus autonomous, text versus work) and even around abstract philosophical issues (the totality as such), are finally, from an allegorical standpoint, not the ultimate ones, and do not identify the political issues that are finally at stake here. In fact, the third term – the collective – does not mark a return to the centred subject after its opposite number, the decentred one; but, rather, the transcendence of both towards something else. I suggest that Cold War anti-Marxian and anti-Communist stereotypes will play their part in certain versions of an aesthetic of heterogeneity, but will limit myself to noting the irony of attributing a 'centred' dramaturgy to Brecht, whose plays – however experimental they once seemed – are considered, in their overfamiliarity, to have been made obsolescent by Beckett (whom he once planned to stage) or, better still, by Robert Wilson, if not by Heiner Müller. The *Lehrstücke* are then appealed to to confirm this formal and conceptual rigidity, whereas in fact (as I hope to have shown) they do just the opposite. The exemplary text for an argument of this kind would be, I imagine, Derrida's attack on Lévi-Strauss,[48] which argues that the structuralism of the latter, however much it wishes to disaggregate older conceptions of meaning based on identity, itself remains centred. Whether in fact the stream or flux, the decentred heterogeneities, of modern works have been able to be as purely decentred as this is also an empirical question; and the discussion would probably also need to raise the question of the media, and in particular of theatre versus film (or radio versus video) as the form in which time is irreversible (and in which the flux in question can thereby be most suitably expressed and dramatized).

The philosophical version of this quarrel then necessarily takes as its centrepiece contradiction and negation; and finds its most authoritative text in Gilles Deleuze's valorization of differentiation over negation; however, dialecticians and Hegelians will already have lost this battle if they initially agree to its terms. I will therefore leave it to the Brecht friends among the Deleuzians (there must be some!) to show that what the playwright (and perhaps even Hegel himself) called contradiction was in many instances only a larger tent or umbrella for rich and subtle differentiations of all kinds. It is more important at this stage to show that, for both, contradiction is a moment in a process rather than a static structure. I want to argue that for Brecht, the dialectic – the 'Grosse Methode' – is defined and constituted by the search for and discovery of contradictions. Perhaps one might even say: by the construction of contradictions – since it is as a reordering process that it is necessary to grasp the dialectical method in Brecht: as the restructuring of juxtapositions, dissonances, *Trennungen*, distances of all kinds, in terms of contradiction as such.

But this is exactly what happens in the work of Brecht's favourite Western philosopher as well: Hegel himself, whom Brecht provocatively characterized as a great humorist, and whose most illustrious 'jumping frog' narrative can be found in the central chapter of the greater *Logic*: the so-called 'Determinations of Reflexion'. The story told by this chapter – is it a classical story or not? Could one estrange this narrative as well? Are its characters or actants reflexive? Self-designating? Self-distancing?, and so on – is something like a *Bildungsroman*, or at least a tale of the fortunes of a phenomenon called Identity, which might be rewritten (in the language of the *Phenomenology*, for example) as familiarity *per se*: how otherwise would we recognize anything, how otherwise would a stable world of things come into being around us (how, indeed, could a stable personality or sense of inner 'identity' otherwise gradually emerge within us, an organization of temporal continuity, or complete actions or projects, and so on and so forth)? But at the very moment at which Identity has begun to make itself at home, and to win adherence on all sides as the dominant or fundamental category, the most necessary one, without which we could not even be human in the first place, it suddenly undergoes a fundamental challenge, which shakes its pretences and claims to the very ground, reducing them to so much flimsy propaganda or ideology. For this is the moment of Difference as such, the moment in which it becomes obvious that *omnis determinatio est negatio*: 'it is identity as difference that is identical with itself'.[49] You can define a thing, say what it is in its innermost identity, only by showing what it is not, thus opening the floodgates to a host of minor and major differences. This is virtually a social revolution among the philosophical categories, the seizure of power of the immense mass of subordinates and subalterns, who dethrone the monarchical figure of Identity as such, and claim to rule in a Deleuzian flux as far as the eye can see.

Perhaps, however, like all 'bourgeois' revolutions, this one is not the last word either: for these innumerable and multitudinous differences are not all 'equally' different from one another: one does not exactly want to say that new hierarchies come into being but, rather, that factions and parties begin to re-form. 'Difference in itself is self-related difference; as such, it is the negativity of itself, the difference not of another, but *of itself from itself*; it is not itself but its other. But that which is different from difference is identity. ... Difference [thus] possesses both moments'.[50] This is the moment Hegel calls 'diversity', in which it gradually becomes obvious – in a kind of philosophical Thermidor – that 'Difference' also depends on 'Identity', and that what has come into being is not the boundless sway of sheer Difference, but, rather, something rather different: the 'unity of Identity and Difference' – if not, indeed, the 'identity of Identity and Not-identity' – out of which, in a most crucial moment of change and turnover indeed, Opposition emerges: as such, as a new actant. Or rather, oppositions emerge, in which the older random multiplicities begin to be recognized as so many provisional dualisms. In Marx, clearly enough, this is the moment of the emergence of modern class struggle from the indifferent equalities and juridical equivalences of the bourgeois revolution; but in some larger or Brechtian sense it is also the moment in which the relationality of differences begins to come to the surface – or, if you prefer, begins to be organized, rewritten, constructed:

> Each [moment, i.e. identity and difference] has an indifferent self-subsistence of its own through the fact that it has within itself the relation to its other moment; it is thus the whole, self-contained opposition. As this whole, each is mediated with itself *by its other* and *contains* it. But further, it is mediated with itself by the *not-being of its other*; thus it is a unity existing on its own and it *excludes* the other from itself. ... It is thus the contradiction that, in positing identity with itself by *excluding* the negative, makes itself into the *negative* of what it excludes from itself, that is, makes itself into its opposite.[51]

This is a crucial moment also for the misreading and misunderstanding of the dialectic, for it is here that the latter's enemies are likely to read the 'unity of opposites' as mere 'unity' *tout court*, and the 'Identity of Identity and Not-identity' as simple old-fashioned Identity in sheep's clothing. Take, for example, one of the grandest observations about character structure in Brechtian theory, a formulation which reverberates on all our allegorical levels simultaneously:

> Die Einheit der Figur wird nämlich durch die Art gebildet, in der sich ihre einzelnen Eigenschaften widersprechen.
>
> (XXIII, 86)

> The unity of the figure is constructed by the way in which its individual properties and characteristics contradict one another.
>
> (Willett, 196)

Clearly, this identification of the relationship of opposites will give us a rather different kind of personage or character to be observed on stage:

using our previous example, it will ask us to construct the character of
Galileo as a combination of sheer weakness (obsession with ideas on the
order of the weaknesses of the flesh, and in particular the lust for food,
scientific passion and discovery as gluttony) and the grand pedagogical
virtues of the seer or wise man, of the generosity of Lao-tse transcribing
the Tao on his way into the peaceful exile of old age, of the perpetual
willingness to disregard one's own immediate aims for the pleasure of
teaching; indeed, the very pedagogical temptation as such (which might
then swing around dialectically into a kind of vice, while reciprocally the
obsession with knowledge and experiment, innovation, might itself be
reorganized into a new kind of virtue).

What has happened in this moment of the emergence of Opposition
as such is thus clearly that two differences have come to be related to
each other – or, in other words, that we have been obliged to construct
some relationship between them: it being understood that any such
relationship is *already* an opposition.

But now the next step is more fatal, and less problematic; already,
indeed, being foreshadowed in the language and terminology of our
previous quotation: for now suddenly, like a force of nature, Opposition
becomes Contradiction as such; and now not only do floodgates burst
open, but the dam itself is inundated and carried away. It is the moment
in which class conflict (Opposition) becomes genuine revolution as such
– or at least the preconditions for revolution which in the Marxian
'classics' is always defined as the emergence of the 'pre-revolutionary
situation', in which – in a virtually Laclau–Mouffe projection of a host
of different codes on a single master-signifier[52] – all the planets line up
in a single row, the random and distinct oppositions that have emerged
from a host of differences of all kinds are now, for one long moment,
explosively synchronous, and in an ominous 'unanimity' which, far from
being the old-fashioned kind of Identity, is the immediate prelude to the
end of a whole world and the explosive emergence of a new one upon
its fragments and ruins. Such, then, is the Hegelian story, and the way in
which all these various conceptual and categorial streams, drifting
downwards from whatever continental divide, carrying with them whatever rainfall that seeks its lowest level – that humble force 'water', to
which all things give way – ultimately flows into that great Orinoco of
the Americas and of the future which Hegel celebrates in his *Philosophy
of History*, modestly effacing himself 'as regards a philosophy having to
do with that which . . . is neither past nor future but with that which is',
and thus obliged to ignore what is 'intrinsically new in respect to their
entire physical and psychical constitution'.[53]

That Contradiction (in Hegel) then goes on to reveal that Ground –

namely, the historical situation itself from which the New will emerge – is no longer a necessary part of our story, even though the causal paradoxes through which so many insights in Brecht are articulated spring from this sense of a historical Ground, just as much as the latter can be momentarily reified into the metaphysical image of a Tao.

But what I have mainly wanted to stress is the process whereby a contradiction is constructed: this is a process which will sometimes appear to be a perception, a deeper probing of a surface hitherto arranged in merely empirical juxtapositions and non-relationships, and which, on closer inspection, proves to rearrange itself into fields of force, and primary and secondary antagonisms. But sometimes what is more evident is a rhetorical procedure (in its most august Aristotelian sense) in which items are rearranged with deliberation in order to bring their vectors into hostile alignment and to help them act out their own unique movements in such a way that the dialectic appears to be demonstrating itself, and offering a veritable allegory of all change.

But in this instance, at least, allegory must include its own theory; the reflexivity of the acting must begin well back before the text itself or its rehearsal; and what the latter must give us to see, besides its own literality, is the dramaturgy of which it is itself an example and an illustration. This is not only to say, as was so often fatuously said in the structuralist period, that texts about a text are also a text in their own right, that criticism is also (like everything else) a text not inferior in aesthetic dignity to what it comments on; that (parallel to the proposition that intellectual workers are also labourers) critics are also creators, or – to reduce the rhetorical shrillness a little – that, following Barthes's formula, *écrivains* of all kinds can sometimes also become *écrivants*, that is, producers of Text in the nobler sense.

More apposite, perhaps, is that peculiarly named sociological current called 'ethnomethodology', whose guiding principle lies in the exploration of what people say about what they do – in other words, about the inherent and verbal knowledge their gestures and actions carry with them, and how they explain these to themselves and to others. In that sense, we may also suggest that for Brecht, too, everybody always acts, and that we ceaselessly tell stories to explain ourselves, dramatizing our points in all kinds of ways, the undramatic as well as the ostentatious and self-parodical. It is thus better to shift the vocabulary of reflexivity, and to suggest that all acts are not so much reflexive and self-conscious as they are already proto-dramatic. Sartre's waiter who 'plays at being a waiter' not only illustrates a theory of being, or of the lack of being, he also dramatizes a whole dramaturgy.[54] Only it is one that does not go in the direction of populism and collect, with reverence, the small acts of everyday life; rather, it seeks out what is unpopulist and uncommon in the common, and spies intently for those instants in which the theoretical content of our everyday movements suddenly intrudes upon us and our fellow 'actors'; in which, as Gramsci liked to put it, ordinary people are all also revealed to be intellectuals, or theorists, in their own right.

The V-effect is this instant of intrusion into the everyday: it is what constantly demands to be explained and re-explained – in other words, it is an estrangement which asks to be further estranged. The accident in the street was one such illustration of arguments in which potential causalities were acted out, and so many dramatic gestures were proffered in opposition to each other. Yet any account of the estrangement-effect, any illustration of it, must itself produce estrangement. The theory of estrangement, which always takes off from the numbness and familiarity of everyday life, must always estrange us from the everyday; the theory is thus itself an acting out of the process; the dramaturgy is itself a drama. It is therefore as astounding as it is logical that at the end of one of his first and most comprehensive essays on the theory of estrangement (which includes an extended illustration about a motor car, today and yesterday), Brecht should add:

> Der Verfremdungseffekt selber ist durch die vorliegende Darstellung in gewissem Sinne verfremdet worden, wir haben eine tausendfache, gewöhnliche, überall vorliegende Operation, indem wir sie als eine besondere beleuchteten, zum Verständnis zu bringen versucht. Aber der Effekt ist uns nur bei denen gelungen, die wirklich ('tatsächlich') begriffen haben, daß dieser Effekt 'nicht' von jeder Darstellung, 'sondern' nur von bestimmten erreicht wird: er ist nur 'eigentlich' etwas Übliches.
>
> (XXII, 657)

> The V-effect itself has in a certain sense been estranged by the preceding presentation; we have tried to bring about some understanding of a frequent and quite ordinary operation that can be found everywhere, by illuminating it in a special way. But this effect will itself have worked only for those who have really ('in fact') grasped that it does 'not' result from every representation 'but only' from certain ones: the operation is only 'really' a familiar one.
>
> (Willett, 145)

For in that sense 'really' means that what is affirmed is not visible on the surface, but it is there, more deeply, and 'in reality': 'really' is a hermeneutic operator, which sends us down below the surface, all the while insisting that it is true of the surface itself and of reality on our first approach, and not only of our second or hermeneutic one. The V-effect is, then, this 'really', which we bandy about so loosely in our everyday conversations; it is the proof not only that reality is theoretical,

but also that Brecht's theory includes his 'literary' works inside o
that it is itself our object of study when we examine that work; it
is 'really' or 'in reality' Brechtian in Brecht.

Notes

1. Tatlow, *The Mask of Evil*, pp. 353–4.
2. Ibid., p. 369.
3. Gerald F. Else, *Aristotle's Poetics: The Argument* (Cambridge, MA: Harvard, 1957), pp. 414–20.
4. See Terry Eagleton, *The Ideology of the Aesthetic* (Oxford: Blackwell, 1990).
5. XXIV, 76–84; Willett, 35–42.
6. XXIII, 65–97; Willett, 179–205.
7. Speaking of the death of the classics in 1929, Brecht observes: 'Wenn sie nun gestorben sind, *wann* sind sie gestorben? Die Wahrheit ist: sie sind im Krieg gestorben' (XXI, 309): 'If they are dead, *when* exactly did they die? The fact is that they died in the war.'
8. Sigmund Freud, 'Notes upon a Case of Obsessional Neurosis', *Standard Edition*, vol. X, pp. 151–317.
9. See, for example, 'Über blaue Pferde': 'Mir gefallen die blaue Pferde. . . . Ich zweifle . . . stark, ob man die Werktätigen durch Kunsterziehung zu Anhängern der blauen Pferden machen kann,' etc. (XX, 350): 'I like blue horses . . . but I doubt if the right kind of art appreciation courses could really make working people into their supporters.' The case of Kafka is more complex: Brecht's rather perverse remarks on Kafka's fascism (to Benjamin, during the latter's stay in Svendborg: Walter Benjamin, *Understanding Brecht* [London: New Left Books, 1973], pp. 108; Walter Benjamin, *Gesammelte Werke* [Frankfurt: Suhrkamp, 1985], vol. VI, p. 527) need to be placed in perspective by his earlier appreciation (XXII, 37–8) of Kafka's anticipation of the Nazi movement; the later remark has something to do with passivity and victimization – still, it affords us the allegedly Chinese parable of 'the tribulations of usefulness': 'In a wood there are many different kinds of tree-trunk . . . of the stunted ones, they make nothing at all: these escape the tribulations of usefulness': 'Im Walde gibt es verschiedenartige Stämme . . . aus den verkrüppelten . . . wird nichts – die entgehen den Leiden der Brauchbarkeit.'
10. These unpublished essays and fragments were collected in *Aesthetics and Politics* (London: New Left Books, 1977), and can be found scattered through the 1938 entries in volume XX (pp. 417ff.).
11. Alain Robbe-Grillet, *Pour un nouveau roman* (Paris: Minuit, 1964).
12. Letter to Gershom Scholem, 20 July 1931: Brecht's *Versuche* (Essays) are:

> 'the first – to be precise, the first of the poetic or literary essays – that I champion as a critic without (public) reservation. This is because part of my development in the last few years came about in confrontation with them, and because they, more rigorously than any others, give an insight into the intellectual context in which the work of people like myself is conducted in this country.' (Walter Benjamin, *Correspondence* [Chicago: University of Chicago Press, 1994], p. 380)

13. It is no disparagement of John Willett's immense service to the Brechtian cause – *Brecht on Theater* concentrated and systemized Brecht's thought fully as much as the classic selections from Gramsci's *Prison Notebooks* or the long-standing Benjamin essay collection called *Illuminations* – to stress what is misleading about his translation (throughout the volume just mentioned) of *Verfremdungseffekt* as 'alienation effect'. The Marxian concept we identify as 'alienation' is, however, *Entfremdung* in German, so that this one had better be rendered 'estrangement' in keeping with its Russian

ancestor (*ostranenia* – a 'making strange'). In any case, the V-effect will be thus translated throughout, despite some support for the more aesthetic term 'defamiliarization'.

14. See the note on XXII, 934. Artistic relations between Berlin and Moscow seem particularly lively and developed throughout this period, something stressed in Willett, *Art and Politics in the Weimar Period* (London: Pantheon, 1978), as well as the magnificent exhibition *Berlin–Moscow, Moscow–Berlin 1900–1950* (catalogue edited by I. Antonowa and J. Merkert [Munich: Prestel, 1995]).

15. XX, 270 ff.; Willett, 157–9.

16. Brecht's attacks on empathy in acting, which can sometimes seem a bit obsessive, might well be repositioned and reevaluated when they are juxtaposed with Plato's attack on imitative art (the recitation and acting of a still essentially oral culture, according to Eric Havelock) in *The Republic*: 'Human nature, Adeimantus, looks to me to be minted in even smaller coins than this, so that it is unable to make either a fine imitation of many things or to do the things themselves of which the imitations are in fact only likenesses' (Book III, paragraph 395); trans Allan Bloom (New York: Basic, 1968), p. 73. In both Brecht and Plato, it is the overarching pedagogical framework which justifies the apparently anti-aesthetic positions.

17. 'Verfremdungseffekte in der chinesischen Schauspielkunst', XXII, 200–210; 'Estrangement Effects in Chinese Acting', Willett, 91–9. This 1936 essay is Brecht's first use of the term (see the note at XXII, 959).

18. Jean-Paul Sartre, *Œuvres romanesques* (Paris: Pléiade, 1981), p. 51.

19. As in recent times, there also existed in the 1920s and 1930s a left-wing political position that advocated the end of art as an essentially anti-political activity and a distraction from *praxis*. Although I hope to show that Brecht's conception of the political function of art (specifically, of literature and theatre) was not the common or stereotypical one, it is important to stress the obvious: that he could not take this kind of radically anti-aesthetic position and, indeed, frequently attacked it: see, for example, his thought about the Vandals (XXI, 288): 'I see them differently' ('ich glaube nicht, dass das so gewesen ist'), etc.

20. See *The Philosophical Discourse of Modernity* (Cambridge, MA: MIT, 1987), particularly Chapter 3.

21. This positioning of the origins of modernity back in the medieval disputes over nominalism is the originality of Louis Dupré, *Passage to Modernity* (New Haven, CT: Yale, 1993).

22. Arthur Schopenhauer, *The World as Will and Idea*, vol. II, Supplement to the Second Book (to Chapter 18 of volume I), (New York: Dover, 1958), pp. 191–200.

23. 'Discours de la méthode', Part II, in René Descartes, *Œuvres* (Paris: Pléiade, 1953), p. 138.

24. Harry Braverman, *Labor and Monopoly Capital: The Degradation of Work in the Twentieth Century* (New York: Monthly Review, 1974).

25. Walter Benjamin, *Gesammelte Schriften*, Band I (Frankfurt: Suhrkamp, 1974), p. 498; *Illuminations*, trans. Harry Zohn (New York: Schocken, 1969) p. 235.

26. *Gesammelte Schriften*, Band I, p. 499; *Illuminations* p. 236.

27. *Gesammelte Schriften*, Band I, p. 495; *Illuminations*, p. 233.

28. *Gesammelte Schriften*, Band I, pp. 495–6; *Illuminations*, p. 233.

29. *Gesammelte Schriften*, Band I, p. 495; *Illuminations*, p. 151.

30. Roland Barthes, *S/Z* (New York: Farrar Straus & Giroux, 1974), p. 82; *Œuvres*, vol. II, p. 609.

31. *S/Z* pp. 82–3; *Œuvres*, vol. II, p. 610.

32. In the *Nichomachean Ethics* (Book III, Chapter 3) Aristotle both identifies and differentiates choice (end) and deliberation (means); while I am tempted to say, with Barthes (as in the old Soviet joke), it is the opposite. Aristotle means that you cannot really be said to choose something about which you cannot deliberate (in other words, something absolutely impossible – to be immortal, for example); you might well, of course, deliberate about something not yet definitively chosen. But in Barthes's narrative deployment of the concept, an intensified modernity makes its presence felt in the identification of choice with deliberation, so that a deliberating hesitation over

alternative means no longer seems very distinct from the alternating weighing back and forth of ends (which probably means that ultimate ends have been bracketed to the benefit of means, which now, as in Weberian rationalization, fill up the foreground). Of Brecht one would then perhaps want to say that it is precisely these confusions and differentiations, and the categories themselves, which are meant to be foregrounded and held up for inspection and for a different kind of deliberations – historical evaluation, political judgement – by his cigar-smoking audience.

33. Erich Auerbach, *Mimesis* (Princeton, NJ: Princeton University Press, 1953), pp. 11 ff.
34. Jürgen Habermas, 'Self-Reflection as Science: Freud's Psychoanalytic Critique of Meaning', in *Knowledge of Human Interests* (Boston, MA: Beacon, 1971), pp. 214–45.
35. See Roland Barthes, *Sade, Fourier, Loyola* (*Œuvres*, vol. II). It might be argued, however, that the *Spiritual Exercises* are, on the contrary, a Stanislavskian text *par excellence*, demanding the most thoroughgoing identification and 'restlos' loss of self; yet note how Barthes describes their structure:

> non seulement la matière ascétique est brisée, articulée à l'extrême, mais encore elle est exposée à travers un système discursif d'annotations, de notes ... dès qu'un objet paraît, intellectuel ou imaginaire, il est brisé, divisé, dénombré. ...
>
> (p. 1089)

This text may be a better one to scan for the last traces of a Brechtian impulse in Barthes's later work than the more famous 'Diderot, Brecht, Eisenstein', which follows it by a few years, and in which Barthes's unhappy consciousness about realism and representation (with which he identifies the formerly avant-garde figures of his title) is more embarrassingly clear.

36. Jean-Paul Sartre, *Situations* I (Paris: Gallimard, 1947): pp. 20–21, 22–23; see also the essay on Camus's *L'Étranger* in the same volume.
37. Simone de Beauvoir, *The Prime of Life*, trans. P. Green (New York: World, 1962), pp. 113–14.
38. This is the central argument (against the concept of negativity as such) of Gilles Deleuze, *Différence et répétition* (Paris: Presses Universitaires de France, 1968).
39. See Prologue, Note 23.
40. Adorno's famous interpretation in 'Versuch, *Endspiel* zu verstehen', *Noten zur Literatur*, vol. II (Frankfurt: Suhrkamp, 1961).
41. See Darko Suvin, *Lessons of Japan* (Montreal: CIADEST, 1996).
42. Reiner Steinweg, *Das Lehrstück* (Stuttgart: Metzler, 1972).
43. See Steinweg's own reply to these critiques, and in particular to Klaus-Dieter Krabiel, *Brechts Lehrstück* (Stuttgart: Metzler, 1993), in the *Brecht Yearbook, No. 20* (1995), pp. 217–37.
44. As, classically, in Alfred Sohn-Rethel, *Manual and Intellectual Labor* (New York: Humanities, 1978).
45. Jean-Paul Sartre's classic objection to Proust, in *L'Être et le néant* (Paris: Gallimard, 1943), pp. 216–17.
46. Alongside *Trennung*, Brecht – not unexpectedly – deploys the concept of 'admixture' [*Vermischung*]: concepts which demonstrate the 'Identity of Identity and Not-identity', if nothing else. See, for example, the suggestive pages on the use of scientific categories in art works (XXII, 479): modernizing categories such as 'flight', 'bridge-building' and 'war' are to be strategically 'mixed' with the psychological categories of 'jealousy', 'selflessness' and 'ambition'. The recommendation underscores the degree to which Brecht, precisely while 'combining' or 'mixing' them in his works, felt such categories to be distinct from each other in the first place.
47. Gertrude Stein, *Four in America* (New Haven, CT: Yale, 1947), p. vii.
48. 'Structure, signe et événement', in Jacques Derrida, *L'Écriture et la différence* (Paris: Seuil, 1967).
49. G. W. F. Hegel, *Wissenschaft der Logik* (Leipzig: Reklam, 1977), vol. II, p. 42; trans. A. V. Miller, *Science of Logic* (New York: Humanities, 1969), p. 413.

50. *Wissenschaft*, pp. 48–9; *Science*, 417, 418.
51. *Wissenschaft*, pp. 68–9; *Science*, pp. 431, 432.
52. Ernesto Laclau and Chantal Mouffe, *Hegemony and Socialist Strategy* (London: Verso, 1985), pp. 111, 182.
53. G. W. F. Hegel, *Philosophy of History* (New York: Dover, 1956), p. 87.
54. Jean-Paul Sartre, *L'Être et le néant*, pp. 98–100. It is a dramaturgy, one might add, out of which Judith Butler's 'performativity' emerges later on (*Gender Trouble*, New York: Routledge, 1990).

Part II

Gestus

9 Pedagogy as Autoreferentiality

Autoreferentiality has long been thought not merely to be a crucial sign and marker of what counts as modernist in literature, but also to be an operator of modernism's inherent aestheticism and the way in which, as a kind of artistic tropism, it inveterately grows inward towards itself, makes its own situation, and forms a new and often unconscious type of content. It can be argued that self-reference is not its only content but, rather, something like a supplementary connotation by which the work seeks to justify its own existence; and the unique historical situation in which autoreferentiality gradually comes into being is constituted – the breakdown of the public, the crisis of the genres, art's loss of status in the market – can itself be documented. But if 'modernism' is a word that characterizes the artist's situation rather than his aesthetic ideology, then it will scarcely be surprising to talk about Brecht in that way. What may be more surprising is the unexpected outcome he has in store for traits and features that may otherwise (like this one) be considered fateful and beyond his control.

Yet Brecht is not often considered a modernist in that sense, and still less autoreferential and absorbed in the construction of hermetic and circular forms (a reluctance we have already had to argue against in discussing the *Lehrstücke*). Indeed, it is often precisely the didactic features of Brecht which are adduced against the modernist ones: experimental staging and costumes, no doubt, yet a set of messages to be hammered home, and generally political ones at that, which are commonly supposed to be the most resistant of all to aesthetization.

Yet our search, in Part I, for a doctrine that might make up the substance of such teaching and supply the messages for such didactic techniques was unsuccessful when it came to positions and philosophies, or even what Brecht liked to call *Absichten* or *Meinungen*: opinions and ideologies, the substance of what you argue about or claim to believe. A contradiction is not an opinion or an ideology in that sense; an estrangement is not exactly a philosophical concept, let alone a system; change may make you act, and even think, but perhaps it is not itself something you can teach.

There are no doubt teaching scenes throughout the classics: the Greek choruses informally offered wisdom and advice of a moral and psychological kind; *Henry V* staged some language lessons; *Hamlet* a brief master class; Molière's *Bourgeois gentilhomme* instruction in linguistics, and Shaw even more famously a specific branch of that discipline. But all these lessons bear on the central themes of the play or advance its plot in one way or another; the lesson is a device to develop the drama, rather than the other way around. But in *Galileo*, the great opening lesson (to which we have already referred) is more or less just that: the audience does not need to learn about the solar system, nor is it really necessary to characterize Galileo as a teacher – the drama turns on his science and his experimentation, his relationship to his new truths and discoveries. From the standpoint of any traditional dramaturgy, this great opening scene is utterly gratuitous (save, perhaps, as a way of introducing a character – Andreas – who will have a more important part to play at the end, in smuggling the new and final manuscript out to Holland).

Meanwhile, it should also be added that even if teaching is not central to the dramatic or on-stage actions of these classics, Brecht's most characteristic way of rewriting imposes the new thematics on them. Thus the formerly tragic heroes Coriolanus and Hamlet find themselves reevaluated on the basis of transitional moments in history; yet where American pop psychology would evoke adaption, Brecht overtly specifies learning. Hamlet and Coriolanus are *incorrigible*; faced with the new, they are unable to learn anything, their habits and thought patterns still locked into the old feudal modes of behaviour and the old obsessions of hierarchy and revenge. Kleist's Prince of Homburg, crushed under the inhuman authority of the Prussian tradition, must go down celebrating it:

> Tot ist er nicht, doch liegt er auf dem Rücken
> Mit allen Feinden Brandenburgs im Staub.
> (XI, 273)

> Not dead, to be sure, but lying on his back
> With all the foes of Brandburg in the dust.

Alexander Kluge's development of the Brechtian motif, indeed, proposes a post-Brechtian afterlife worthy of its origins, when, in the title phrase 'Lernprozesse mit tödlichem Ausgang' (deadly pedagogies), he reminds us that the learning process can also take fatal directions. Meanwhile, immense pedagogical volumes – most notably *Geschichte und Eigensinn*[1] – propose a variety of collective pedagogies; and, learning from the concept of Maoist reeducation and Cultural Revolution (if not from the execution of these projects), extrapolate deeply Brechtian tendencies and currents on to a larger historical surface. But in Brecht what is fatal is always the failure to learn: as witness the alleged tragedy of Mother Courage, for Brecht a fundamental illustration of the deadliness of the idea you can't give up (the little nest-egg, the capital of the wagon that cannot be lost, hanging on to your investment no matter what happens).

The fundamental difference between 'adaptation' as a value – and one in the light of which *Mother Courage*, but also all Bradley's Shakespearian 'tragic flaws', might well provoke the standard 'pity and terror' – and the very different Brechtian combination of the celebration of the *Novum* and the delight in learning, lies ultimately in the *gestus* of showing as such. The opening scene of *Galileo* is, after all, less a mimesis of scientific knowledge – its models and complexities, its value as a unique solution to peculiarly knotty problems – than it is the representation of how you go about transmitting and conveying such knowledge: 'the stool is the earth'. Teaching is thus showing, as has already been remarked; the dramatic representation of teaching is the showing of showing, the showing of how you show and demonstrate.

No doubt the complexity of the theory also poses representational problems, and nowhere so intensely as the 'science of society': indeed later on we will examine the problems Brecht faced in attempting to stage economics – or in other words, as he at first thought, to find a

Technik, die es ermöglichte, große finanzielle Geschäfte wahrhaft auf der Bühne darzustellen.

(X, 1074)

technique that made it possible to give an accurate representation of great financial operations on the stage.

Yet in the fragmentary notes on *The Life of Einstein*, the complex scientific theory is dramatized as a social function, and the scientist's famous remark 'God does not play dice with the universe' is glossed as follows:

Der Protest des Arbeiters, der noch weiter zuhören will, wenn am Ende herauskommt, es gebe genug Gesetzmäßigkeit, daß Voraussagen und Planen

möglich bleiben. . . . Ihre Theorie ist ein Aufstand, und für Aufstände benötigt
man eine gute Kausalität.

(X, 984)

The worker's protest – he wants to hear more when it turns out at the end
that there is still enough lawfulness in the universe for plans and forecasts to
be possible. . . . Their theory [that of the new physics] is an uprising, and you
need the right kind of causality for uprisings.

What is implied here, and throughout the *Galileo*, is not so much an
analogy between the advances of the natural sciences and our capacity
to think and resolve socioeconomic dilemmas; indeed, the late fragments
on Einstein and Oppenheimer suggest just the opposite: a lag between
the social institutions and the innovations and discoveries of modern
physics (and indeed, the performances of *Galileo* in the DDR will
incorporate this general contextual and political idea by framing the play
within a general anti-war and anti-nuclear politics). But this does not
exclude another historical perspective, the one in which movement in
the social order itself enables the conceptual breakthrough in science, a
preparatory relationship underscored throughout the play. We may thus
also posit the dependence of new ideas in science on the emergence of
new forms and structural ideas in the social order. In any case, Brechtian
possibilities of representation in such areas are predicated on an allegorical movement back and forth between these 'levels', where sometimes
the scientific idea is conveyed by a social reality, and sometimes the other
way round: the emergence of new social possibilities is suggested by the
excitement in sheer intellection itself.

One is tempted, therefore, to pursue this line of speculation even
further, and to assert that in Brecht, what is taught, what is shown, is
ultimately always the New itself, and thus somehow, modernity in its
most general (rather than specific and technological) acceptation. Learning thus displays the breaking in of the *Novum* upon the self: a dawning
both of a new world and of new human relations. It thereby becomes
inseparably associated with the great theme of change as such, and
reinforces Brecht's insistence that change always brings the new, and his
unwillingness to conceive of a change that would be purely retrogressive
or degenerative. At the same time, the thematic binding works the other
way as well, and underscores the need, in change, for pedagogy as such,
projecting the latter outward on an immense collective scale, and thereby
anticipating the fundamental discovery of cultural revolution – the
conviction that objective transformations are never secure until they are
accompanied by a whole collective reeducation, which develops new

habits and practices, and constructs a new consciousness capable of matching the revolutionary situation.

Now we must develop a sense of the omnipresence of these themes and motifs throughout Brecht's work, in order to come to understand that pedagogy is more than a mere theme or motif, and begin to appreciate the structural originality of its relationship to form as such. It is significant, for example, that *The Three-Penny Opera* also begins with a lengthy lesson that could be mistaken for some ingenious exposition (of Peachum's character, of his establishment, of the nature of the interchange between 'middle-class morality' and crime in this work), were we not forewarned and alerted to suspect that the pretext may be more significant than the ostensible motive. For Peachum's guided tour of his firm, 'The Beggar's Friend', utilizes the occasion of a new recruit (Filch) to enumerate the various beggarly costumes, 'the five fundamental forms of suffering', and the way in which each appropriate costume is to be used. This, no doubt, also illustrates the nature of a business, and the relationship of the good businessman to his work: it thus constitutes one of the earliest exercises in what will become a fundamental Brechtian 'number': the demonstration of capitalism and how it functions, which can be seen to go at least from the selling of the alleged elephant in *Mann ist Mann* all the way to Mother Courage's prudent husbandry of her little capital, but culminating clearly enough in the central *St Joan of the Stockyards*. Indeed, it will be clear enough in the sequel, *The Three-Penny Novel*, that all the activities represented in *The Three-Penny Opera* tend towards capitalism, and that Macheath's sinister glamour as a highwayman will later be expiated or expunged by his life in that alternate world as yet one more capitalist among others.

But in fact Peachum's lesson is not only a sermon on moneymaking and a satire on religion: it is that also, to be sure, but the topic itself becomes enlarged and transcended – quite literally estranged – if we remember Brecht's fascination with the Salvation Army as a kind of proto-political party, and the way in which religion here generally stands for the cultural level as such, as well as for the misguided and illusory values of idealism and philanthropy. Religion is, to be sure, also a literary matter and an occasion for eloquence, as the place and function of the sermon testifies in literary works from Melville to Joyce. It is also the very locus of rhetoric, and the space of a strategic deployment of the emotions, and in this case very specifically those of pity and fellow-feeling.

For if Peachum's opening morning hymn wishes to reinforce the universal guilt of Calvinism by rehearsing the great and terrifying prospect of the Last Judgement (and this is itself a theatrical anticipation, which prepares and directs our anticipations of what function as climaxes in this play, most notably the final 'execution'), his more immediate preoccupation lies in the generalized lack of feeling that accompanies this universal godlessness: and this seems attributable less to sin itself than to sheer habit and the wearing out of novelty.

> In der Bibel gibt es etwa vier, fünf Sprüche, die das Herz rühren, wenn man sie verbraucht hat, ist man glatt brotlos.
>
> (II, 234)

> The Bible has some four or five sayings that speak to the heart; when you've used them up you're out of luck and out of bread.

So it is that a spectacle that relies on producing certain kinds of emotions is mistaken in believing in content as such. There are no eternal verities and foolproof timeless situations that can always be counted on to wring the heart and bring on tears.

> Denn der Mensch hat die furchtbare Fähigkeit, sich gleichsam nach eigenem Belieben gefühllos zu machen.
>
> (II, 233)

> For man has this horrible capacity to extinguish all feeling in himself at the drop of a hat.

Nor does Peachum really solve this particular problem later on, for all the cleverness of his staging and his long experience of the *métier*:

> Zwischen 'erschüttern' und 'auf die Nerven fallen' ist natürlich ein Unterschied. . . . Ja, ich brauche Künstler!
>
> (II, 258)

> There is a big difference between shaking people up and getting on their nerves [he tells another practitioner]. Oh, how I need artists!

And we will understand why when we return to the Brechtian aesthetic as such, and examine the matter in the light of the theory of estrangement. At any rate, here we need only note the concomitant surfacing of an aesthetic of innovation or the *Novum* – 'Es muß eben immer Neues geboten werden' (II, 234): 'We always have to have something new to offer our customers' – and to recall the ambiguity of the relationship of 'empathy' with 'sympathy' more generally, and more specifically with 'pity': in Rousseau these last are identified, but as constitutive of his historically original theory of the Other; while in Oscar Wilde, pity becomes an argument for socialism, but in a uniquely negative sense, virtually Brechtian *avant la lettre*.[2]

Here, however, Peachum's aims may very specifically be identified with those of 'culinary theatre' and of what Brecht characterized as the Aristotelian aesthetic: to inspire feelings, whether of pity, fear or something else, to mesmerize an audience and put it in a trance; above all to produce empathy, so that whatever the character feels on stage the audience also feels along with him, weeping when he weeps and laughing when he laughs, and so forth. But Peachum's problems are precisely those of the aesthetic of empathy itself: it wears out, and leaves the audience in a state of non-feeling which necessarily scuttles a play based on the arousal of feelings (this failure can then, as with Peachum, be associated with commercial failure: loss of income). We are even treated to a Diderot-like lesson in acting, when Peachum is horrified to find Filch himself feeling pity (for the industrial accident case): 'Er hat *Mitleid*! Sie werden in einem Menschenleben kein Bettler' (II, 236): 'He feels pity himself! You will never become a proper beggar as long as you live.'

To say, then, that Peachum's demonstration incorporates some of the basic lessons of the theory of estrangement is not only to show how, once again, Brecht presents this last by estranging it, but also to raise the question of autoreferentiality with renewed urgency, in some new ways. For one thing, the matter of feeling will itself be 'estranged' in a second and different way, in which, alongside these Calvinist images of sin and terror, the *Three-Penny Opera* also vehiculates stereotypical images, of love and romance. Polly and Macheath act these clichés out, in a style heightened and ennobled by the music; and thereby not only cast further doubt on conceptions of natural emotion, but inflect the theme of estrangement in the direction of issues of mass culture, the simulacrum, commercial imitation and influence, and the like (already present in the inaugural texts of modernism: in Flaubert's *Madame Bovary*, for example, where it is no longer clear whether Emma Bovary feels anything herself any longer or is simply imitating the feelings transmitted to her by the novels and romances she has absorbed). In Brecht, however, this notion of artificiality is inflected somewhat differently: it does enable a loftier, self-chosen kind of love in *Mahagonny* – a love ritual more akin to allegedly Eastern practices (in which the gestures are everything, the 'sincerity' of the 'feeling' is nothing) than to Western romanticism. Finally, it endorses the ultimate images of the multiple personality, the good cousin and the bad cousin, the two sides of Puntila (drunk and sober), Mauler's 'two souls in one breast': where the very conception of sincerity becomes meaningless, since the grounding of the personalities in question – which absorb the more local issues of love or even 'friendliness' into larger 'world-outlooks', not to say ideologies – is now attributed back to the situation itself and the socioeconomic.

But the Peachum episode also restages our problem at a higher level
by suggesting that there is a thematic conflict between the interpretive
alternatives of dramaturgy and capitalism. Is this work finally about the
estrangement-effect, or is it about the criminally commercial culture of
the bourgeoisie? Does autoreferentiality rule out references of other
kinds? Is there some allegorical link between the theory of estrangement
(as work on aesthetic ideology) and the theory of capitalism, as that
centres on what Eagleton calls 'general ideology'?[3] Or does the former
merely remain a kind of purely aesthetic appendage and decoration to
the serious didacticism of a focus on capitalist real life?

Mahagonny allows us to turn this screw yet another dialectical notch,
since it purports to take the very matter of the 'culinary' and of old-style
opera as its subject-matter by way of the mediation of 'pleasure' itself as
what capitalism sells its consumers. 'Pleasure' as a theme, indeed, allows
for a rather different kind of structuration than the polemic target of
'empathy', which requires a very special interpersonal situation for its
rehearsal. But *Spaß* (fun) can both criticize and justify itself:

Was den Inhalt dieser Oper betrifft – *ihr Inhalt ist der Genuß*. Spaß also nicht
nur als Form, sondern auch als Gegenstand. Das Vergnügen sollte wenigstens
Gegenstand der Untersuchung sein, wenn schon die Untersuchung Gegenstand
des Vergnügens sein sollte. Es tritt hier in seiner gegenwärtigen historischen
Gestalt auf: als Ware.

(XXIV, 77)

As for the content of this opera, *its content is pleasure*. Fun, in other words,
not only as form but as subject-matter. At least, enjoyment was meant to be the
object of the enquiry even if the inquiry was intended to be an object of enjoyment. Enjoyment here appears in its current historical role: as merchandise.

(Willett, 36)

But a trick is being played on us here by dialectical mediation: for
presumably the fun portrayed as subject matter in the various orgies
celebrated in this operatic version of the founding of a pure capitalism is
perhaps not altogether the same as that fun Brecht assures us we will
find in true learning, in the work of Galilean science, and in the
contemplation of change and productivity itself.[4] Do we have an interest
in enlarging this gap, this interpretive distance, or in reducing it, and in
admiring the way in which the Brechtian dialectic solves its problems by
an ingenious fiat?

The privileged position of pedagogy as both form and content is then
reconfirmed by the repeated figures of the teacher or sage throughout
this work: the ambiguous figure of Azdak, meanwhile, suggests that here

sage and trickster are at one, so that the cortège of teachers can be seen to range all the way from Schwejk himself to the Chinese sages who underlie Brecht's passion for the Chinese imaginary (never particularly, as Antony Tatlow insists, to be sharply distinguished from the realities of classical Chinese literature). Thus Lao-tse becomes the strong form of the good teacher (as distinguished from aberrant forms, such as the eighteenth-century 'private tutor', Lenz's unhappy Hofmeister, who has to castrate himself to prove his fitness for instructing the German upper classes); and the story of the writing down of the Tao is as basic to the analysis of the didactic in Brecht as is the related and symmetrical version of the Buddha's parable of the burning house. Both have content, and it is a content which is not perversely and ingeniously extracted from the text by inversion and estrangement, as when *Hamlet* is made to function as an object-lesson against feudal violence. Rather, the Buddha's teaching is that of desperate impatience with the world (Brecht's characteristic addition would then merely be the phrase: 'as it now is'). The lesson of Lao-tse is also consistent with the Brechtian version of Marxism: 'Dass das weiche Wasser in Bewegung/Mit der Zeit den mächtigen Stein besiegt' (XII, 33) – flowing water overcomes the hardest stone in time: a doctrine that underscores the temporal change in the process – the water must be in movement, and time must be allowed to pass – at the same time as external power relations are shown to be illusion. It is thus a doctrine of process, but also of overturning and reversal ('revolution' in the literal sense): a conception which could also recapitulate the pedagogical process in its 'mise en abyme'. But the narrative itself moves in a different direction, and underscores the active role of the learning in the process: the Tao is written down not out of some ambition in its philosophical progenitor but, rather, owing to the request of the marginal figure who hears about it in passing, who shows curiosity and interest, drawing on his own life experience. There are no students or disciples in the picture, only the boy who drives the ox and makes the practical arrangements (he knows the teaching, to be sure, and gives the summary quoted above); the learner is thus, so to speak, an amateur rather than a pedagogical professional. It is the customs man – a professional, no doubt, of curiosity as such, but no representative of the ruling classes ('Flickjoppe. Keine Schuh. Um die Stirne eine einzige Falte': 'Worn tunic. Got no shoes. And his forehead just a single furrow' [Poems, 315]). And the poem concludes with a plea to honour not merely the sage himself, but the listener and learner who drew his wisdom out of him, who insisted on it in the first place. This, then, is precisely the pedagogical ambivalence Brecht underscored in his remarks on Galileo: was it that the teacher was so full of his subject he couldn't help talking about it, or did the student know in advance how cunningly to draw it out of him?

Yet it is also obviously no surprise to find that pedagogy becomes reflexive by shuffling its own categories: so that the paradox that results from the initial twist – teaching itself is actually what you teach – becomes inverted by the substitution of the non-teaching parts of teaching for the identified and specialized activity as such. This, no doubt, is a way of extracting pedagogy from everything, and very emphatically from non-pedagogy; but it is also a way to strip official pedagogy of its respectability and to undermine the institution by comparing it with itself, all the while preserving the truth of the process. So it is that one of the interlocutors of *The Refugees' Dialogues* admits that his finest lessons were indeed learned in school:

> Die Lehrer haben die entsagungsreiche Aufgabe, Grundtypen der Menschheit zu verkörpern, mit denen es der junge Mensch später im Leben zu tun haben wird. Er bekommt Gelegenheit, vier bis sechs Studen am Tag Roheit, Bosheit und Ungerechtigkeit zu studieren. Für solch einen Unterricht wäre kein Schulgeld zu hoch, er wird aber sogar unentgeltlich, auf Staatskosten, geliefert.
>
> (XVIII, 212–13)

> Teachers have the richly self-sacrificing task of embodying those fundamental types of the human species with which the young person will have to do in later life. He has the opportunity from four to six hours a day of studying vulgarity, evil and injustice. No price would be too high to pay for such lessons, which are however gratuitous and provided at the state's expense.

Of course, the account of these lessons – as well as their formal framework, teacher in front of a group of spectators – makes one at once suspect the kinship with that other vocation of acting (which is, however, as we also begin to suspect, at the heart of all the other vocations as well). Thus, describing his best teacher, whose sharpest pleasure lies in exposing the stupidity and ignorance of his students, the informant explains that the content of the lessons is utterly irrelevant:

> Er brauchte den Unterichtsstoff, wie die Schauspieler eine Fabel brauchen, um *sich* zu zeigen.

> He required the subject matter in question only as actors require a fable, in order to show *himself* off.

So even in the satiric inversion of the relationship we end up confronting the identity of acting and pedagogy, and their omnipresence throughout the societal continuum. These multiple models demand that we do not now speak of pedagogy merely as an interpersonal process, but that the two-way street of a genuinely dialectical relationship be articulated within it, such that it becomes problematical to whom we owe the doctrine, which can now emerge on its own right with a certain independence from the one who 'first' conceived it (for to discover the properties of the stone is not to invent them), and also from those who 'first' recognized and acknowledged it as a doctrine. Alongside the characteristic description of the Brechtian audience, therefore – sitting back comfortably, judging the outcome as you might watch a boxing match and comment on the skills of the participants, smoking the well-known cigar with a certain calm detachment – is now also to be added this ever-so-desirable property of wanting to learn, of eagerness for the doctrine. And yet, we have said, the doctrine is simply the method itself.

10 Parable

Much ink has been used up in arguments and counter-proposals about Brecht's larger narratological concepts: *gestus* is certainly a favourite one, but only, in my opinion, if we keep it in the original, with a Latin pronunciation (Willett's suggestion, *gest*, is something of a joke; otherwise the adjective might work in English – gestural, for example – but the noun is quickly reabsorbed into the too-restrictive *gesture*). Etymology, and particularly folk or artificial etymology, is a form of philosophical exposition in its own right,[5] as well as a form of articulation, so that we can use the difference in French, between *le geste* as gesture and *la geste* as epic, decisively to separate a meaningful physical movement from an achievement celebrated in narrative form, while the Latin even more usefully allows us to set a purely verbal and grammatical form – the *gerundive* – in place beside the bodily gesture and the epic or legendary deed. In fact, it is a whole sliding scale we want to bring out here: for the epic *geste* (as in *chanson de geste*) is clearly diminished when we get the scurrilous anecdotes of the *Gesta Romanorum*; and in the novella even a physical gesture – particularly some of the more florid Italian bodily signs tabulated in the great Sicilian catalogues, for example – could be a story in its own right. As for the original *gerere*, my dictionary translates it as nothing more lofty than 'to carry on', which, even if it is suggestive, does not seem particularly definitive (it also means: to wear, to bear, to wage, etc.).

The exercise is immediately clarified, however, when we understand that *gestus* is the operator of an estrangement-effect in its own right; and in particular that the estrangement derives from the superposition of each of these meanings on one of the others: showing us, for example, how an involuntary movement of the hand, say, could under certain circumstances (when executed by Louis XIV during a particularly decisive interview, but also when performed by an insignificant shop-keeper during the elaborate and unforgivable negotiations of village life) count as a fateful historical act, with momentous and irreversible consequences. Indeed, Proust combined both the high style of the chronicle and the common one of the everyday when, in an elaborate simile, he attributed the despotic jealousies of the court to his bedridden great-aunt: it is a superposition and an estrangement which not only makes us grasp the specific narrative element in a new and transformed light, but also changes our conceptions of what a simple physical gesture is, and what counts as a historical event at the same time. The 'usefulness' of Brecht's term – something both a little more and a little less than a concept – lies, perhaps, in the way it keeps the procedure open. We do not always need the other, Proustian, dimension of the juxtaposition; sometimes the physical movements of the actor on stage are enough – as when the Chinese player, showing himself his own gesture, sets it apart for us as well, as in a frame, and obliges us to name it and endow it with heightened significance. Brecht's own favourite definition tries to square this circle, by identifying the heightened and the everyday with each other:

Er wandte eine Sprachweise an, [here he describes his own practice in the third person, as characterizing the poet Kin-jeh] die zugleich stilisiert und natürlich war. Dies erreichte er, indem er auf die Haltungen achtete, die den Sätzen zugrunde liegen: er brachte nur Haltungen in Sätze und ließ durch die Sätze immer die Haltungen durchscheinen. Eine solche Sprache nannte er gestisch, weil sie nur ein Ausdruck für die Gesten der Menschen war. Man kann seine Sätze am besten lesen, wenn man dabei gewisse körperliche Bewegungen vollführt, die dazu passen.

(XVIII, 78–9)

He developed a manner of speaking and using language which was stylized and natural all at once. He achieved the combination by paying attention to the stances that underlay the sentences: only turning stances into sentences, only writing those sentences through which stances could show through. He called this a *gestisch* or gestural language, as it was simply an expression of human gestures. You can read these sentences best by completing those specific physical movements that correspond to them.

Thus the identity between the 'stylized' and the 'natural' is already a way of differentiating them; nor is one's instinctive feeling that *gestus* marks some radical simplification of the movements or the action – that

'formidable erosion of contours' Gide quoted Nietzsche as recommending – always reliable either: one could imagine excessive complication as
a decorative emphasis equally calculated to arrest the attention and
invite closer scrutiny. I will argue in a moment that such scrutiny is
bound, in one way or another, to be allegorical.

But it is important to note first the peculiar and even paradoxical
relationship of such narrative concepts to philosophical abstraction as
such: a relationship which will go a long way towards accounting for
our difficulty in defining *gestus* in any hard-and-fast way, even though it
is probably readily comprehensible to the layman. Even before semiotics,
in the West it was Northrop Frye's reinvention of narrative archetypes
in *The Anatomy of Criticism* (1957) which renewed the theorization of
storytelling and the various narrative forms; along with the 1953 English
translation of Vladimir Propp's *Morphology of the Folktale*, which
offered a rather different way of abstracting from concrete events in the
form of narrative functions. In Propp as well as in Frye, however, some
basic irreducibility of narrative content is to be observed: the archetype,
for instance, in whatever version it is deployed, will always carry a kind
of proto-story with it, an abstracted and simplified version of the
ultimate story- or tale-type, but none the less one to which vestiges of
narrative still necessarily cling: the solar hero, the ogre father, the
princess in the tower, Christ, and so forth. Even in these examples, it
remains clear that there is a kind of equipoise between the situation and
the narrative actor (whom Greimas will later usefully reduce to the
notion of *actant*, and which Propp designates as 'function'[6]): that is to
say, we can identify the 'solar hero' either from his own characteristic
deeds within a situation which his own presence suffices to redefine as
the mythic one of the test and the trial, the ritual overcoming of obstacles
and the ultimate confirmation; or we can deduce his presence, under the
rags and unprepossessing mien and subaltern behaviour of a peasant
youth, say, by the characteristics of that same situation which we first
identify as the one calling for the solar hero in the first place. Much the
same is true of Propp's *Morphology*, despite his efforts at further
abstraction: for even terms like 'adversary' or 'helper' already sketch in
a proto-narrative to which little enough concrete content has to be
added. This is to say that character function and situation are in narrative
– and thereby in narrative analysis as well – virtually inseparable; and
therefore that in narratology it is impossible to complete the act of
abstraction, and to reduce either of these twin and mutually implicating
faces to a terminology and a conceptuality which is itself radically non-
narrative. One might go on, from this point, to argue the ultimate
irreducibility of narrative as such; or, taking it from a different angle,

the inevitable anthropomorphism of even our most seemingly abstract conceptual categories: Althusser might have evoked the inevitable ideological investment in our most scientific notions and vocabulary, ideology being ultimately for him also a narrative process, as his Lacanian formula – the subject's 'Imaginary Relationship' – suggests.[7] Or, should the prospect of some ultimate philosophy of narrative prove too forbidding, we might simply fall back on Marx and Engels's notion of the concrete, and remind the Brechtian reader what he or she knows only too well already – that

> Morality, religion, metaphysics . . . have no history, no development; but it is men . . . who alter . . . the products of their thinking.[8]

The narratives of change and development will therefore first and foremost be narratives about people – characters, actants – and not yet even the personifications their products, acts and institutions could eventually be turned into for narrative purposes. The problems such a narrative obligation raises for the teaching and the learning about the nature of capitalism itself – not least for Brecht as a storyteller – will be examined later on.

For the moment, it is enough to draw the consequences for *gestus* and to admit that no matter how abstractly we are able to formulate a given example of this kind, it will remain a narrative abstraction, and carry some general hint and whiff of human action about it, whether of an archetypal or, on the other hand, a purely common-sense type: either people always do things like this, or, hidden away in the collective unconscious, are a few primal acts and a few primordial stories. It would seem, therefore, that we have wedged Brecht in between these two equally unacceptable alternatives, both of which, in their different ways, suggest that human nature has always been fundamentally the same, yet the one limits us prosaically to the surface of daily life, while the other intimates deeper sacred mysteries behind our seemingly ordinary actions and gestures. The alternative is, in fact, a rather precapitalist one, which offers the choice between the village life of the everyday and the tremendous things hidden away in the sanctuaries of priests. I think that Brecht was indeed interested in such an alternative, and in the precapitalist social relations it presupposes; and I will try to show later on how this interest coexists with very different ones. For the moment, it suffices to invoke the social and the historical for the picture to change entirely: once the *gestus* is identified as a historical one, we are evidently liberated not only from an eternal human nature, but also from archetypes as well (or at least, from the archetypes of the past: perhaps utopian archetypes, not-yet-existing archetypes, from out of the future, might be better accommodated).

What has not yet been added is that *gestus* clearly involves a whole process, in which a specific act – indeed, a particular event, situated in time and space, and affiliated with specific concrete individuals – is then somehow identified and renamed, associated with a larger and more abstract *type* of action in general, and transformed into something *exemplary* (even if archetypal is no longer the word we want to use about it).[9] The theoretical viewpoint required by *gestus* is therefore one in which several 'levels' are distinguished and then reassociated with each other: but this is precisely the process we wish to identify as an allegorical one, inasmuch as allegory, unlike other rhetorical figures, is a mode uniquely frustrated of abstraction, and one in which, in the absence of the concept, various narratives – some quite different from each other, some mere versions of the same story – are called upon to comment on each other, in a circular process in which each level none the less enriches the previous one.

But in order to grasp the complexity of these forms, we need to disentangle some of the tensions and oppositions in their theory: one of those runs from the notion of *gestus* to the question of contradiction; another, which intersects that line of tension, from the parable to the juridical 'case' or *casus*. Yet these oppositions already betray a more general opposition between observation and judgement, between the registering of a fact or situation and the reaching of some ethical or political decision about it; between realism and some other literary mode – political vision, for example, or science fiction, perhaps even certain modernisms – in which it becomes possible to imagine radically different situations, or at least radically modified versions of this one; between empiricism and the utopian.

That it might well be possible to reconcile both alternatives is illustrated by the play like *The Good Person of Szechuan*, where the duality of the protagonist registers both the empirical nature of a fallen society that requires violence and 'unfriendliness', and thereby, at one and the same time, the immanent or utopian presence of one that does not. The gods themselves short-circuit their function of judgement, as we shall see later; for by reducing the latter to the merely ethical, they demonstrate its ineffectuality, at the same time calling for a different kind of judgement by virtue of their existence as outside observers and their actantial position as judges in the first place. (In much the same way, the duality of Shen Te and her 'bad' cousin rectifies the 'realistic' or empirical world in which people are either one or the other, and in which they either succeed or fail.)

We must therefore begin all over again – not with the *gestus* as such, but with the *Grundgestus*: 'Jedes Einzelgeschehnis hat einen Grund-gestus.' (XXIII, 92): 'Each individual happening has its *Grundgestus*, its fundamental or basic *gestus*' (Willett, 200). The examples are mostly classical ('Richard Gloucester courts his victim's widow'), although *The Chalk Circle* is slipped into the series with all due false modesty; but what seems to characterize the *Grundgestus*, as opposed to the *gestus* itself, is its paradoxicality. Something in the situation seems to designate or to call for the Salomonic solution, the cutting of the Gordian knot, the unexpected identity of opposites; whereas the *gestus* simply identified the nature of the act itself, revealing altruism to be aggressivity, for example, showing private emotion to be socially and economically functional, and in general revealing the basis of individual psychology in social dynamics, in such a way that the only too familiar everyday world of the personal feelings and reactions is both estranged and explained by equally familiar social and economic, collective, motives which, however, have not hitherto been identified in this context.

But these satiric unmaskings do not quite seem to be of the same order as the larger contradiction which, in the form of the *Grundgestus*, sets the programme of the whole play itself. In fact, they seem for the most part to combine two distinct kinds of *gestus*, as here, for example, the slaying of a victim and the wooing of a bride; thus suggesting on the one hand that in one or the other case the term is a misnomer and *gestus* has little enough, structurally or functionally, to do with *Grundgestus*; while on the other that the latter aims to underscore some fundamental tension, contradiction, irresolvable antinomy, where the former simply subsumes a particular under a universal: one act under a more general heading (wooing or courtship: courting the victim's widow). At the same time, the nature of the *Grundgestus*, not merely that it applies to the play as a whole, but also that it requires a much more obvious verbal and poetic labour – finding the formula which will most strikingly yoke together the two irreconcilable parts of the dramatic situation – points us in a somewhat different narratological direction.

To be sure, it immediately recalls the great aesthetic of *Trennung* or radical separation, as that presided over the construction of song and scene titles, and other elements and deliberately heterogeneous features of the Brechtian musical and/or epic theatre. Now, however, it brings to mind procedures of the fable, or at least the parable on its way towards becoming a fable: namely, the tendency of the narrative material to split in two and to go in two different verbal or semiotic directions – on the one hand, into a narrative proper, an anecdote, in which either human or animal characters are shown doing something with certain results or outcomes; on the other, a relatively more abstract linguistic formulation, on the order of a saying or proverb, in which a kind of abstract lesson (or 'moral', to use the technical term) is juxtaposed with the preceding narrative and offered as the latter's meaning or 'lesson'. But this abstract and quasi-proverbial status is not at all on the level of abstraction of La Rochefoucauld's Maxims, say, of which it has been observed that each one might be expanded into a miniature novel, or perhaps several versions of one (for example: 'Les vieillards aiment à donner de bons préceptes, pour se consoler de n'être plus en état de donner de mauvais exemples'[10]). The position of the moral at the end of a fable, however, does not at all incite us to think up various other instances or narrative versions of the 'meaning' thereby outlined: it probably does not even cause us to go back over the story, to rewrite and simplify it in our mind's eye according to the hints and direction thus peremptorily given. I think it encourages us to a kind of production: to change the raw material that precedes it – the narrative text – into a different kind of verbal object; to replace the former with the latter, as you would turn it into something more portable that is easier to carry around with you and store up. This new object is no doubt still made of words, like the first one; but its discourse is utterly different, and one might just as well try to get some consolation out of the argument that a tree and a slab of roast beef are both forms of matter. But then, of course, the visual titles on stage are very different kinds of objects from the songs or the dramatic situations they are supposed to name and to sum up.

11 *Grundgestus*

But does the Brechtian *Grundgestus* come first or last? Does it sum something up or, rather, suggest the parameters in which the staging can take place? In the event – for the most part classical plays (or the adapted legend of the *Kreidekreis*) – it does both; for it summarizes the classic raw material with a view to reworking it along the lines of what may now be called the fundamental tension or contradiction. Yet in the sense in which it has been affirmed that everything in Brecht is plagiarism in one way or another – whether from past or present, from other people or the classics – the *Grundgestus* also suggests the uniqueness of some Brechtian 'mode of production' in which there is always a preexisting raw material that requires a reworking based on an interpretation. In that sense the Brechtian readings of the classics (whether in the outrageous sonnets called *Studien*, the new stage productions of *Coriolanus* and other Elizabethan plays, or the *Hamlet* interpretation that follows) are paradigmatic of his 'textual production' as a whole.

Thus, *Hamlet*[11] turns out to be a patchwork of tensions between the new peaceful commercial ways (settling of the dispute over fishing rights between Norway and Denmark, the 'new science' in Wittenberg) and the survival of the bloodiest archaic habits of feudalism. *Hamlet*'s famous hesitations ('sicklied o'er with the pale cast of thought', etc.) are not to be attributed to some heightened, 'modern', individualistic psychology or subjectivity emerging from the formulaic Middle Ages but, rather, the other way round: to the interference of these two cultural patterns, themselves the force fields of two distinct modes of production. The play is thus the moment of their overlap and coexistence, its peculiar temporality that of a 'transition from feudalism to capitalism' better thought synchronically, as a peculiar structure in its own right, than as a mere chronological succession.[12] One may even suggest that the various interpretations of Hamlet's uniquely modern psychology (from Goethe and Coleridge to Mallarmé and Joyce) are themselves part of the play and of its subject matter (just as Lévi-Strauss suggested that Freud's conception of the Oedipus complex was to be added in as one more version of the ancient myth), for in that sense they amount to the ideological justifications furnished by an emergent modern bourgeoisie to a transitional and objective situation of a wholly different kind, in which neither of the alternatives (the feudal baron's violence, the businessman's negotiations) has anything positive about it. But what the modern interpretations do is to turn a situation into a psychology, into some new mode of subjectivity, itself then reallegorized as a struggle between various 'values' or psychic instances. What Brecht wants his (imaginary) production to bring out, however, is the determinant role of the distinct modes of production in this seemingly individual drama: the fact that Hamlet reverts to the ideal image of feudal 'action' in the final hecatomb, then, scarcely constitutes a last judgement on the part of either dramatist, nor even an ethical position on the alternatives; but, rather, a means of articulating them in their qualitative difference.

Thus, finally, we return to judgement as such: the dramatist is not concerned with drawing a 'moral' exactly (or if he has done so, it is at the beginning of the process, when he deduces and explicates the *Grundgestus* required to give its slant and perspective to the new staging of the play):

Die neue Vernunft . . . kommt ihm bei den feudalen
Geschäften, in die er zurückkehrt, in die Quere. . . .

(XXIII, 94)

In the feudal business to which he returns, [the new approach to Reason] simply hampers him.

(Willett, 202)

Thus ultimately Brecht seems, rather, concerned with leaving that process open, and allowing the audience to have its own opinion and to frame its own moral, all the while attempting to suggest strongly – nay, even insist – that it cannot not do so. But perhaps we do not have to make a judgement as such – if, indeed, in our minds 'judgement' is always felt to be an essentially ethical matter in which ultimate values of right and wrong are somehow bestowed, and positives and negatives meted out appropriately. To ask us 'merely' to register the structural of the historical situation itself, and to articulate the feelings and acts of the play in the light of its more 'objective' tensions – is this still judgement in the sense in which the bourgeois tradition has transmitted the concept? Or perhaps, rather, it is something closer to the so-called Great Method or, in other words, the dialectic itself, as Marx and Engels developed it in the *Manifesto*: as an inseparability of progress and violence all at once, as the impossibility of separating a positive from a negative, both of which we can none the less identify in a well-nigh existential fashion?

In fact, there is a place in Brecht's work where all these issues come together, and the formal questions – the structure of the form of fable or parable, the function of the *Grundgestus* – meet those of content – the nature of the dialectic, the didactic substance and narrative and the nature of the judgements we are called on to make, if any. These, of course, are the political parables, mostly contained in the collection *Me-ti, or, The Book of Shifting Ways*, in which political events and historical figures are transposed to an imaginary ancient China and endowed with Chinese names.

But before we cast a glance at these important texts, it would be well to take some account of their formal predecessors, written at much the same time (in the late 1920s and early 1930s, and then again after the war); for the evolution of the form – as from the oratorio-cantata to the learning plays – is crucial for us, who seek not merely what Brecht tried to represent but his means of doing so, and how those means themselves reacted back and modified their ostensible content. The predecessor-form can be identified as the stories of Herr Keuner – the name has sometimes been thought to be a modern analogue of Odysseus' Outis or Nobody, since in some German dialects the sound is very close to that word Keiner; on the other hand, the figure already so named comes from Brecht's incomplete play *Fatzer*, about returning veterans, a kind of post-*Baal* attempt to posit nihilism now within political and national history. (*Fatzer* can be thought to embody that side of Brecht closest to his 'disciple' Heiner Müller, who in fact 'completed' and staged the fragmentary drama.)

'Herr Keuner' is at any rate a series of anecdotes, which would be parables, if we had any confidence in the authority of their eccentric hero. Here Brecht dramatizes himself incongruously, yet with slightly more dignity than the dirty old men Godard chooses to incarnate in his later films; both, however, use these figures as the mouthpieces and spokesmen for what may best be called *Absichten*, or in other words (not altogether accurate ones) opinions – what Schlick offered to buy from Garga in the opening scene of *The Jungle of Cities*. Are not *Meinungen*, or *Absichten*, then, what intellectuals generally sell – critics, in particular, who are kept around precisely for this purpose? The long debate between opinion and knowledge or philosophy as such (which passes importantly through Hegel, but is surely still around in the present day) involves on the one hand the conditioning by the subject and his psychology of the stray thoughts that get called opinion and must therefore be classified as variable or private, not generally or universally binding, only of anecdotal interest (but Herr Keuner's opinions are precisely given to us in anecdotes); and whatever gives the thinking and writing of the philosophers their impersonal, or at least their suprapersonal, validity – universality, perhaps, or abstraction from the situation, logical rigour (but then, of course, there is the problem of the starting point or premiss), deep metaphysical insights, even perhaps 'estrangement' from the dreary paths of the stereotypical 'what has best been thought and said'. The tension between these two poles – they are supposed to have been united at the dawn of philosophy, when Socrates interrogates various *Absichten* with a view to extracting from them the sheer gold of the Platonic Idea – can only be exacerbated by the twin modern discoveries of ideology and the Unconscious, which tend now to call even the certainties of the philosophical pole into doubt, and – at least, for those who are populistically inclined – to send the lovers of truth over in the direction of *Absichten*, where, under the guise of Gramscian good sense or Wittgensteinian general usage – not to say class consciousness as such, or various other forms of popular wisdom – a different kind of validity seems to emerge from the mouths of babes.

In the Herr Keuner stories, those opinions, which seemed to have most closely bordered on ideology, now tend to swing back towards the exemplary and the recommended, but not necessarily in the direction of the philosophical treatise: rather, in that of the dramatic figure. Herr Keuner, indeed, shares aspects of the trickster and the sage, of the militant and of the 'heroic coward'; and, as has been observed about other characters in Brecht, the pleasures of his representation also lie in the decentring of his subjectivity – that is, in the perpetual transformation of 'character' as such, which is determined by the relationship of traits to changing (and here, for the most part, incomplete) situations. Thus abstract ideas, by way of their appearance as opinions, begin to draw their enunciator into themselves, to the point where it becomes unclear if it is the idea which is to be cherished in its own right or, rather, the character who is to set an example.

At this point, then, we have reached the formal presentation of *Me-ti* itself, where the enunciation tends to involve the authority of the sage – even though his status as sage also derives from the value of the opinion, both finally initiating a reciprocally valuating interrelationship with that third thing which is the Method, in this case the Great Method (or the dialectic). But the Brechtian figure stands midway between two precedents: the ancient Chinese sage who gives these anecdotes their traditional narrative form, and the great strategist or political tactician, who is of course here and always Lenin (and who also has his place in the *Me-ti* as a named character with sayings and advice of his own). Yet the association is important to the extent to which it draws a hitherto traditional and primarily ethical form of advice and counsel in the direction of the collective or, in other words, of military and political tactics. In thus infusing the ethical with the political, Brecht perhaps reinvents the very spirit of ancient Chinese philosophizing; just as Tatlow showed that he reinvented the spirit of classical Chinese poetry.[13] For the pleasure in the Chinese anecdotes is at least in part a political pleasure which, since Machiavelli, the West has separated off, specialized, consigned to other disciplines, at the same time as it created what is called private life – an isolation from which even the limited forms of Greek counsel on action and *praxis* were gradually expunged. It is this, no doubt, more than anything else, that has led critics to see in this seemingly supplementary Brechtian production something like the emergence of an ethic from his politics, and the recommendation of a way of living consistent with the Great Method. If so, it would be an occurrence relatively unique in the Marxian tradition, where ethics are mostly borrowed from elsewhere, and whose originality always seemed to be its insistence on a collective logic distinct from the individual kind (along with a willingness to consign most inherited or traditional ethical systems to mere class ideology).

It is evident that the form of these parables – short anecdotes, which suggest pointed lessons that the reader must deduce – is characteristic enough of the episodization and systematic fragmentation we have attributed to Brecht (and to the modern more generally): 'fragment', to be sure, is the wrong word for these self-contained paragraphs, which often seem to fulfil something of the function of the journal, to comment punctually on a matter that has caught your attention. Yet Brecht also kept journals, for much of his life; and the parables equally evidently constitute a work of second-degree reflection, which one hesitates to call abstraction, since it moves, rather, in the opposition direction of the concrete and the dramatized. Yet here, too, a dual or two-level structure is persistent, in which an empirical starting point, observation or *Einfall* is cancelled and taken up into some more vivid form in which the gesture of the demonstration is retained. Indeed, one needs a word for this specific *gestus*, on the analogy of *deixis* in linguistics for the act of pointing. The narrative is not empirical: it includes with it the You see? and the Do you understand now? Implicitly it corrects a mistaken opinion, an all-too-comprehensible popular misconception: but what it replaces the latter with is no longer an opinion, exactly (we must come back to the function of this word in Brecht, whose third play begins, as has been noted, with the offer to *buy* the protagonist's 'opinions'). If we can tell its story or narrative, in other words, that is a kind of proof, and it is better than the opinion: the narrative articulates the conceptual position, and thereby proves that it can have historical evidence – it is an alternative form of argument, implicitly as valid as the abstract philosophical.

Coming back to the matter of ethics: some of these anecdotes, to be sure, merely dramatize the way the revolutionary militant ought to live, not the way everyone should (under socialism). To recommend, as Herr Keuner does (XVIII, 439), that we always check the escape route and the various back doors when we enter any building, is no doubt also useful in aeroplanes and public places, and constitutes more generally part of the useful lessons for dwellers in 'the jungle of cities', but does more to stage his picturesque personality than to offer material for thought (nor would it have been suitable for rewriting in the Chinese mode). But it already represents an estrangement of the ethical proposal: a 'you ought' (or *Sollen*) which has been distanced like an anthropologist's view of a strange collective mode of life. And thematically, no doubt, it offers yet another view of heroic cowardice, the fundamental sly and tenacious materialism of the Brechtian view of life itself. But in other instances, the Keuner anecdotes turn around the judgements of Herr Keuner himself. We are not asked to 'like' Herr Keuner any more than we are called upon to like the deliberately and ostentatiously dislikeable features of Brecht sometimes foregrounded in his own persona; but we are asked to notice the paradoxicality of his viewpoints, so different from the standard ones. They do not necessarily add up to a system of some kind; but the aggressive eccentricity itself underscores the central imperative of cultural revolution – namely, that the objective transformation of institution be accompanied and completed by radical changes in subjectivity.

We have already seen that later and more definitive collection of anecdotes and parables – *Me-ti*, or *Das Buch der Wendungen, The Book of Turns* – remarks on the relative paucity of ethical teachings in the (Marxian) classics themselves: 'nur wenig Fingerzeige für das Verhalten der einzelnen' (XVIII, 188): 'few enough indications as to behaviour of individuals'. Perhaps it is this very deficiency that makes for the boldness of the complementary suggestion:

> Es ist vorteilhaft, nicht nur vermittels der großen Methode zu denken, sondern auch vermittels der großen Methode zu leben.
>
> (XVIII, 192)

It is advantageous, not merely to think according to the Great Method, but to live in accordance with it as well.

Yet this posthumous volume would seem at best to offer political and topical reflection, whose subjects and objects are thinly disguised under Chinese names (thus, Lenin is called Mi-en-leh, Stalin Ni-en, Marx Ka-meh, and so forth): short episodes composed from 1934 onwards, whose principal protagonist was fashioned in homage to Mo-di, a critic of Confucianism of the classical period. The resultant sage-like figure Me-ti does not share the Brechtian personality traits of a Herr Keuner; indeed, in this cycle it is, rather, the poet Kin-jeh who fills this role (and even acts out various features of Brecht's love affair with Ruth Berlau, here called Lai-tu).

The Book of Turning Ways, long thought of as Brecht's principal work in the dialectic, is also, but not exclusively, a set of political commentaries on the left politics of the period; its 'dialectic' then turns characteristically on the contingent fact of the existence of the Soviet Union and the effects of that existence on a more general theory of political strategy, and also on something like a 'philosophy' of the party itself, and of party structure. These topics, which can also be tagged with the names Lenin and Stalin respectively, would seem to outmode this thought from the outset, for a period in which the Soviet Union has vanished into the past and the very conception of the vanguard party (Leninist or not) scarcely seems a current matter any longer.

In retrospect, indeed, it can be suggested that much of left dialectics, from 1917 onwards, was generated by the conceptual dilemmas offered by precisely this conflict between the particular and the universal, between a specific historical fact or datum – the Soviet Union, with its own local and national requirements – and the universalism of a left class politics which aims at abolishing even the specificity of class itself, and lays claim to a general validity across national borders. (It is a conceptual tension of this order, for example, that Brecht rehearses in

'Über mögliche Kriege' [XVIII, 85–6], when he accuses those who call
for a revolt of all national workers' movements against their capitalist
ruling classes of undialectical thinking: such movements should not
revolt in the countries which are allied with the Soviet Union, since the
triumph of the latter is their best guarantee for future development.) The
dialectical casuistry which thereby became part and parcel of the left
intellectual culture of this whole period, and found ready material for
ingenious exercises in the problem of the show trials (the ethical
paradoxes rehearsed from Koestler to Merleau-Ponty) and later in the
contradiction between Stalinism and the progressive left or revolutionary
movements in the world that were supported by the Soviet Union, is
now perhaps to be separated from the history of the dialectic itself, and
regarded as no more than one of its crucial episodes.

At best, it can motivate us to return to the earlier history of the
dialectic, in order to determine whether in its earlier stages, as well, this
thought mode was not always provoked and exacerbated, if not inspired,
by just such contradictions between the particular and the general which
cannot be handled by analytic thought or Aristotelian logic. In particular,
in Hegel's own period, the contradiction between the specificity of
capitalism as a historical form and the universalisms of bourgeois
thought would seem to be the goad that stimulates the dialectic into a
productivity that will go on to infuse Marxism itself.

Yet alongside the various arguments against anti-communism (which
even include some of Lenin's own 'parables' – most notably that of the
mountain-climbers who must constantly retrace their steps in order to
find the right path to the top [XVIII, 63–5]), there are also metaphysical
reflections, particularly on the eternal 'flowing of things'.

On the whole, however, it may be said that the wisdom transmitted
by these fables is a political kind in the most general sense, sometimes
strategic and sometimes tactical; as in the story of the peasants and the
barons, with its dialectical opening premiss: 'Die Brandschatzung war
zugleich ein Schutz, der Schutz eine Brandschatzung' (XVIII, 68): 'the
sacking was at one and the same time a defence, the defence a sacking'.
The explanation lies in the fact that the troops of their own lord do as
much damage to the individual peasants as those of the neighbouring
enemy. The ultimate recognition of this contradiction is then at one with
its reversal and resolution. Indeed, the barons do not only fight among
themselves, but sack and lay waste 'in general', in their very nature:
allowing the peasants, 'die schlecht getan hätten, nur ihre eigene Barone
zu verjagen, dazu überzugehen, all Barone zu verjagen': 'who would
have erred in simply driving out their own lords, to reach a policy of
driving them all out'.

The language of this fable, however, suggests that some more general picture of the Great Method is at stake throughout the various demonstrations. It can perhaps best be approached through a passing remark of Brecht during the rehearsals for his *Coriolanus*. (We have, incidentally, the record of these rehearsals, and they make it clear that as has already been said, the fundamental theatrical work for him was something like a master class, in which detail is discussed in detail, and alternatives are endlessly proposed and debated. Thus when Ernst Busch, horrified at the length of the *Galileo* rehearsals, objected that at this rate it would take four years to put it all together, Brecht slyly replied that four years would not be so bad at that; and in general, observers have always remarked that the benefit of state sponsorship for the Brecht theatre was very precisely this lack of any time pressure, this ideal of thoroughness in which no problem is too small for discussion, no gesture too insignificant for explication and criticism/self-criticism. Indeed, what we have said above about the analytic nature of the Brechtian aesthetic suggests that in some ways the individual gesture is likely to be even more significant than the overall form and the overall effect. Here too, then, the text includes all commentaries on the text: the idea of estrangement is greater than any individually performed estrangement; and the final performance is also a pretext for all the theoretical inquiries that necessarily precede it in practice, and ought then to follow it in theory.)

At any rate, on this particular occasion (which centred on the crucial transformation of the first mob scene of *Coriolanus* into something more closely approximating a revolutionary conspiracy), the actors give their observations as to the character and determination of Shakespeare's rabble (they don't think much of their decisions), at which point Brecht mildly interjects: 'Ich glaube, Sie verkennen die Schwierigkeit einer Einigung der Unterdrückten' (XXIII, 387): 'I don't think you realize how hard it is for the oppressed to become united' (Willett, 252). This is surprisingly untriumphalistic, and an excellent motto for a historical situation like our own, in which the very disappearance of the idea of the party seems to put problems of unification and organization back at their origins (it is true that there are now many more specifically capitalist or business-oriented techniques for the creation of collective organizations or institutions, some of which have filtered down to the surviving left movements as well). But what this means for Brecht is that we are perhaps wrong to see his work and his thematics as simply presupposing the Leninist idea of the party (just as we were wrong to think that it presupposed any dogmatic evaluation of Stalin): indeed, *Me-ti* itself looks rather different if one sees it as a set of preliminary arguments and demonstrations about the necessity of something like a party, rather than its simple defence and apology. In that case, if you like, the Great Method might indeed be said to constitute a very philosophy or metaphysic of the party as such, to the degree to which the latter is now understood as a figure for unification and the aggregation of particulars. It is a rather different philosophy from the superficially analogous moment in Lukács, in which 'party' comes to be substituted for class as such: in Brecht, rather, party is made to be synonymous with the emergence of syndicates and labour unions, with workers' organizations. In the spirit of Leninism, 'union' (in its more general sense as 'soviet') is supposed to mark the synthesis of these two relatively distinct things, whose tensions and contradictions a (not only bourgeois) critique of workerism will perhaps always reemerge to question and to interrogate. But in a situation like our own, where both party and labour union are enfeebled as forms of social organization, the critique is perhaps no longer so imperious and urgent as it was in the Stalinist period.

In any case, it is precisely as a figure for unification as such and in the abstract that the specificity of the Great Method (or in other words, the dialectic itself) is defended here:

> Die große Methode begreift man am besten, wenn man sie als eine Lehre über Massenvorgänge auffaßt. Sie läßt die Dinge nie einzeln, sondern sieht sie in einer Masse sowohl ähnlicher oder verwandter als auch andergearteter Dinge, und außerdem löst sie selber in Massen auf.
>
> (XVIII, 184)
>
> The Great Method can best be grasped when you understand it as a doctrine about aggregates [*Massenvorgänge*]. It never takes things individually but, rather, sees them within a mass or aggregate of other things, similar or related ones fully as much as those different in kind, and then it goes on to dissolve these groups or masses into larger ones.

This, of course, is one superficial reason why ethics – the problem of individual cases, and even of the individual himself – is not central to the dialectic; but it is preferable to put this positively rather than negatively or privatively. In that case, it means that one of the central tasks of the dialectic will be a search for the most 'minimal unity' – 'die kleinste Einheit' (XVIII, 79) – a formula that emerges as a critique of the emphasis of Confucius and others on the family as just such a fundamental collective unit. Characteristically, the discussion becomes a struggle between the good old things and the bad new things: the family, Me-ti responds, may well have constituted such a unit in the past, under another mode of production. Today the minimal unit

entsteht, wo gearbeitet wird, oder wo Arbeit gefragt wird. Sie legt alle
Erfahrungen mit der Umwelt in einen Topf. Sie ist klüger als alle ihre
Mitglieder.

(XVIII, 79)

arises wherever people work or wherever work is sought for. This unit puts
all the experiences of the outside world into one pot. It is more intelligent
than any of its parts.

And such small working collectives will themselves be the components
of Mi-en-leh's invention, the party (here called the *Verein* or union). But
even existential 'units' – two lovers, for example – are better united by
some third thing, which is work on the common project ['Die dritte
Sache': XVIII, 173]).

Once this 'metaphysical' basis of the dialectic in the dynamics of
aggregates and collectives is grasped, its other features – historicism and
pragmatism, the primacy of the situation, and the role of contradiction
– follow logically enough. Contradiction – in the larger philosophical
sense we have attributed to it here – is the name for the very relationship
that obtains within groups, between their components, and between the
groups themselves.

Zu der Praxis Mi-en-lehs [Lenins] gehörte es, in einheitlich erscheinenden
Erscheinungen den Widerspruch aufzuspüren.

(XVIII, 100)

One part of Mi-en-leh's [Lenin's] *praxis* lay in the search for the contradiction
in seemingly unified appearances.

The fact that such 'appearances' then at once turn out to be groups
suggests, however, a further consequence: that for this thinking, group
dynamics are the strong form of relationship as such, the form on which
everything else is patterned. Thus the atoms obey the logic of social
groups, but so do works of art and philosophical systems when they are
analyzed and broken up into their smallest parts. Or better still, that
such things have 'smallest parts' is itself a metaphysical presupposition
which is grounded on the prior existence of the social groups themselves,
and their dynamics. This, then, is a fundamental social materialism, as
opposed to a physical kind (such as the mechanical materialism dear to
eighteenth-century Enlightenment philosophy).

But what holds 'synchronically', as it were, must also obtain for
diachrony or the flow of things in time. We have often enough insisted
on the supreme value of change as such for Brecht to enter at this point
his basic qualification: the dialectic must not be reduced to some mere

lament and elegy over the transitoriness of all things. Everything flows: the Tao, yin and yang, the stream of time – all these are stirring images, but only under certain circumstances: better than some dwelling on the ephemerality of life and the things of this world, the Great Method 'verlangt, daß man davon spricht, wie gewisse Dinge zum Vergehen gebracht werden können' (XVIII, 83): 'demands that we also discuss how certain things can be brought to ephemerality, can be made to disappear'. The ephemeral – for example, Hitler – 'can still kill': 'auch Vorübergehendes kann töten' (XVIII, 113: wisely enough, this particular reflection is identified as 'Gefahren der Idee vom Fluss der Dinge': the 'dangerous aspects of the notion of a streaming away of things').

Thus, it is better to grasp Becoming as a mixture of the old and the new; and the dialectic as consisting in understanding how the latter can be made to emerge from the former: 'Das Neue entsteht, indem das Alte umgewältzt, fortgeführt, entwickelt wird' (XVIII, 106).

But this is precisely the context in which something like a narrative evaluation of the situation becomes indispensable: indeed, everything depends on the length of the narrative units within which a given thing exists.

> [Meister Hi-jeh/Hegel] meint, daß man diesen Satz oder einen ihm entsprechend gebauten Satz zu lange sagen kann, daß heißt, daß man zu einer bestimmten Zeit und in einer bestimmten Lage recht haben mit ihm, aber nach einiger Zeit, bei geänderter Lage, mit ihm unrecht haben kann.
>
> (XVIII, 102)
>
> Master Hi-jeh [Hegel] thought that you can say such a sentence or a similarly constructed sentence for too long, that is that you can be correct at a given time and in a specific situation with such an enunciation, but after a while, and when the situation is altered, can then be wrong again.

This is why Me-ti liked tales of rogues:

> Mich belustigt Kraft und List. Wenn ihr ein Land habt, in dem die Listigen und Kräftigen Gaunereien verüben können, dann muß ich mir das Vergnügen an List und Kraft dort verschaffen, wo sie für Gaunereien verwendet werden.
>
> (XVIII, 62)
>
> I enjoy strength and cunning. When you have a country in which strength and cunning can only be exercised in trickery and knavishness, then naturally enough I must indulge my pleasure in strength and cunning in their application to such things.

It is a saying which goes far: both to the estimation and evaluation of the virtues preferred and cultivated in a given national context (such as the German one), where they are the compensation for other kinds of failures, and to the very role of antisocial forms of energy in Brecht's work in general. But above all this observation serves to drive home the basic lesson of historicism in *Me-ti*, the situation-specific evaluation of everything, which must necessarily alter in its judgements as the situation itself is drawn into change.

But now, perhaps, we can best appreciate the concentration of Brecht's own lapidary definition:

> Die große Methode ist eine praktische Lehre der Bündnisse und der Auflösung der Bündnisse, der Ausnutzung der Veränderungen und der Abhängigkeit von den Veränderungen, der Bewerkstelligung der Veränderungen und der Veränderung der Bewerksteller, der Trennung und Enstehung von Einheiten, der Unselbständigkeit der Gegensätze ohne einander, der Vereinbarkeit einander ausschließender Gegensätze. Die große Methode ermöglicht, in den Dingen Prozesse zu erkennen und zu benützen. Sie lehrt, Fragen zu stellen, welche das Handeln ermöglichen.

(XVIII, 104)

> The Great Method is a practical doctrine of alliances and of the dissolution of alliances, of the exploitation of changes and the dependency on change, of the instigation of change and the changing of the instigators, the separation and emergence of unities, the unselfsufficiency of oppositions without each other, the unification of mutually exclusive oppositions. The Great Method makes it possible to recognize processes within things and to use them. It teaches us to ask questions which enable activity.

But it is a discussion which cannot be concluded without a final word about intellectuals, who come in for their share of observations here as elsewhere in Brecht (on art and artists, these notations are much poorer, and for the most part aggressively anti-aesthetic, perhaps because the bulk of positive reflections had already migrated into the dramaturgical theory). But thoughts are like groups of people:

> Gewisse Gedanken ordnender Art, Gedanken, welche die Ordnung zwischen den Gedanken herstellen, kann man ganz gut mit Beamten vergleichen in ihrem Verhalten. Ursprünglich als Diener der Allgemeinheit aufgestellt, werden sie bald zu ihren Herren. Sie sollen die Produktion ermöglichen, aber sie verschlingen sie.

(XVIII, 71)

> Certain thoughts, of the ordering kind, thoughts that institute order between various other thoughts, can be compared to bureaucrats in their conduct and function. Originally created as servants to the generality, they soon become the latter's masters. They were to make production possible, and instead they stifle it. . . .

and so forth: one already sees the kinds of developments Brecht will work out on the basis of this 'observation'. It is an estrangement of intellectual activity (to call it intellectual 'work' is itself already to estrange it in another way) which is based on the allegorical structure demanded by the 'dialectical' primacy of social groups over other kinds of phenomena: thus here, individual thoughts are also like certain kinds of social strata or professional guilds.

12   *Casus*

But we have not yet come to any formal conclusions about these anecdotes, which seem to oscillate between the 'showing' of pedagogy and the rather different drawing of a moral from the fable or the parable. Indeed, the tension now seems to run between showing and judging: does the 'moral' shown by a given parable-like or exemplary situation ask us to make our own judgement, to sit back and consider, reflectively, as Brecht so often liked to describe his workers' theatre, or does it simply offer us the judgement already made, and at best ask us to judge the judgement, whether it was not the wisest or the most appropriate?

The question of judgement and the Law is surely a very hot one at the present time, and the distaste for all kinds of judgements, let alone punishment itself, is a class and political question, from which a body of work which includes *Die Massnahme* cannot be expected to remain exempt. These are indeed part of a larger body of attacks on the legal and intellectual structure of the system itself, which largely transcend those now antiquated and oversimplified matters of power so prevalent in the 1960s. To be sure, these attacks can take a wide variety of forms, and we will touch on others later on: above and beyond the matter of judgement as such, about which Deleuze has been the most eloquent, there also exist ideals of this or that norm as such (as in Derrida's analysis of Searle, for example), and finally notions of various essentialisms, of which the idea of nature, and in particular a human nature, as well as natural meaning or law, are the strong forms and, as one might say, the 'foundation' – itself often formally open to attacks of the same kind. These attacks express democratization of an increasingly widespread type, no doubt: but as this political term has been the private property of American rhetoricians, it seems preferable to create the more Brechtian neologism of plebeianization, to account for the coming to voice of groups hitherto kept in subalternity both legal and intellectual; but also for a levelling which is the result of the sweeping away of elite culture – partly because of the way a bourgeoisie now itself in the throes of class-cultural self-destruction held to an inheritance from its prede-cessors the upper classes, and thus is in the process of losing a way of life that never belonged to it in the first place; and partly because the media have hastened that process and have not replaced it with anything else besides their own commercialization. The refusal of judgement and the law, however, clearly enough springs from the fact that people do not feel that they made these institutions, and thus have no loyalty towards them: in an initial Enlightenment moment of the emergence of bourgeois culture, Kant insisted on the way in which the subaltern must learn to treat emergent law as though it were their own choice and production.[14] But that situation was one of emergent popular power, in which people could be expected to feel that, and to welcome their possibilities of *praxis*; our own, which is characterized by loss of popular power and by increasing incomprehension of what *praxis* might be in the first place, cannot be expected to feel the same way about it, however much the institutions imposed on subaltern groups are decorated with democratic slogans and encouragements.

But it does not seem certain that all appeals to judgement necessarily ratify the Law as such: appeals to the latter tend to have a Stoic or even a tragic character, reconfirming some inevitable failure of desire or of the utopian, a breaking against inevitable limits, the need for renunciation and a submission to order. This, however, is the moment to remind ourselves that Brecht made a significant move when he decided to substitute for Me-ti's Great Order, which was to characterize socialism as opposed to the chaos of capitalism (the Depression, the jungle of cities, war itself), a new slogan to characterize the postwar construction of socialism, namely the Great Production. (Indeed, to imagine the creator of *Baal* in some final form as the glorifier of order as such is rather to imagine those lives which, out of conversion and renunciation of their youthful spirits, can truly be described in Dante's phrase as 'great capitulations'.)

And yet the great final plays all offer images of judgement: the Church's judgement on Galileo is redoubled by what we have seen to be complex and ambiguous appeals to the public to pass a different kind of judgement on this seemingly broken figure (who can under certain circumstances make one think of Dante's expression). In the case of Mother Courage, it is life itself and History which passes the judgement and abandons her to the hollow business of a lonely old age. But in *The Chalk Circle* and *The Good Person* the act of judgement is placed on stage: in Azdak's drunken wisdom and in the presumed reliability of the gods who come to earth to find the 'one good person'. In any case, it has often been noted that from the *Oresteia* on down, the playhouse has

much in common with the courtroom, and acts and acting seem to call
out for that response we call judging and judgement.

One way out of this dilemma may be afforded by André Jolles in his
remarkable and still too little known book *Simple Forms*, which offers
an alternative to the traditions of French and Russian or Czech narratology, and a very different path from that of Frye as well.[15] for among his
'simple forms' – these are turns of thought which initiate elementary
verbal formations that are later on, in some but not all cases, elaborated
into literary genres – he includes a quasi-legal category for which it is
best to retain the Latin word *casus* (which German reproduces): the
English word 'case' has to be explicitly qualified and restricted in order
to designate a legal situation, and is probably even then not altogether
specific enough, failing, for example, to exhibit its kinship with 'casuistry' as such: namely, the arguing back and forth, the attempt to specify,
particularly thorny legal issues and matters of judgement. Jolles gives us
several of those, particularly paradoxical and savoury ones, which direct
our attention to the form but do not particularly need to be repeated
here.[16] Initially it seems clear that the problem of *casus* deploys and
exacerbates a fundamental philosophical problem: the relationship
between the universal and the particular – in other words, is this fact an
instance of that larger classificatory concept, does this act fall under this
particular category, what is the status of the existential uniqueness of a
given action and its special claim on our sympathy, and so on? Literature
seems generally to have staked out the realm of the individual and the
concrete; and matters of the universal intrude merely as 'philosophical
issues' or very specifically as so many identifiable *casus*; but ideological
analysis has made it clear enough in recent years that abstract categories
and hidden universals are always at work beneath the surface of a
narrative, and best examined particularly where they seem most absent
and best concealed. The judgement on Shen Te (in *The Good Person of
Szechuan*) is thus scarcely some special case in literary form, but is
probably being exercised and inflected whenever we identify characters
as heroes or villains, or respond to the evaluations an author prepares
and suggests for us.

But in the case of Jolles's *casus*, these judgements are brought to the
surface of the text and made, as it were, self-conscious, by a certain inner
tension or conflict between various features and standards which are not
normally challenged by the ordinary stances of courtroom activity, and
in these special or unique 'cases' become veritable scandals and stumbling blocks. In place of Jolles's instances, I will cite a remarkable *casus*
from the work of Alexander Kluge, which can also illustrate what this
extraordinary writer was able to inherit and transform from Brecht in

his often interchangeable short stories and filmic episodes. This one is from a film, *Die Macht der Gefühle* (*The Power of Emotions*),[17] in which opera's powers to move us are juxtaposed with a variety of very different, and mostly criminal, episodes. In the matter that concerns us here, we follow the story of a depressed young woman who determines on suicide and, parking her car in a relatively isolated public space, passes into unconsciousness after taking a quantity of pills. There now arrives the repulsive figure of a middle-aged and respectably dressed male in search of adventure: the spectacle of the unconscious woman arouses him and, dragging her body into the nearby woods, he proceeds to rape her. The police notice two suspiciously empty cars, and apprehend the rapist, at the same time rescuing his victim, whom the hospital is able to revive and save from death. The legal question is then the following: is the man in question a criminal or a hero? He raped his victim, to be sure; but without his attentions she would never have been saved. Is he to be punished for one crime without being rewarded for the other, good deed of her redemption or salvation? The anecdote (which Kluge leaves in the form of a question) can clearly enough be read as a parable of many different forces and situations; but it is also a *casus*, by the nature of its structure; and this not merely because two kinds of laws are in conflict here – one of physical violence, the other of life itself – but also – and it is a point strongly stressed by Jolles – because the judgement is suspended (at least in Kluge's narrative). For once a *casus* is settled and a judgement made, the 'case', as it were, drops out of the form, and we have merely a simple empirical narrative. It is the contradiction which makes for the uniqueness of this simple form, and keeps it in being – for the *casus* represents a judgement about judgement as such: the passage of a sentence not with respect to a given norm but, rather, with respect to the very validity of norms as such, in juxtaposition with each other:

> In the *casus* itself the form derives from a standard for the evaluations of various types of conduct, but in its fulfilment there is also immanent a question as to the value of the norm in question. The existence, validity and extension of various norms is to be weighed, but this very appraisal itself includes the question: according to what measurement or what norm is the evaluation to be performed?[18]

This is the sense in which the Brechtian revolutionary *casus* does not reaffirm the norm or Law but, rather, challenges it; in which the Brechtian dramatization of contradiction calls for a judgement which is not a choosing between two alternatives but, rather, their supersession in the light of a new and utopian one: 'nehmt zur Kenntnis die Meinung

der Alten, dass da gehören soll, was da ist, denen die für es gut sind'
(VIII, 185): 'be mindful of the thoughts of the ancients, that the
belonging of what is there should be to those who are good for it'. It will
already be seen that the ethical value of this 'good' is here infused with a
historical value: production, which includes change and the New;
thereby displacing older kinds of ethics altogether.

We ought also to mention Jolles's conclusion: that 'what we are
accustomed to call *psychology* in the literature of the eighteenth and
nineteenth centuries – the weighing and measuring of the motives for an
action according to internal and external norms . . . seems to me to have
a great kinship with casuistry in the Roman Catholic tradition'.[19] The
break with the psychological, in the modern, then restores these inner
movements of categories to the surface, and places the very acts of
decision and judgement on stage. Such, at least, is their narrative
structure; yet the tempting designations of fable and parable remind us
that we must also examine their vertical or allegorical one.

13   Allegory

Allegory consists in the withdrawal of its self-sufficiency of meaning
from a given representation. That withdrawal can be marked by a radical
insufficiency of the representation itself: gaps, enigmatic emblems, and
the like; but more often, particularly in modern times, it takes the form
of a small wedge or window alongside a representation that can continue
to mean itself and to seem coherent. The theatre is once again a peculiarly
privileged space for allegorical mechanisms, since there must always be
a question about the self-sufficiency of its representations: no matter
how sumptuous and satisfying their appearance, no matter how fully
they seem to stand for themselves, there is always the whiff and suspicion
of mimetic operations, the nagging sense that these spectacles also
imitate, and thereby stand for, something else. Even if that standing-for
is what is generally referred to as a realistic one, then, an allegorical
distance, ever so slight, is opened up within the work: a breach into
which meanings of all kinds can cumulatively seep. Allegory is thus
a reverse wound, a wound in the text; it can be staunched or controlled (particularly by a vigilantly realistic aesthetics), but never quite
extinguished as a possibility.

I am tempted to say that every interpretation of a text is always proto-
allegorical, and always implies that the text is a kind of allegory: all
positing of meaning always presupposes that the text is about something
else [*allegoreuein*]. In that case (having extended the meaning of this

phenomenon so universally as to make it already seem less useful), attention will be turned to the way in which controls are placed on the text to limit those meanings, to restrict their sheer number, to direct the pervasive and omnipresent interpretive activity; to make of the allegorical a specific signal that comes into play only when it is desirable.

The historical play is peculiarly allegorical and anti-allegorical all at once, for it certainly posits a reality and a historical referent outside itself of which it claims, with greater or milder insistence, to be an enlightening and thereby interpretive representation: at the same time the sheer fact of historical existence seems to square this circle, and to close off the process, by suggesting that if the representation does minimally mean something else – namely, the actual historical event – then that is all it means, and nothing more is to be added in the way of supplementary interpretations. (It was only an older religious historiography, for example, which claimed that history was also a book, that of God, and that its events therefore had their own allegorical meanings.)

On the other hand, there must also be a question about the gratuitousness of any historical representation: why this one, why now, what is the point of exhibiting this particular historical episode from out of the innumerable anecdotes of the past? It is a question Brecht is swift to answer, and not merely in the programme notes to the East German *Galileo Galilei*, but in hints and allusions within the text itself: this play is to raise questions about the scientists and their responsibilities. If we go back to Galileo himself, then, it is because of Oppenheimer and the atomic bomb; and the play thereby insensibly becomes an allegory of the anti-nuclear movement (as that was refracted through the various disarmament and anti-NATO campaigns in East and West alike, and found rich material in the wartime settings of any number of Brecht's plays – indeed, most ingeniously, his first European production after the war, the *Antigone*, performed in Switzerland with Helene Weigel in the title role, was able to be staged as an anti-war play.

But this is only the beginning of a more general allegorical proliferation: if Oppenheimer's acquiescence in the making of the bomb comes to be suggested by Galileo's renunciation and submission to the power of the Church, surely a number of other topical analogies can also be found: the most obvious (yet the least mentioned, no doubt for all kinds of reasons, although Brecht himself mentions it) is the submission of Bukharin in Stalin's show trials.[20] The general parallel in left culture was already established by Dimitroff's use of the Galileo reference in his defence in Goering's show trial in 1934: something which makes the later 'confession' all the more scandalous.

If, as St Augustine says (not an unscandalous saying in its own way), a thing can mean either itself or its opposite,[21] then we have here the signifying mechanism of allegory, which can play on Identity and Difference indifferently, with the expectation that these will move on to Opposition, and finally to Contradiction. This mechanism explains why we do not have to decide whether Galileo (or Bukharin, for that matter) was justified: all we have to do is to note the issue itself, and debate it: is this cowardice to be reckoned among the forms of 'heroic cowardice' we have heard so much about, or is it cowardice plain and simple, and then in that case, how does the latter ever become 'heroic' in the first place? It is a question that moves on to include materialism itself in its ambit; for what is heroic about the slyness of Schwejk or the tricksters was precisely their commitment to the body itself, and to life.

This Hegel already saw in the dialectic of the Master and the Slave:[22] the Master is willing to sacrifice his life for Honour (for a Recognition that will later include power and material privilege as a bonus and a supplement). It is this willingness to sacrifice his own life and living body that distinguishes him from the Slave, who is supremely unwilling to lose that one good he already has. The Slave is the materialist; the Master the idealist: materialism, then, is this ultimate unwillingness to let go of the body as such, no matter what the promises of reward (and those are, in any case, generally paid out in idealistic rhetoric and in a hollow language of honour a good deal less 'materialist' in the long run than the Master's feudal privileges).

Included in this attachment to the body's here-and-now is a cherishing of its pleasures: Brecht, who ingested ascetically, here endows Galileo with an imperious concentration on his food, particularly in his old age: not gluttony exactly but, rather, the affirmation that nothing is more important than physical satisfaction, and certainly not the quarrels of ideas and theories so apt to make him neglect his meals and his interests, his appearance, in the earlier discovery stage of his life. No doubt it is this contrast, between the earlier and the later Galileo, which inflects the culinary feature (remember the contemptuous connotation given this word in the V-effect essays) in the direction of a specific evaluation. Still, we need to retain the ambivalence of the matter, which seems to position a desperate contradiction and tension somewhere between body and soul, between physical satisfaction and mental or scientific excitement; such that one or the other is always on the point of being 'renounced' or sacrificed – in a situation in which the modern, Brechtian person is no longer in any mood to swallow the value of 'sacrifice' as such just because the authorities urge it on him. In the name of what? Such is the age-old subversive question that echoes back into the *Realpolitik* of the

Renaissance as it rearticulates itself in the various refusals of contemporary existentialism and beyond: what is worth the loss of the present, of the here-and-now, of an immediacy whose incomparable worth – obvious in itself – can scarcely be outweighed by anything else that is proposed to us?

Meanwhile, it is then on the other scale or balance of what is to be sacrificed that a different but related allegorical process sets in. The act of submission was what was topically allegorized in the preceding moment; now it is what was betrayed which comes into focus, and here neither Oppenheimer nor Bukharin is of any great immediate help to us, since both of those instances presuppose a value – scientific inquiry as such, or revolution as such – which remains to be analyzed and grounded. (Yet we will want to retain this dual system of levels – science and politics – in what follows.)

What the play makes plain, with abundant energy and overflowing delight, is that Galileo's fundamental abnegation consists in a sin against the New itself, against the *Novum*. Not yet the new science as such, not yet 'physics' in the form of an experimental method, of the newer use of Reason and testing, of Bacon and systematic doubt and inquiry, but, rather, something more vast – itself significantly conveyed through the very literal figuration of revolution as a turning of the great wheel, a mighty rotation in the river of time and that process of change in all things which is the dawning of a new age. Nothing, indeed, is more magnificent in this play than the passage from prose to verse (and no doubt from words to music) in the first great scene – a shift in levels marked by staging itself and put into the mouth of a babe, when Galileo gives the boy Andreas the printed volume to read, and the latter recites the beginning of the great poem itself:

> O Lust des Beginnens! O früher Morgen!
> Erstes Gras, wenn vergessen scheint
> Was grün ist! O erste Seite des Buchs
> Des erwarteten, sehr überraschenden! Lies
> Langsam, allzuschnell
> Wird der ungelesene Teil dir dünn! Und der erste Wasserguß
> In das verschweißte Gesicht! Das frische
> Kühle Hemd! O Beginn der Liebe! Blick, der wegirrt!
> O Beginn der Arbeit! Öl zu füllen
> In die kalte Maschine! Erster Handgriff und erstes Summen
> Des anspringenden Motors! Und erster Zug
> Rauchs, der die Lunge füllt! Und du
> Neuer Gedanke!

(XXII, 811)

Oh joy of beginning! Oh early morning!
First grass, when none remembers
What green looks like. Oh first page of the book
Long awaited, the surprise of it. Read it
Slowly, all too soon the unread part
Will be too thin for you. And the first splash of water
On a sweaty face! The fresh
Cool shirt. Oh the beginning of love! Oh wandering glance!
Oh the beginning of work! Pouring oil
Into the cold machine. First touch and first hum
Of the engine springing to life! And first drag
Of smoke filling the lungs! And you too
New thought!

                                                      (Poems, 337)

So the poem generalizes all the empirical changes Galileo has just enumerated: the new construction methods of levering blocks of stone, the new chess rules that open up free movement of the castle across the board in a new conception of the straight line stretching out to infinity – the concentration of all these examples gives us the vision of the New itself, the incomparable excitement of the breaking of a new dawn and the coming of a new time.

This will now be the allegorical vehicle in the second interpretive movement of the play: here it is no longer 'science' as such which is the focus, although in Brecht science always knows its own form of a kind of subordinate allegorization. Thus science, along with learning as such, is assimilated to play and sheer pleasure, to the fun of manipulation and experiment, to the delight not only in change but in the very ability to provoke changes and make new things happen. But in a larger sense the New, as *Galileo* uniquely in Brecht's work stages it, must clearly bring with it its own multiple allegorical reference, of which it seems clear that we must articulate at least two levels. One is the emergence of new human relations, and thereby a whole new kind of society itself: this is clearly the level of social revolution as such; and it thereby identifies the Renaissance scientific revolution with the twentieth-century political revolutions inspired by Marxism (where the notion of Marxism as a science and, indeed, as the well-known 'science of society' is a secondary signifying move which also corrects and limits itself: it says, yes, Marxism really is a science in that sense, but *only* in that figurative sense of what accompanies and theorizes the New).

It is an allegorical operation which then at once releases its own specific determinations and consequences; for in that case we must also add that this Renaissance 'revolution' was short-lived, and that the story of Galileo also illustrates a counter-revolutionary moment in which, in response, it is quickly contained and controlled, its first impulses and excitements systematically thwarted and disappointed:[23] even in the utopian space of a free bourgeois Holland, the moment of the opening in which Spinoza could think his materialist and utopian thoughts is shut down after a few years and replaced by a modified form of hierarchy and aristocratic government.[24] Is this, then, a reflection on the supersession of Leninism, and the great moment of the Soviet cultural revolution in the exuberance of the Soviet 1920s, with their limitless experimentation, followed by the reimposition of Stalinist discipline and order, the closing off of innovation? And to what degree, following the Oppenheimer reference, can some allegorical allusion to the emergence of the Cold War in the West not also be detected, with the new postwar strictured and systematic extinction of all the rich impulses developed by the Western (but in particular the North American) Left during the 1930s? These, to be sure, are now secondary elaborations of the primary allegorical level: the New as the revolutionary *Novum*.

But the very movement of these suggestions, from political revolution as such and Marxism as a form of 'science', to cultural revolution and the efflorescence of a host of new cultural forms, suggests a second moment in the process which we must now make explicit. For if political and social revolution is one level of the allegorical structure of this *Novum*, then the aesthetic is the other, and here Galileo's innovations are to be read as the analogy with what we call modernism as such. Here indeed we touch – in so far as Brecht's work is also modernist but, as we have argued above, not simply one form of modernism among others but, rather, the strong form, the only legitimate form, of modernist innovation as such – on yet another central example of autoreferentiality: Galileo's scientific-aesthetic innovations are here implicitly related to the Brechtian aesthetic itself. (And to that extent, perhaps, also some of the hesitations about the development of the new aesthetic – the need to compromise with current theatrical conventions, to offer the solace of a new version of a V-aesthetic that underscores pleasure and consumption – in the postwar *Short Organon*: the spectacle-oriented richness of the so-called 'great plays' themselves. Perhaps second thoughts about all this, including those which others have expressed about the very radicality of the new style of acting explicitly demanded by the Brechtian theory, themselves get registered in the allegorical movement thereby opened up.[25])

As an allegorical artifact, *Galileo* thereby gives off at least two distinct messages besides the 'literal' one (which is, if you like, the allegorical message of the historical reference as such): that of political revolution, as a kind of anagogical level, and that of aesthetic revolution, as a moral level. I am tempted to complete these with the fourth level of medieval allegory, the properly 'allegorical' one, in which the specific topical references we mentioned first of all (Oppenheimer and Bukharin) function to inaugurate the allegorical process itself. Thus the medieval four levels of meaning are both retained and complexified in the new scheme: they rose, as will be remembered, from the literal level, the historical fact (let us say, of the people of Israel coming up out of Egypt), to the allegorical level, of Christ rising out of the grave and returning from Hell, and on to the twin signifying levels of the moral and the anagogical: the soul cleansing itself from sin in its conversion, and the human race facing its own collective resurrection in the Last Judgement.

Here we may say that it is Galileo and his historical situation which is the first literal level, to which the whole conception of the New and of revolution corresponds: a properly allegorical level, which on the moral level is inflected by the betrayal of the New: the diversion of the new physics into the Cold War and the making of the bomb; the misappropriation by Stalin of Bolshevism and its travesty (and literal extermination) in the purge trials; while at some anagogical or collective level, perhaps, remembering the identification of theatre with cultural revolution in general, the evolution from the stark purity of the original learning plays to the more culinary pleasures of this spectacular *Galileo* then offers a kind of commentary on itself, and a kind of sly autoreferentiality on its own style and compromises.

If so, the form of the *casus* is there to keep the matter open, on appeal: the repeated attempts, on the literal as well as the allegorical level, to urge a position of judgement on the audience, to divert the more 'natural' first-person judgements promoted and encouraged by the allegorical frame itself. Yet a tension persists, in Brecht, between the judicial and the pedagogical instances. T. S. Eliot is more consequent and dramatically more shocking as well, when, at the end of *Murder in the Cathedral*, he has the assassins address the public directly to accuse them and to declare that they themselves bear ultimate responsibility for Thomas à Becket's martyrdom, as citizens of a secular society: 'If you have now arrived at a just subordination of the pretensions of the church to the welfare of the state, remember that it is we who took the first step.'[26] At the very least, it is a reversal that would be appropriate only in a capitalist society and before a public committed to the market and private property. Yet even in the anti-Nazi works, Brecht's attacks on his own German audience and readership are satirical ones which aim to foster guilt and shame, and thereby ultimately to constitute the first step in collective reeducation they are to learn to teach themselves. But

Galileo navigates this dilemma and this tension only with the greatest difficulty, finding its ultimate resolution in time and change itself, in the voyage of the book into the future: the message in the bottle to be opened on the utopian shores of other seas and other worlds.

Notes

1. Oskar Negt and Alexander Kluge, *Geschichte und Eigensinn* (Frankfurt: Zweitausend-eins, 1981); see also my discussion in *Valences of the Dialectic* (London: Verso, forthcoming).
2. 'The majority of people spoil their lives by an unhealthy and exaggerated altruism – are forced, indeed, so to spoil them. They find themselves surrounded by hideous poverty, by hideous ugliness, by hideous starvation. It is inevitable that they should be strongly moved by all this.' Oscar Wilde, 'The Soul of Man Under Socialism'.
3. The allusion is to Terry Eagleton's important distinction between 'aesthetic ideology' (the set of the work towards representation as such or, in other words, the ideologies of form) and 'general ideology' (positions on the social as such or, in other words, what is generally called 'content'): *Criticism and Ideology* (London: Verso, 1976).
4. Aristotle is not always an adversary in such arguments: thus, the *Poetics* tells us that 'learning is a very great pleasure, not for philosophers only, but for other people as well, however limited their capacity for it may be'. It is true that this observation is meant to support the position that mimesis or imitation is an 'inborn instinct'; yet alongside the account which enlists the recognition provoked by mimesis under a general philosophical training in universals (an account which clearly strengthens the status quo), we find this observation of a more Brechtian and defamiliarizing cast: 'if by any chance the thing depicted has not been seen before, it will not be the fact that it is an imitation of something that gives pleasure, but the execution or the colouring or some other such cause' (paragraph 48B4; English trans. T. S. Dorsch, from: Aristotle, Horace, Longinus, *Classical Literary Criticism* [Harmondsworth; Penguin, 1965] p. 35).
5. Jean Paulhan's little book *La Preuve par l'étymologie* (Paris: Minuit, 1953) explores just such formal questions, surely with Heidegger in mind.
6. A. J. Greimas, Part III ('Le récit') of *Du sens* (Paris: Seuil, 1970).
7. Althusser, *Lenin and Philosophy*, p. 162: 'Ideology is a "Representation" of the Imaginary Relationship of Individuals to their Real Conditions of Existence.'
8. See Prologue, Note 31.
9. I want to distinguish this rather unBrechtian terminology of the types and the typical from its official Lukácsean usage: in Lukács, the 'typical' operates chiefly as a classificatory category for *characters* – a restriction which clearly enough locks the great Hungarian critic into a rather traditional realism of stable subjects and centered psyches. What is 'typical' in the Brechtian *gestus* is, rather, the action itself, and even, as we have seen already, the various henceforth unrecognizable components or building blocks of an action: here the stable and recognizable subject is gone from the outset.
10. La Rochefoucauld, *Maximes* (Paris: Folio, 1976), no. 93, p. 59.
11. See the *Kleines Organon* (XXIII, 93–4), or Willett, 201–202; also the sonnet in Studien, 'Über Shakespeares Stück "Hamlet"', XI, 269.
12. See, on the concept of 'transition', Etienne Balibar's contribution (Part III) to Althusser/ Balibar, *Reading Capital* (London: Verso, 1970).
13. See Prologue, Note 15.
14. See, for example, Section E ('The Right of Punishment and the Right of Pardon') of the *Metaphysics of Morals*: 'Any undeserved evil which you do to someone else among the people is an evil done to yourself', and so on: *Kant's Political Writings*, ed. Hans Reiss (Cambridge; Cambridge University Press, 1970), p. 155.

15. Tübingen: Niemeyer, 1982. On the analysis of the parable in general, however, see also Louis Marin, *Sémiotique de la passion* (Paris: Aubier, 1971); and his fundamental essays in Claude Chabrol, ed., *Le récit biblique* (Paris: Aubier Montaigne, 1974); see also Paul Ricoeur, 'Biblical Hermeneutics', *Semeia* 4 (1975), pp. 29–148.

16. For example, the thief who gives his accomplice the stolen money: if he changes it and 'breaks' the large bills first, she is, according to German law, not guilty of receiving stolen goods. In literature, one may also think here, and when I recount Kluge's virtual reworking of it below, of Kleist's *Marquise von O*.

17. The Kluge film dates from 1983; see also the collection of the same name (Frankfurt: Zweitausendeins, 1984), which includes the screenplay, among other things:

> Zeugin, ich frage sie ernstlich: es hat also Ihrem Gefühl nichts ausgemacht, von dem Angeklagten, der einerseits Ihr Retter, andererseits Ihr Nitzuchtiger ist, vergewaltigt zu werden?

> Witness, the most serious question is this: have you no reaction to the fact that the accused, who is on the one hand your rescuer and on the other your assailant, raped you? (p. 102)

The symmetry of Kluge's interrogation of emotions here with Brecht's strategic suspicion of the emotional reaction makes for even more interesting historical differences between the two projects, the one offering a method for analyzing and distancing the immediate; the other attempting to measure the role and power of sheer affect in our decisions and our daily life.

18. Jolles, *Simple Forms*, p. 190.

19. Ibid., p. 199.

20. See Roy A. Medvedev, *Let History Judge* (New York: Knopf, 1971), pp. 174–9.

21. *De doctrina christiana*, Book III.

22. G.W.F. Hegel, *Phenomenology of Spirit*, trans. A. V. Miller (Oxford: Oxford University Press, 1977), Chapter 4, section A, pp. 113–19.

23. I believe a parallel is to be drawn here with the short-lived opening of Rabelais's moment, as Mikhail Bakhtin tells the story in *Rabelais and His World* (Cambridge, MA: MIT Press, 1968). For Bakhtin, Rabelais is a breath drawn between the traditional or customary restrictions of the Middle Ages and the imposition of a new and elaborate man-made cultural and political discipline by the baroque Counter-Reformation: the allegory aims clearly enough at a celebration of the great Soviet cultural revolution as that erupted between the moment of a well-nigh medieval Tsarism and the repressive orthodoxies of nascent Stalinism in the early 1930s.

24. See Antonio Negri, *The Savage Anomaly* (Minneapolis: University of Minnesota Press, 1991), Chapter 1.

25. Yet another and different, yet related, posthumous allegory might then be afforded by equating Galileo's and Brecht's 'modernist' discoveries with those of Einstein, whose relativity drew the line at accepting radical indeterminacy ('God does not play dice with the universe'), and to whose modernity, therefore, some more thoroughgoing and consequential postmodernity of the newer physics may be opposed. This is the sense in which a post-Brechtian dramaturgy might accuse the modernist Master of compromises (with Marxism, with Leninism, with the state), and propose some freer Holland of the decentred aesthetic and the heterogeneous. Here too, then, Brecht's own allegorical parable remains 'useful', even though I myself would prefer not to use it in this way.

26. T. S. Eliot, *Complete Plays* (New York: Harcourt Brace, 1967), p. 50.

Part III

Proverbs/*Sprüche*

14 Proverbs and Peasant History

Il y a quelque chose de paysan dans l'histoire.

(Gilles Deleuze)

The proverb is presumably the other face of the parable, and what concentrates the latter's narrative wisdom into a single lapidary formula; it is, to be sure, an already acquired wisdom, whereas fable or proverb offers wisdom to be acquired, even if it also springs from someone else's previous experience (or from the experience of the collectivity). The difference in perspective is no doubt determined by the effacement of narrative as such, which persists in the fable but is here reduced to a grammatical minimum. As we have shown above, the connection with *gestus*, narrative, the representation of events and action of some sort, no matter how abstractly retailed, can never be expunged altogether, since even proverbial discourse takes human events and human fortunes as its object. But perhaps history can offer an analogy here, and in particular Arthur Danto's powerful argument that however non-narrative a given historiographic text may seem (statistics, economics, etc.) it can always be translated back into narrative form (of an allegedly old-fashioned kind); it carries narrative at its very heart.[1] In much the same way, La Rochefoucauld's maxims have often been characterized as miniature novels, as the minimal structure of situations, conflicts and dramatic outcomes still to be fleshed out.

Certainly the proverbial structure of the Brechtian verse or enunciation has often been remarked (and sometimes attributed, along with the so-called 'simplicity' of his language, to the Bible, of which he was an avid reader in his youth[2]). 'Erst kommt das Fressen; dann kommt die Moral'!: 'Food first; sermons later!' Literally the German reads: 'First comes eating – or gobbling up; then comes moralizing, or the moral'. What is untranslatable is the form of the proverb itself and its concision in the national language; meanwhile, the 'saying' designates itself by adding its 'moral' in at the end in the manner of a genuine parable or fable. The proverbial is, at the very least, a presupposition for any number of narratives (and many Brechtian ones at that); but its resonance fans out into many other dimensions, from ethics and politics to psychology and aesthetics. This is to insist on the way in which language has here been arranged so as not to be completely subsumed under any of the discursive or cognitive or generic categories, but to be capable of development in any number of them; it is the proposition we attempt to defend in our notion of triangulation: namely, that there existed a Brechtian 'stance' [*Haltung*] which was not only doctrine, narrative, or style, but all three simultaneously; and ought better to be called, with all due precautions, 'method'. That the proverbial can be a method is perhaps not a particularly daring or outrageous proposition; one can be intent both on turning experience into proverbs (or on recognizing their persistence throughout experience) and on allowing one's actions to be guided by a proverbial view of things. Yet it is not so easy to pin such a method down.

I believe that it has to do with substantives and with definite articles: in a sense, these insist on that very 'already said' and 'already known' which we have seen it to be the deeper vocation of estrangement to undermine. For the definite article names a particular action, event or experience: it lends it a familiarity in advance, *avant la lettre*; we may even say that the process of naming which is at one with the very category of the definite article as such constructs its object and creates the first familiarities, the first organized recognitions as those become sedimented in language. But at the same time, this very characterization makes it clear to what degree any attempt to grasp the nature of the definite article opens up some Ur-perspective of a linguistic past, of the verbally archaic, the beginnings of time, the organization of the world into names and familiar categories. And it also seems to project those categories initially, and against all the ideologies of contemporary linguistics, in the form of substantives. The definite article thus grounds Aristotelianism in the first habits of language itself, rather than in that process-oriented movement which philosophy has had painfully to discover after the long reign of Aristotelian common sense. We eat concretely, many times over, but 'das Fressen' is now a kind of essence, an atemporal Idea (which, by ricochet, makes 'die Moral' back over into an activity, yet one of a named and familiar – only too familiar – type).

Yet this reification was very precisely the technique proposed by the V-effect: not to construct some archaic experience, but to destroy the ideological images of experience handed on down by society's masters and intended to sap any nascent sense of history or of change, by persuading people that life has always been this way, and has always involved these renunciations, these proverbial sacrifices. The V-effect then proposed something like a poetics of reification, in which new and, as it were, unsuitable, inappropriate devices of reification were brought to bear on these immemorial stereotypes: the insignificant individual or personal event being treated like a famous historical action, known to everyone; a characteristic mode of personal or family behaviour being made over, anthropologically, into the official costumes and rituals of a whole primitive tribe. Even if this is a homeopathic method, in which reification is used to dereify and to bring change and new momentum to customary behaviour and stereotypical 'values', it would seem inconsistent with any initially 'biblical' or proverbial style principle, which sought to create familiar and reified entities by way of the definite article:

> Erst muß es möglich sein auch armen Leuten
> Vom großen Brotlaib sich ihr Teil zu schneiden.
>
> (II, 284)
>
> Poor people have to first be able
> to slice their own slice from the great big loaf.

'The great big loaf', with its definite article, assures us that we have known this idea all our life: the figure itself – save for the magnificent subsidiary verb that is its consequence: 'to cut off a slice' – is less important as metaphor or 'poetic language' than for what it does to the idea of social prosperity, of the so-called 'wealth of nations', of what the market economists today call the 'breadbasket', about which it affirms a zero-sum wisdom: first, that the production of a given population is somehow a unified entity, one big loaf, not the scattered products of individual farms and isolated villages; second, that when the unmentioned other people, the rich, slice their piece off, there is that much less to go round. The figure thereby constructs a form of recognizable 'proverbial' wisdom which carries class struggle within its own internal operations: to recognize, as the action of the definite article recommends we do, that we are all dependent on the single great loaf, is to unify the 'us' in question; it is to take those isolated peasants (of whom Marx said that they were like potatoes in a sack) and enforce their solidarity, if not as actors or subjects of history, then at least as the poor, as history's sufferers, as what Liberation Theology calls 'the body of Christ'. But as it is a unification based on need, the other group, left out of the formula, is there to become the enemy if the process of perception develops any genuinely political fashion. Even the modest 'taking your own share', which could in a pinch simply mean the agreement for an organic participation of all the social classes, does not really make any binding pledges for the future ('erst muß es möglich sein') or promise obedient commitment to social peace and order; no one can really tell in advance how the process of cutting your own slice will develop.

To replace Brecht in the tendencies of poetic modernism, then, is to grasp a strategic originality in his work; for the modern in general grasped modernity's languages, as they issued forth from the industrial era and were then multiplied and amplified by media no less industrial, as inauthentic degradations of some earlier and purer speech: 'Donner un sens plus pur aux mots de la tribu.'[3] The various modernist styles were also estrangement-effects after their fashion, and sought to dispel the familiarity of the inauthentic and reinvent a kind of freshness of language, which could at least connote authenticity, could serve as an equivalent or a sign, or symbolic marker, for an authenticity really to be concretely realized only in social life itself. This work on language is always and everywhere the socially symbolic dimension of all modernist poetry, no matter how hermetic and seemingly apolitical.

To reintroduce Brecht back into that story, then, means to reconstruct the pallor and the sparsity of his earliest work: the insistence on the washed-out quality of the world's colours, the sky as 'fahl': a characteristic private word and a stylistically preeminent Brechtian tactic for insisting on poetic perception at the same time as you deny the presence of anything vivid to perceive; reduction of the object world, even in the late poems – the Buckow Elegies, for example – to the few poor items: the stick tree, or the lonely single cloud in the early 'Memory of Marie A.' – a poverty and singularity of objects which, as in Beckett, empty the stage out and leave the surviving items ready for their definite article: *the* tree, *the* leaf, *the* rope, and so on. We do not often think of Brecht in terms of this kind of minimalism, for it strikes out in a different and more 'East Asian' direction in the learning plays (as these include *the* young comrade, *the* businessman, *the* aviator, and so forth); yet as Adorno's taste for Beckett and Alban Berg alike – for radical impoverishment and impure richness and excess – testifies, both minimalism and excess are dialectically related features of the modern as such. In Brecht, however, it is nature which is minimal, and the city, with its jungle and grim profusion, which will offer an opposing yet related richness.

What happens to poetic language, however, is precisely this movement of the impoverished in the twin directions of the definite article and the Eastern/traditional. Clearly, this new language will stand for and figure the old authentic lost one; but how is this substitution to be understood? For we have in any case learned from current regimes of time that in that sense the past never survives; that it is a reinvention by the present (to use Hobsbawm's strategic term for the persistence of 'traditions'). It was the resistance of older life-ways to modernization that generated for a time the mirage of some stubborn tenacity of the past, now almost wholly dissipated by what we call postmodernity. Brecht could thus not tap into, let alone resurrect, sources of the past within the German language; or rather, had he done so, archaism being itself one of the stereotypical resources of a desperate modernist stylistic renovation, his work might at best take its place alongside those now-antiquated mannerisms. For in the latter, it is the odd and unfamiliar word or turn of phrase, it is sheer verbal decoration, added on to the sentence structure, that stands as the sign and connotation of the past. In Brecht it is somehow, rather, the thought itself. But, how does thought offer anything of the past? Thoughts can at best be old-fashioned; only their language can be antiquated (to use this verb in a strong or active sense):

> Da war Mittag nicht mehr die Zeit zum Essen
> Da war Mittag die Zeit zum Sterben
>
> (VIII, 29)

> On that day noon was no longer the time to dine
> On that day noon was the time to die

But this stillness of death, the imperceptible withdrawal of the guards, the prudence of foreknowledge, the emptiness of the ceremonial halls, desertedness as a prelude to the great dynastic strokes – the murder of Agamemnon, the approach of the enemy armies, betrayal, conspiracy, vain warning and portents – all this is the doing of the Singer: he is the space of an archaic tradition which thinks and speaks the older thoughts about things. Or perhaps it is the things themselves that are archaic.

> Wenn das Haus eines Großen zusammenbricht
> Werden viele Kleine zerschlagen.
> Die das Glück der Mächtigen nicht teilten
> Teilen oft ihr Unglück. Der stürzende Wagen
> Reißt die schwitzenden Zugtiere
> Mit in den Abgrund.
>
> (VIII, 21)

Is the second sentence of this verse paragraph a saying of some kind, or even the artificial construction of a proverb? It has at least the symmetry and the latter's rhythm, but it is still insufficiently absolute. 'Sometimes' cannot replace the definite article; 'viele' and 'oft' are not stark enough, they still merely designate bad luck, being in the wrong place: to their realities applies, no doubt, Jolles's example of a *Spruch* – 'man muß

Glück haben'[4] ['you have to be lucky'] – but Brecht's language has not
yet taken on that form. But now, in the last line, the definite articles
appear: 'the' falling cart, 'the' oxen, 'the' abyss. A narrative form, a
fable, is already implicit here, with its paradoxical turns: the very weight
that makes the oxen sweat, defines the work they are given to do, is
what makes for their destruction, what pulls them over the edge:

> When a great man's house collapses
> Many little people get crushed.
> Those with no share in the mighty's fortune
> Often share their fate. The wagon's downfall
> Tugs the sweating oxen with it
> Into the abyss.

But what gives this language, this sentence, its authority? The adjectival
gerundives, with their half-rhyme ('stürzende', 'schwitzende'), make for
a parallel between subject and object; the catastrophe comes first in time
– the cart – and then its terrible consequences, far more tragic than the
loss of the cart itself; but the temporal sequence still remains absorbed
in the syntax of the sentence; it is not until the climactic 'Mit' that the
thing really happens, that the time of the event separates itself from the
sentence and, as it were, happens above and beyond it, if not in 'reality',
then at least in yet another dimension produced by *Trennung* itself. But
even this eventfulness of the storytelling, which expertly positions the
parts of speech for its narrative demonstration, is not yet what we are
looking for. It carves with clean large strokes; even the adjective itself –
the shame and scandal of any modernist stylistics – is verbalized, and
ceases to be some mere decorative property. We find ourselves again
confronted with the mysteries of the definite article – 'the' oxen, where
the article is no longer even *cataphoric* in the newly discovered sense of
modern text grammar, where the unnamed 'he' of the first sentence of a
novel places us in a unfamiliar 'middle of things', yet also produces an
'hors-champ', a preceding world before that arbitrary beginning, which
we hope eventually to be shown more of and to have identified for us.
These particular oxen have no previous history, no farm to describe, no
family ownership or paths to market, precisely because they are not
'particular' oxen at all, and are perhaps not even oxen in the first place
(since they are also the 'viele Kleine', the camp-followers, the small
merchants and suppliers – indeed, the peasants themselves).

I think we must look behind these ostensible characters, these extras
and supernumeraries of the scene – who are its protagonists by virtue of
the very fact that they are supernumeraries – to the thought mode which

sees them as such, and identifies them in its great flat homogeneous categories. For as has already been observed, these syntactical items have been crystallized and reified into the tokens of an experience everybody knows and recognizes in advance, in a tacit collective experience that need not be explained. The definite article therefore presupposes a kind of peasant history – that is to say, the paradoxically changeless and immemorial, stagnant history, which is not yet history in our modern sense, and which Marx associated with the notorious 'Asiatic mode of production' in the *Grundrisse*. Indeed, Marx's description (and the very concept he invented for this particular mode of production) has been stigmatized for any number of features: its identification with the notion of 'Oriental depotism', in the way in which many peasant collectives are grouped together under a single sacred or imperial figure; their lack of development ('they vegetate independently side by side', he says contemptuously; and related to that, their imperviousness to change ('the Asiatic form necessarily survives the longest and the most stubbornly'5). All of which has been taken to mean that Marx was Eurocentric and vilified the people of the 'Orient' (their societies have no innate dynamism, and are thus unable to develop into capitalism, as in the West; they have an affinity for tyrants) and that their peasant societies (despite the great classical civilizations of China and India) were subject to simple repetition: in short, that their history is to have no history, and that the changes registered in these very long periods of stasis are merely 'dynastic' ones: they affect only the people at the top, who come and go, are swept away in palace coups or by nomadic incursions, and are simply succeeded by different dynasties with the same dynamics. They thus do not even have the possibility of genuine revolution – that is, of the overturning of one mode of production and its supersession by another – because their agricultural system is not susceptible of a development of the feudal type that led into capitalism in Europe and Japan. And finally, related to these two things, they do not know genuine or even emergent democracy, presumably because they do not have genuine individualism. The theory embodies Eurocentric contempt only if we assume that for Marx, individualism and the development into capitalism is a good and desirable thing. But it is more complicated than that, since his dialectic (above all, in the *Manifesto*) presupposed that this was both bad and desirable: harmful, yet necessary for development into socialism.

At any rate, it seems to me that this general view of peasant life – as cyclical, as rife with catastrophes of all kinds which cannot, however, lead to genuine historical change – is also that of Brecht; but that at the same time it constitutes only one of several visions of History that coexist in his work (and no doubt in him as well, and perhaps also for some of the rest of us). Perhaps it would be better to say this the other way round, and to suggest that it is the vision of the peasantry which enables a certain crucial view of and access to History (but not the only one). For in the peasant works – and above all in the *Chalk Circle*, from which we have been quoting here – peasant time is *par excellence* the time of oppression: in the great class struggle of human history as a whole, now defined not by the specific modes of production as such but, rather, as the immemorial relationship between exploiters and exploited – yet not a relationship of sheer power and domination only, as in the anarchist tradition, but as a very general economic relationship between those who produce and those who enjoy the products of that production – in this vision of human history, as Brecht sees it and is able to represent it, or perhaps as he sees himself able to represent it, peasant life is the great vehicle through which one is able to represent the experience of the exploited and the oppressed; while the life of the capitalists is the form through which one can best represent the exploiters (we will come to them shortly).

This, therefore, is a 'vision' of history based on a mismatch or mixture of socioeconomic categories: it is theoretically incorrect and misleading, while poetically true.[6] And surely Brecht's secret Maoism (after 1949) prolongs this 'theoretical' error into the realm of politics as such. The enthusiasm for the emergent Chinese revolution is on the one hand a category mistake not unlike that witnessed in Lukács's first enthusiasm for the Soviet Revolution, in which Lenin is seen as the ultimate product of that Russian or Slavic mystical culture which flowered in Dostovesky. So here the Maoist revolution is felt (perhaps with a little more justice) as the ultimate development of the classical Chinese culture and philosophy Brecht so admired. It is finally the truth of a peasant culture, rather than a capitalist one; and yet of course this mistake is not only Brecht's, but that of reality and history as well. For Mao Zedong's was a peasant revolution of the type unforeseen not merely in the Leninist doctrine of revolution but also in the Marxian analysis of modes of production. Thus, to describe the double standard of the Brechtian vision of history as poetic is not to accuse it of being merely poetic; it also requires us to acknowledge and sense the historical resonance of the 'representational error'. This is not done by those who think of Brecht as a Stalinist, because he chose with passion and commitment to associate himself with the construction of socialism in the Soviet East: he was not the only one (compare also Althusser) to feel that the new Maoist revolution of the 1940s and 1950s offered a return to revolutionary authenticity after Stalin, and promised a redemption of the socialist spirit within the nominally socialist industrial system that it was the 'usefulness' of Stalin to have built.

The temporality of the working class, then, is utterly different from this one of the peasantry, as we shall see: strikes, unemployment, the frantic bike rides of the unemployed to Eisler's music in *Kuhle Wampe*, as opposed to the innumerable palace revolts that change nothing, and the generations of peasants passing through the rhythms of the seasons; peasant avarice as well, and resistance to innovation, as opposed to the intelligence of the machine-builders. Yet one great redemptive moment is held open by the view of History from a peasant perspective – and it is a very different one from the great depressions and the highly mechanized and industrially destructive wars of the capitalist era: this is a way of grasping change. It is a vision of change as a kind of immense window, not unlike Bakhtin's theorization of Rabelais as a brief moment of freedom between a scholastic Middle Ages and a counter-revolutionary baroque dictatorship: an allegory of the great Soviet cultural revolution of the 1920s, as we have seen, wedged perilously between Tsarism and Stalin. (It is an allegory Brecht himself deployed on one level of the *Galileo*, as we have also said.) So now the dynastic revolt, which Marx saw as the only event of this non-history of Asian and peasant history, and which then, very much in Marx's spirit, meets its end in the restoration of the ruling dynasty, and the return of the Governor's widow to seek to wrest the heritage of this revolt – the child itself – from its peasant saviour Grusha: this revolt is none the less the moment of Hope in the immemoriality of peasant life: 'O Wechsel der Zeiten! Du Hoffnung des Volkes' (VIII, 21): 'O vicissitudes of time, you ultimate hope of the people!'

This is the moment of freedom, the redemptive moment, in one of Brecht's temporalities: the moment of provisional change, the moment in which an Azdak can appear, no matter how briefly, before vanishing again into the mists of time and the immemoriality of peasant labour and oppression. It is the Xairos of Brecht's peasant history, and a temporality of precapitalism that is most often associated with the 'populist' features in Brecht, and determines the chronologies of the great plays: the Thirty Years War in *Mother Courage*; a peasant Middle Ages shaking off its timeless lethargy in the new science of *Galileo*; the Oriental despotism of the *Chalk Circle* (if not also the Chinese precapitalist merchant urban setting of the *Good Person*), this last overlaid by the quarrel of the two Soviet industrializing peasantries in the frame of the same play or fable. These settings are no doubt 'unreal' in the sense of being unhistorical: but Brecht always warned us, with annoyance at our inveterate incomprehension, that here we were most often still thinking of naturalism and its photographic ideals of reproduction; nor do the references to

Shakespeare's romance settings do much good either. I would prefer to commemorate Ernst Bloch's generic reclassification of Wagner's *Ring* and his proposal to rethink these operas, whose associations with the Nazi period make them so ambivalent and problematical, as fairy-tales, thus reemphasizing the popular and utopian, folkloric elements, at the expense of the nationalist-racist ones.[7] It is indeed the fairy-tale – or, better still, the untranslatable German term *Märchen*, 'little story' – which is a better generic reference here, for everything it includes of the fable-like and of collective wish-fulfilment, which does not exclude the baleful, bad luck, oppression and death, but strikes all this with a magic wand that also includes hope along with them:

> Verehrtes Publikum, los, such dir selbst den Schluß!
> Es muß ein guter da sein, muß, muß, muß!
>
> (VI, 279)
>
> Now, honourable public, the finding of an ending is passed to you:
> There has to be a happy one out there somewhere, has to, has to, has to!

Nor is the fairy-tale unreal or unrealistic either; provided you are not locked into oppositions such as the real and the false, or the realistic and unrealistic. For the redemptive mentality of the fairy-tale is itself at one with the *mentalité* of a peasant world: that is the price we must pay for this particular utopian register (others are also possible), and why we must cherish and choose it. And this is the sense in which Brecht's inclusion of a dimension of peasant history was not some ideological blockage or limit on his part; rather, that dimension was necessary in order to recapture and represent the note of Hope it could alone afford. Yet the peasant world, and Chinese culture, were also real, and a part of human history in some way still available to us.

15   Registers and Generic Discontinuities

Returning to the proverb for one last moment, we must note the rather different interpretation Jolles offers us: observing its presence in all classes and walks of life, by way of the traces of content from a variety of trades and occupations from the blacksmith's ('strike the iron while it's hot') to the farmer's ('shutting the barn door after the horse has gone'), he proposes a more metaphysical reading of the form – that is to say, one which posits some more timeless and universal human experience. In fact, this experience resembles nothing quite so much as a well-nigh Deleuzian or Bergsonian flux:

When we grasp the world as a manifold of individual perceptions and individual experiences, these perceptions and experiences – grasped successively and then held together simultaneously – do, to be sure, constitute *experience* as such, but at the same time their sum remains a multiplicity of individual entities.[8]

The dynamic of the *Spruch* or proverb thereby remains a formal one: it seals off a segment in the flow, affords a momentary kind of closure in what can never be stilled or arrested:

In this morphology therefore [that of the so-called 'simple forms'] the proverb names that literary form which shuts off and closes out a story, without divesting it of its nature as a particular world of specificities and disjunctions. The proverb pulls its world together, without thereby absolutely lifting it out of its empiricality.[9]

From our current perspective, this view sends us back to the conditions of possibility of the 'proverb' in the flow of experience itself, the materials which allow for such closure – or, in other words, precisely that social texture Jolles himself has excluded from the outset. But even more interesting from our perspective is the way in which the 'proverb' offers a kind of arrested abstraction – indeed, a resistance towards going all the way to the concept itself:

We might even say that the proverb here wards off its generalization into the concept as such; it would be only a slight exaggeration to affirm that it is structured so as to be usable only here and in this particular place, and not elsewhere.[10]

The same is true for the other, more generalized uses of the abstract concept as such:

In the world of the proverb we ward off all those infantilizing consequences and conclusions to which experience forces us at all those points at which it calls for conceptual thought and attempts to become a form of knowledge.[11]

This is indeed why Jolles concludes his discussion of the proverb with the peculiar figure of a material entity; another smaller yet independent physical object is inserted into the principal one as a kind of adornment – what the ancients called an emblem, *emblema*. The emblem thus, Jolles explains,

does not incorporate the meaning of a whole in the mode of its content, and of the whole *qua* whole, but, rather, dramatizes the way in which the meaning of this whole can be grasped only as a coexistence of distinct unities.[12]

But this is precisely the direction in which we now propose to move. For we must reconcile the mirage of some simple and homogeneous peasant language with the heterogeneities and impure mixtures of Brecht's city poems and of the various other aesthetics which radiate from his work, whose juxtaposition even with just such peasant proverbs makes them into random pieces of an assemblage, rather than serene glimpses of a pastoral world. But Jolles himself luminously demonstrates how the proverb fails to be even an abstract sentence; it is somehow an object language beyond normal syntax.[13]

In short, an emphasis on the closure of this object-like form brings us at once to that 'poetics of quotation' which is evident, not merely in Brechtian dramaturgy and in construction of *gestus*, but within the very language itself. But the result of these floating, quoted lines – they are also presumably 'already known', 'already heard', as cultural objects floating through the collective mind – is not always, as one might have expected, satirical. Brechtian lyricism is also grounded in such dissociation, as though 'sincerity' were as out of place in love as in acting, and quoting one's lines lifted one out of time better than all the timebound ideologies of passion.

Whence, alongside the 'peasant' proverbs, a rather different type of verbal isolation and timelessness that can be observed in the great lyrics, such as the duet of the cranes from *Mahagonny* ('Sieh jene Kraniche', XX, 364–5), in which clouds (as in 'Marie A.') are both in movement and at rest with respect to one another. Here the Tao of perpetual change – 'So mag der Wind sie in das Nichts entführen': 'So the wind may well carry them off into nothingness' – is perpetuated, yet also unexpectedly overcome. It moves them, yet the fact of the twin movement (both of the cranes with each other, and of cranes and clouds: and then in the performance the two lovers' voices, now alternating separately, now singing in unison) also lends them their timelessness, beyond all change:

> Und keines andres sehe als das Wiegen
> Des anderen in dem Wind, den beide spüren.

> Seeing no more than that rising and falling
> of the other one, rocked by the wind both feel together.

This is the sense in which the final line – 'So scheint die Liebe Liebenden ein Halt': 'So love seems to the lovers to arrest them in full course' –

wins its significance, is somehow 'paid for' and proven by the very movement of the verses themselves, in motion and yet still in their parellelisms: and a strange dialectic is enacted in which these opposites also become unified, and stillness proves to be the same as that perpetual change or movement so frequently celebrated elsewhere in Brecht, and theorized as the fundamental feature of his dialectic.

This also explains those moments of elevation in Brecht in which characters – like these of Joe and Jenny – are separate from their context, and even their own specific personalities, and lifted up in one long wondrous momentary suspension: 'Aus einem Leben in ein andres Leben': 'From out of one life into another'. The momentary abstraction and transformation is perhaps even more striking in the love scenes of the *Three-Penny Opera*, where Mac and Polly have satiric contexts that must be neutralized, and where even their language ('Can you feel my heart beating?') has already been preempted by the Peachums and marked as sheer mass-cultural stereotype. The presupposition is that love is a state and, as such, independent of the quality and nature of the persons who inhabit it momentarily: in other words, that there is a distance between the element itself and its momentary contents. But it still falls to the language (and its music) to perform the act of radical separation which will lift Mac and Polly into this new and transitory element. This is done by one of the more paradoxical formulations in Brecht, in which the kind of mutual neutralization (swiftness and motionlessness all at once) takes place in the enunciation itself, in its positive and negative. It may also be said that here high style and comedy also neutralize each other, to the extent to which the ethereal echo may seem either nonsense or the very cancellation of love itself, about which it also seems to be affirmed that it can end in the next minute without anyone caring:

> Die Liebe dauert oder dauert nicht
> An dem oder jenem Ort.
> (II, 254)

> Love lasts or doesn't last
> In this place, or else in that.

It does or it doesn't; it is or it isn't: here or there, somewhere or nowhere. These effects themselves would not, however, be possible without that initial and fundamental internal distance about which we have already spoken. Unless 'love' were not already somehow at distance from these characters, there would be no mechanisms in place to realize this fuller separation; but it is precisely just such mechanisms which are at stake both in supreme and mystical moments of this kind, and also in the line-to-line movement of the plays in time.

I want to show the ceaseless transformations of the latter in a characteristic example, the finale of Act I of the *Three-Penny Opera*, in which Polly philosophically confronts her parents on the question of marriage: Is happiness really too much to ask? Why can I not simply marry Macheath, the man I love? What is to be examined here is not merely the V-effect itself, as that already takes place by virtue of the elevation of a plot necessity into a metaphysical issue. For the Peachums, this unexpected elopement means a loss of income (Polly as capital); for the play, this hostility will lead on into the plots against Macheath that spell his downfall; yet for some other level of interpretive activity, it also means a reflexion 'Über die Unsicherheit menschlicher Verhältnisse': 'On the uncertainty of human relationships' (the title which is lowered to announce this finale-number). Even this interpretive focus is misleading, however, since for one thing, *Verhältnisse* will have a different meaning within the song itself. The title means something like a mutability in human relationships, love or otherwise; the song takes *Verhältnisse* – 'Doch die Verhältnisse, sie sind nicht so': 'But things don't work that way' [literally, relationships/circumstances/situations are not like that] – as life itself, the way life is, the relationship of human beings to the world and to destiny: the title thus uses the word in an interpersonal, the song in a metaphysical, acceptation. More than that, however, it is not mutability which is underscored in the song but, rather, 'the right to happiness on earth', and the reasons why happiness is not to be expected. That, however, is not 'uncertain' but, rather, only too certain and inevitable. There is thus even an initial distance between the title of the song and its content, let alone between this 'philosophical' level of the new text and its context.

Now, however, we must briefly enumerate the distances within the text themselves: they are clearly enough given in advance by the mere fact of its music, about which, we remember, Brecht had already insisted that it should clash with the words, such that 'Musik, Wort und Bild müßten mehr Selbständigkeit erhalten' (XXIV, 79): 'words, music and setting must become more independent of one another' (Willett, 38). This *Trennung* is then inscribed in the actor himself, and his relationship to the ensemble:

> Indem er singt, vollzieht der Schauspieler einen Funktionswechsel. Nichts ist abscheulicher, als wenn der Schauspieler sich den Anschein gibt, als merke er nicht, daß er eben den Boden der nüchternen Rede verlassen hat und bereits singt. Die drei Ebenen: nüchternes Reden, gehobenes Reden und Singen, müssen stets voneinander getrennt bleiben, und keinesfalls bedeutet das

gehobene Reden eine Steigerung des nüchternen Redens und das Singen eine solche des gehobenen Redens.

(XXIV, 65)

When an actor sings he undergoes a change in function. Nothing is more revolting than when the actor pretends not to notice that he has left the level of plain speech and started to sing. The three levels – plain speech, heightened speech, and singing – must always remain distinct, and in no case should heightened speech represent an intensification of plain speech, or singing of heightened speech.

(Willett, 44)

We already know how these differentiations are to be achieved: through quotation, such that plain speech is quoted from the character the actor is demonstrating; heightened speech quoted within that plain speech; and singing quoted as yet another type of gesture of expression to be foregrounded and separated from any context in which it might be felt to be somehow 'natural'. This is the sense in which Macheath's and Polly's romantic exchange is somehow rescued from the prose opprobrium whereby it can be identified as the stereotypical kitsch it represents in the real world; for, quoted, it takes on its own semi-autonomy which can be realized in a kitsch music whose qualities are at one with kitsch itself, as in the artificial moon so admired for its very artificiality in 'Moon over Alabama'.[14]

This description thus far underscores the discontinuities effectuated by quotation as such: but it does not account for content in any other than purely formal ways. We therefore need a supplementary description to account for the nature of these effects, something that will try to convey the idea of a perpetual transcendence of registers, as the text passes from one tone to another: this process of transcendence thus involves a shifting of contextual frames around the lines, the individual sentences, and even the words themselves. It is a process for which I am tempted to revive that much over- and misused term the 'sublime', in a rather different sense from that in which it has normally been appropriated:[15] here, some immense liberation from context as such, as we pass from one register to another – to be fundamentally distinguished from the traditional notion of the liberation within the sublime by way of its cancellation of internal limits, by either immense size or immense power. And although Kant reserved that term for something else as well, the notion of a 'mathematical sublime' is not irrelevant here either, in so far as it can suggest the variability of the meaning and content of an equation depending on precisely the shifting content given to its variables.

The music here (in the concluding trio of Act I) allows us to deal with these subtleties in a relatively tangible and accessible manner; for its solemnity underscores the religious character of Peachum's first stanza. It is very precisely this religious *Weltanschauung* or metaphysic which first enlarges the frame or context beyond Polly's simple, plot-level question (why can I not marry Macheath?), and makes of it a matter for philosophical disquisition: 'man's right to happiness on this earth'. But already this proposition, which contradicts conventional notions of original sin, is transmitted with a gloomy inward-turning reservation that concentrates this 'right' into a veritable inner tabernacle, an ultimate hidden principle, which should scarcely be enunciated at all without the most elaborate religious precautions: 'Das ist des Menschen nacktes Recht auf Erden': 'This is man's right on earth, plain and simple.' Here, awe is gesturally conveyed by the withdrawal of the music into its innermost mysteries: the voice is concentrated, made hushed, perhaps as much by the blasphemy of the sentiments as by the mystery of religious 'right' itself.

Then, in one of the shifts in question, the whole register changes, the music bursts out again; it is now energetic and ferocious as it attests to the failure to receive this due: 'unfortunately/regrettably' [*leider*], no one has ever observed that anyone got what they were supposed to ('that people get what they have a right to'): 'who would not have wanted to get one's due?' [*einmal Recht bekommen*], but 'things are not that way' [*die Verhältnisse*]. Several things must be observed about this language of rights and wishes: the latter ('Who would not have liked to . . .?') allows a modulation for Frau Peachum's more maternal intervention ('how I would have liked to give you what you want'), before yet another, even more fundamental turn in Peachum's own mediation: 'Who would not have wanted to be a good man?' – a return in which the same solemn organ tones of the opening are repeated, preparing yet another raucous outburst in which the final reply to this forlorn hope is delivered: things are not like that, because finally 'the world is a miserable place, and people are rotten!' It is a generalization which the spectacle of Peachum's own business tends to corroborate, along with all the other surroundings of Macheath's existence, with the possible exception of the highwayman himself, who exhibits a certain contagious energy in the midst of this truly eighteenth-century dreariness, an energy we will examine in a moment.

But first a little word, a seemingly unconsequential adverb, must detain us: the word 'leider' (unfortunately), which operates the shift from strophe to antistrophe, from the hush of awe to the outburst of rueful and malign celebration. It returns in the refrain, in which Polly and Peachum accept the diagnosis: 'da hat er eben leider recht'; 'he's right, and it is unfortunately only too true' – a formulation in which the word 'recht' returns yet again in a strange echo of the earlier claims and rights, as though the verse were demonstrating how our 'right' to happiness has mockingly been reduced to this scant consolation of being 'right' after all (in lower case, at that).

The entire formulation will now be triumphantly quoted by Peachum in his retort: Naturally I am 'unfortunately correct' [*Natürlich hab ich leider recht*], in which the adverb, slight as it is, operates the entire shift on to another register by separating Peachum's language from the character himself (the 'leider' belongs to the women, not to him) and reifying it at some 'higher level' in which the finale plunges on to its predictable conclusion ('Und darum ist das alles Kitt': 'it's all garbage').

The result is related to a phenomenon I have elsewhere[16] called 'generic discontinuities': in other words, the slippage of the frames, the way in which each thematic context is transcended, also constitutes a transgression of the generic boundary. It is what allows the moments of elevation peculiar to this 'beggars' opera' and already present in Gay's original version, which shares the metaphysical possibilities developed in the satires of his friends and contemporaries Pope and Swift – namely, the unexpected passage from topical satire into an evocation of the Absolute (albeit, as in all these cases, the negative Absolute of a vision of animality and degradation). In Brecht (and Weill) the religious mode of the music develops immediately out of the well-known Protestant–ethical strain essential to Western capitalism as such; there is thus a triangular figure, in which crooks and gangsters are being compared to businessmen on the one hand, while on the other the secret connections between Protestantism and money are articulated. But we have also seen a range of other 'generic' expressions – a grotesque moment of maternal love in Frau Peachum's song; more ferocious and even sadistic accents (reminiscent of the imperialist cannon-song) in Peachum's celebration of man's inhumanity to man; hymns of repentance; the bourgeois family drama and 'generational' conflict; a view of the human condition from Montaigne's 'épicycle de Mercure' ('auf diesem Sterne': 'on this star') – in short, a variety of distinct tonal levels any of which is capable of crystallizing into what we call a genre (particularly if we think in terms of the 'kinds' of lyric poetry or of song). Still, the effect properly character-izable as 'sublime' derives not from this general generic movement, but from the specific one whereby the frame and focus of the representation suddenly enlarge to include the world itself, and Being. This does not make Brecht over into a 'philosophical' poet (although he admired Lucretius, and tried to do something similar in his abortive epic versification of *The Communist Manifesto* [XV, 120–56]), but it underscores the availability of the metaphysical note among the range of his voices and tonal modalities, as well as reconfirming the old secret and unholy kinship between farce and the tragic (on which Socrates himself was heard to begin a disquisition in the early-morning hours at the very close of Plato's *Symposium*).

But it is precisely Macheath's energy we need to interrogate now, as it is registered in the antistrophe of the finale, in the brash worldly confirmation that vigorously answers the gloomy forebodings of the strophe, full of religion and sin. What we have to ask is why the music – and the words, and the singing, the gesturality, of this finale – should take such joyous satisfaction in the outcome, and how we are to interpret this ferocious jubilation about the hopeless corruption of the world.

The answer lies, I think, in Brecht's relationship to capitalism itself – or rather, in that of a certain Marxism generally: the right-wing disdain for business and middle-class culture which Marxism inherited from the first anti-capitalist critiques of the Romantic period, although it persists as one tendency within a later Marxism, is rendered ambiguous, not to say ambivalent, by the more complex relationship of the working-class movement to an industrial development which is in its own fundamental presupposition, and which it must therefore judge to be as progressive as it is harmful and wasteful.

At any rate, it is precisely a certain delight in surprising and redramatizing the very inner and outer workings of capital, the schemes of the businessmen (not excluding Peachum's own, particularly as that exfoliates into the *Three-Penny Novel*), the somersaults of the market, which, like History itself, convulsively turn over from the positive to the negative and back again – it is this fascination with capital itself, and business as such, that we find everywhere in Brecht – beginning, no doubt, with the sale of the elephant in *Mann ist Mann* (or even the 'buying' of opinions in *The Jungle of Cities*), and reaching one kind of climax in the foundational myth of capitalism in *Mahagonny*, and another in St Joan's journey to the depths in the eponymous play (written between 1929 and 1932), which has so often been taken as Brecht's most comprehensive initiation into Marxian analysis. But the perspective of the later plays should not be forgotten either. Mother Courage is herself a business-woman (as is the 'good person' of Szechuan), and her objectively ambivalent relationship to moneymaking is not foreign to the ambivalence so many readers have attributed to this 'tragic' drama in general. (One should, however, specify this ambivalence more sharply: it is not the appeal of money that is at stake in her sacrifice of her children, but her terror of losing her modest capital, the wagon – a loss one can never make up again: money comes and goes, but a capital can never be restored. It is this distinction between money and capital which is the heart of Marxian doctrine, and constitutes the conflict, tragic or not, of this great play.)

The celebration of capital, then – a joyous gesturality in which its tricks and lore are performed and demonstrated in front of an amused public, for which such acrobatics are supposed to be more entertaining than a boxing match or any other sportive exhibition of strength-cum-skill – is what is at stake here, from the wording of the song all the way to the trammelling of whole intrigues based on Gustavus Meyers's *History of the Great American Fortunes* (1909): it is the investment of libido in what is supposed to be repulsive (or 'negatively cathected') which is acted out and raucously performed before us here. A Marxist aesthetic which does not make a place for this fundamental ambivalence, this fascination with and excitement at everything perverse and suspicious, unclean and scurrilous, about the beast itself, will alway strike outsiders as unacceptably puritanical or prim and excessively decorous, as repulsive as middle-class respectability itself. The Brechtian aversion to respectability in general is richly documented in the early works – with *Baal* as its virtual allegory: the Marxian turn is thereby able to tap those 'antisocial' energies for a new and more productive engagement with the negative.

16 Representability of Capitalism

Yet we must also examine the question from the standpoint of the representational issues that surface here for Brecht as he struggles with the staging of this other fundamental temporality of History: the industrial capitalist one, so different from that of the peasantry and of the older precapitalist modes of production. It is a problem about which he complained repeatedly from the late 1920s onwards – first in the form of understanding how capital works, something which in Brechtian pedagogy is obviously inseparable from the showing of how it works. Yet even before we get to this point, at which theatrical and staging problems lead him on to the reading of Marx, it is important to grasp the temptations along the way, and the representational dead ends.

The first of these is money itself, which offers representational problems in its own right, and stands at some first representational crossroads between the poor and the rich. For interested as Brecht was in productive or industrial labour as such, as raw material it is a stumbling block for which only documentary seems to offer a solution; but he did not believe in photographic realism of that kind.[17] Money thus appears negatively at the moment of unemployment: it is not the workers' work that is representable but their poverty; and finally the suicidal panic of *Kuhle Wampe*, the depression of the jobless – the bicycle wheels rolling towards jobs advertised and then snapped up, the sheer weakness and exhaustion of the queues at the food kitchens (compare Jean Renoir's *La Vie est à nous* [1936]). But in the case of the people who make money and get rich, money is equally unrepresentable, for it has become capital. Thus, in its absence for the poor, and its presence for the rich, money as such is peculiarly unsuitable as a starting point (something Marx himself can be observed to discover at the beginning of his preparatory notebooks for *Capital*, published as the *Grundrisse*). Here is an enlightening sketch of Brecht on the subject, as he tried to put together a first 'social' drama in *Jae Fleischhacker in Chicago* (around 1926):

> Der Hurrikan, in den die Familie Mitchel kommt muß so nüchtern und kalt wie möglich sein. Ohne Romantik. Die Schicksalsschläge durch Gummiknüppel, ihr Untergang vollzieht sich durch Wörter, flach und abgenutzt und unpoetisch wie Geldmünzen. Überhaupt dürfen die durch das Geld hervorgerufenen Katastrophen nicht denen gleichen, die durch kriegerische Leidenschaften oder durch Liebe veranlaßt werden. Diese Katastrophen vollziehen sich viel dünner, stimmungsloser und trockener. Es ist gerade diese dünne, unsichtbare, zerstörende Macht des Geldes zu zeigen, die so furchtbar ist, mangelnde Information.
>
> (X, 279)

> The hurricane encountered by the Mitchel family has to be as cold and prosaic as possible. Without any romanticism. The hammer-blows of fate with rubber truncheons, their downfall, is fulfilled with words alone, as flat and depleted, as unpoetic as gold coins. Above all: catastrophes provoked by money must be absolutely unlike those occasioned by martial passion or by love. These catastrophes take place in a far thinner, non-atmospheric and drier fashion. What has to be shown is precisely this thin, non-visible, destructive power of money which is so frightful, particularly when you lack information.

But precisely this uniqueness in the nature of money seems to shut off any possible representation; for if it is a valuable object or substance – like gold to the miser, or greenbacks to Dreiser's Sister Carrie – it is no longer really a token of exchange; and if it becomes capital, it takes on an incorporeal value which equally can be represented only in its effects.

Thus Brecht stands between two kinds of representation, both of which have already been exploited by the naturalist novelists from Zola to Frank Norris and Upton Sinclair: on the one hand the 'Schicksalsschläge' ('blows of fate') of the very poor, who migrate in family units from one big city to another; on the other, the 'malefactors of great wealth', whose rise and fall, fortunes and downfall, also register 'the fists of destiny' in a way virtually correlative to the first group. But in the great representations of capitalism – particularly in the two fundamental Brechtian works *St Joan* and the *Three-Penny Novel* – these last are reduced to Dickensian misery, lumpen-status (Peachum's beggars) or desperate objects of charity. It is as though in Brecht's works that radically different temporality of peasant life had absorbed the actantial position of the 'proletariat', the position of the oppressed and exploited in capitalism, of the dominated class. The remnants left out of it in the 'capitalist' works then turn out to be the objects of charity, whence a new kind of actantial position: Shaw's Salvation Army or Peachum's 'beggar's store' – the nature of liberal philanthropy may be very different in the two cases, but the narrative position is identical, and tends to slip into the related one of the party itself, most centrally in *The Mother*.

We are therefore left with the very different temporality of the capitalists as such, with whose lives Brecht toyed, showing them again and again (Dan Drew, Jae Fleischhacker, even Mac the Knife himself). But these lives are as subject to catastrophic reversals as the lives of the poor: it is the other side of the great wheel of fortune. If the catastrophes of the peasant world could open up a brief golden age, here they can only lead to disaster; and even success is the prelude to more disaster. What Brecht now has to learn is the secret of this temporality, rather than the psychology of those who are submitted to it. This is his account of his efforts:

Dann half mir eine Art Betriebsunfall weiter. Für ein bestimmtes Theaterstück brauchte ich als Hintergrund die Weizenbörse Chicagos. Ich dachte, durch einige Umfragen bei Spezialisten und Praktikern mir rasch die nötigen Kenntnisse verschaffen zu können. Die Sache kam anders. Niemand, weder einige bekannte Wirtschaftsschriftsteller noch Geschäftsleute – einem Makler, der an der Chicagoer Börse sein Leben lang gearbeitet hatte, reiste ich von Berlin nach Wien nach – , niemand konnte mir die Vorgänge an der Weizenbörse hinreichend erklären. Ich gewann den Eindruck, daß gerade diese Vorgänge schlechthin unerklärlich, daß heißt von der Vernunft nicht erfaßbar, und das heißt wieder einfach unvernünftig waren. Die Art, wie das Getreide der Welt verteilt wurde, war schlechthin unbegreiflich. Von jedem Standpunkt aus außer demjenigen einer Handvoll Spekulanten war dieser Getreidemarkt ein einziger Sumpf.

A kind of occupational accident helped me out. For a certain play I needed Chicago's wheat exchange as background. I thought I would be able to acquire the necessary information quickly by making a few enquiries of

specialists and practitioners. It happened otherwise. No one, neither well-
known writers on economics nor business people – I traveled from Berlin to
Vienna after a broker who had worked all his life at the Chicago exchange –
no one could explain the processes of the wheat exchange to me adequately.
I won the impression that these processes were simply inexplicable, i.e. not to
be grasped by reason, i.e. unreasonable. The way the world's wheat was
distributed was simply incomprehensible. From every point of view except
that of a handful of speculators this grain market was one big swamp.[18]

But as with the case of money itself, the stock market is not capital
personified either – or rather, it is merely one way among others of
attempting to personify something that is too complex for representation, because it involves not only so many distinct lives and points of
view, but also a world of things – technical processes as well as raw
materials, and final products to be sold and used: the three great branches
of production, distribution and consumption, which scarcely intersect at
all, and on which there can be no unifying viewpoint. Eisenstein's
projected film on *Capital* was alternately projected as a series of lessons
on the dialectic and as the demystification (exfoliation) of simple
everyday lives (the woman's of consumption, the man's of production),
in which presumably the commodities would be translated back into
their original materials and turned into so many narratives.[19] But
Eisenstein was more interested in the nature of dialectical abstraction
than Brecht, and film seemed to him both the supreme embodiment of
this new kind of abstraction and also the most obvious vehicle for
demonstrating its structure. I think that this lesson would have been far
too static and academic for Brecht, even leaving aside the prodigious
differences in media: one does not simply want to say that Brecht was
more 'humanistically' interested in people and concrete social situations.
In that respect, it is worth remembering that both were attacked for cold
intellectualism and a preference for ideas over emotions. Rather, it seems
better to say that Brecht's pedagogy always involved pedagogy itself;
that it was self-referential as well as referential. One may certainly say
the same for Eisenstein's writing and theorizing (and perhaps we should
go on to make the same point we tried to make above about Brecht
himself: that the theory is part of the artistic production itself, *Potemkin*
or *October* including all the tireless and extensive commentaries Eisenstein made on each of them, etc.). Yet the mediation of the machine in
Eisenstein (the camera apparatus) complicates the picture; we will look
at Brecht's relationship with machinery (and with modernity) later on,
and certainly, following Piscator, he was deeply interested in the
inclusion of documentary film segments in his production; early projects
like the unwritten *Ruhrepos* of 1927 (XXI, 205–6) suggest a flirtation

with the representation of production as such, not merely the invention of stories and narratives that have production as their background. At any rate, the two greatest practitioners of an artistic dialectic are different enough from each other to warrant a much more extensive comparison (and differentiation) than can be offered here; it being sufficient to note that in Eisenstein's achieved work, and besides this or that glimpse of pre-revolutionary bureaucrats and managers, only *The General Line* attempts a full-dress representation of production as such; and it is the industrialization of agriculture under socialism that is aesthetically at stake there, not any of the features of capitalism that Brecht tried to grapple with.

At any rate, the juxtaposition makes it clear that the stock market offers only one possible figure for capitalism, and scarcely exhausts the complexity of the phenomenon even on an intellectual and analytic level. It certainly affords some characters, and they are representationally useful in three ways: first, they are isolated from working-class characters even more absolutely than the managers of a plant, say, and can thus be exhibited in a virtually zoological way. Second, each one of them is a vehicle for a certain kind of very specialized energy – making deals, evolving combinations, acquiring secret information, gaining a 'corner' on a given commodity, and the like: skills and activities which seem to have nothing to do with that production, distribution and consumption which would also characterize the industrial modernity of a socialist system. And third, they offer the prospect of duels and struggles of the type Brecht loved to witness and stage, since his boxing days and projects like the *Jungle of Cities*: the *agon* is, after all, the fundamental dramatic event, and at the same time nothing can become quite so abstract as these duels to the death between opposing figures; the situation thus partakes of the diagrammatic quality of the *Lehrstück* as well.

Brecht came to do this kind of plot very well; my sense is that in this respect the opening of *Arturo Ui* is the best he achieved along these lines, because instead of offering a rather sterile outcome, in which one businessman necessarily wins out over another (or in which the loser is then able to recoup, as in Mauler's situation in *St Joan*) – a dramatic situation in which we will necessarily be asked to interest ourselves in the psychology of the robber baron in question (again, as in the case of Mauler) – here, in *Arturo Ui*, the entire mechanism of the *agon* between businessmen and the agitation of the stock market is transcended by something which is much more monstrous and no longer belongs in that category at all: namely, Hitler. (I find the rest of the play, in which Nazi history is ingeniously replicated as the Chicaco gangster milieu, amusing, but in the long run much more tiresome.)

As for the representability of this particular institution of capitalism –

brokers roaring like beasts on the floor of the Bourse

– it is familiar enough, and full of a drama that can easily become stereotypical, which is to say visual: Antonioni's great scene from *Eclipse* is only the most vivid modern version; Zola's great novel *L'Argent* the most comprehensive and exciting novelistic treatment. But Zola, like Brecht, was forced to reflect on the nature and possibilities of that representability: 'Donner quelque part la sensation de cela, sous le soleil, la palpitation même de Paris, cette forge des grandes spéculations, au centre même de l'agitation, au coeur de la vie intense, du mouvement, du bruit . . . Paris, de 1 heure à 3 heures, là.'[20] Already highly cinematographic, one would say, except that in the final version it is vitalism and the accompanying metaphoric system that triumphs: '. . . ce quartier de toutes les fièvres, où la Bourse, d'une heure à trois, bat comme un coeur énorme, au milieu'.[21]

This premium on visuality and its figural systems is surely not calculated to serve any demonstrative or pedagogical ends (even though Zola's extraordinary preparations and planification make the project itself pedagogical to a degree); and, finally in that respect, Brecht is both behind and ahead of Zola, more closely related to Balzac on the one hand, and more deeply influenced by Norris and the later naturalistic 'futures markets' on the other.

For the futures markets – the famous 'corner' on wheat, Mauler's meat-packing industry (his stock market ventures have no particular equivalent in Sinclair's *The Jungle*) – have the advantage that in them the abstractions of money can be given a shadow content. Simmel showed us, in the *Philosophy of Money*, that money has a specifically dialectical relationship to the value of its substance: if the substance is too valuable in itself, the very function of money disappears; if money's value becomes too abstract, it becomes an empty set of figures. The situation of the futures markets does not solve the problem of this oscillation, which is structural; but it permits the momentary triumph of an artistic ruse, allowing flashes of the actual production to be glimpsed, and making money over momentarily into a consumable thing you hunger for, like a sausage or bread. Otherwise there remains only the libidinal, the fetish, as in Dreiser: 'greenbacks. They were soft and noiseless and he got his fingers about them and crumpled them up in his hand . . . two soft, green, handsome ten-dollar bills'.[22]

Balzac is, however, fetishistic in a different, precapitalist sense, with his naive pride in his spurious acquisitions and his mania for collections of valuable objects which have to be famous as well. On the other hand, the Balzacian narrative of money – against the background of various proto-stock markets, *Le Livre d'or* (government bonds), and so on, all of which are still too rudimentary to be mapped out with Zola's supreme authority – is much closer to the Brechtian *agon*, the struggle between larger-than-life figures, each of whom feverishly flails and flounders in the net, trying the most ingenious combinations, in frantic agitation. This is why Lukács is right again in this context, and Balzac's characters are far closer to social *praxis* than the types and human furniture of the naturalisms; but Brecht's figures in the *Three-Penny Novel* and in *St Joan* are equally endowed with never-ending momentum, brain-racking intelligence, and an inexhaustible imagination for schemes and escape-hatches, for tricks to outwit the competitor and the energy necessary to sustain a virtually lifelong struggle.

Balzac suggests another feature of Brecht's representations as well; for his principal novella on the subject, *La Maison Nucingen*, is one long breathless tale of intrigue and cutthroat financial duelling narrated by various Parisian hangers-on, and what it betrays above all is supreme Balzacian passion, which is that of insider information, of know-how, of being in on the secrets. As a novelist Balzac is a supremely irritating know-it-all, constantly buttonholing you to offer information that nobody else has but he knows for a fact. Never mind that he was never personally able to make a killing on all this familiarity with the inner workings: the novels represent the attempt to prove it all to you, to show the inner mechanics, to demonstrate his knowledge of the system. Balzac thus stands not only for the representation of money and business but for the passion to know about them – something which, by Zola's time, is an affair of specialists and which requires not the steamy barber-shop or pub-corner whispers and explanations but, rather, simply serious hard work, visits to the *lieux*, documentation, questions for this or that expert, and so forth. With Brecht, however, we are back to the uncovering of secrets again (the trip to Austria): how to get in on the secret of the stock market – as though it had a secret to begin with, and as though, if you knew it (we are by now in the time of Lenin, after all), you could also use it as a revolutionary weapon. This, then, is the place of libidinality, it is this excitement that Brecht associates with the City and its goings-on and with capitalism in general, at least as a representational raw material: this is one side of his 'Marxism' and, indeed, one of the more ambivalent sides, as his hesitant and perplexed notes from 1930 suggest:

Die Größte und unumgänglichste Schwierigkeit: festzustellen, wieviel der Marxismus vom Kapitalismus abhängt. . . . Wieviele seiner Methoden kapitalistische sind oder nur auf kapitalistische Zustände passen. Sie verändern den

Kapitalismus, ihn erfassend? Die Dialektik erklärt ihn, erledigt ihn? Ist also kapitalistisch in ihrem Bezirk bestimmt? Auftauchte sie als Übererscheinung zu ihm. Gibt sie ihm seinen Sinn?

(XXI, 407)

The biggest and most unavoidable difficulty: to determine to what degree Marxism depends on capitalism itself. How many of its methods are capitalist, or at least work on capitalist conditions? Do they change capitalism by understanding it? Does the dialectic explain it or liquidate it? The dialectic thereby being capitalist in its field of application? Does it arise as capitalism's epiphenomenon? Does it give capitalism its meaning in the first place?

In our present context, this question (also addressed by both Lukács and Gramsci in their fashions[23]) is also one of representation: to what degree will it still be necessary to represent capitalism under socialism – or, as I prefer to put it, in a situation of socialist construction? To the degree to which *Arturo Ui* supersedes the stock market, one can suppose that considerations about war will supersede those of money; and this is certainly the case for the more official and governmental 'campaigns' with which the *Berliner Ensemble* will be associated (Picasso's dove, for example). But perhaps war is not so interesting and productive a topic when it is approached in that way: *Mother Courage*, for example, takes it as a setting and, instead of war, dramatizes the petty-bouregois desperation about the difference between capital and money. Meanwhile, *The Affairs of Mr Julius Caesar* shows how war becomes another card you play in the various stock-market-like capitalist and business struggles. But 'warmongering' is a psychological matter, raising issues of authoritarianism, a more psychological or psychoanalytic view of Nazism as sadism, and so forth – it seems clear that Brecht was never much interested in this psychological side of things.

Which brings us to the figure of Mauler, unique in Brecht's work as a full-dress portrait of the psychology of the capitalist, along Goethean or Faustian lines: 'two souls dwell in my breast'. Patty Lee Parmalee has indeed observed that such 'parodies are intended not to make the classics look ridiculous but to show how once progressive forms become an ideological cover for reaction'.[24] Brecht was certainly interested in the workings of pity in a figure like Mauler: the opening speech dramatizes his moments of nervous crisis, of a kind of access of melancholy or depression (or mourning, as we would say today), which are not meant to be merely farcical. How to know, not merely that you make people suffer, but that you slaughter oxen? How to know this, and to carry on?

Erinnere, Cridle, dich an jenen Ochsen
Der blond und gross und stumpf zum Himmel blickend

Den Streich empfing mir war's, als galt er mir.

(III, 129)

Canst hearken, Cridle, back to that great ox
So blond and massive with his gaze on heaven
As the axe struck home: and seemed to strike me too.

It is in reality, looked at dramatistically, a Peachum-like problem: how
to speak to the ever more unfeeling hearts? Mauler is ready-made for the
Aristotelian theatre of sympathy and fellow-feeling, as well as for
Peachumite beggars' strategies. Like Brecht as well, he must renounce
that part of himself, and do away with that weakness ('we who wanted
to prepare the ground for friendliness could not ourselves be friendly'),
but this time in order to do business. Hitler/Ui is a delirious sociopath;
Mauler is a tragic hero, but a tragic hero rewritten by Brecht.

Businessmen are thus a significant actantial category for Brecht, whose
representations of capitalism are mainly, as we have seen, organized
around speculation and the stock market. The category of the oppressed
and exploited is then largely filled with a figuration from another system
altogether, namely the peasants; what is added to this category from the
realm of industrial modernity is not labour – machines will, however, be
a significant substitute, as we shall see below – but, rather, the unemployed. Perhaps, then, we may also suggest that the time-honoured
Marxian category of the petty bourgeoisie is in Brecht displaced by the
rather different one of the city-dweller, as witness his *Lesebuch* (or
Primer) *für Städtebewohner*. But there is also a category of liberal
philanthropy, whose representatives range from Peachum to Joan herself
– or, in other words, from philanthropy as a kind of business to
institutional pity and fellow-feeling (empathy) as a tragic space for
pedagogy and an approach to political commitment, which, internally
conflicted, ends badly. These figures then begin to approach that other
basic actantial category in Brecht, namely the intellectuals, or in other
words the so-called *Tuis* ('Intellek-tuellen'), later for him largely identified with the Frankfurt School. This is not a class category for Brecht,
and it is the moment to insist that his political judgements were never
based on empirical class affiliation, and that he often attacked the
mechanical use of such sociological and family information, just as he
repudiated that frequent infantile-left denunciation of art as such (as
current in the 1920s as it was again in the 1960s).[25] Artists can be, but
are certainly not necessarily or inevitably, *Tuis*: as witness those theatre
people who participate in socialist construction, and whose work is itself
already a symbolic social construction.

Thus, in order to determine the nature of a *Tui* more closely, it will be necessary to see what Brecht thinks ideology is. I want to advance a scandalous proposition at this point, which I do not have the space fully to defend: namely, that in fact Brecht himself comes to eschew classical and modern theories of ideologies altogether – indeed, that for him, it is precisely the preoccupation of leftist thinkers with the various complex ('Western-Marxist') theories of ideology that marks them as *Tuis* in the first place. This is not to say that *Tuis* must always be on the left; in fact, he thinks the Nazi 'revolution' itself was also an affair of *Tuis*, or in other words of disgruntled intellectuals, full of *ressentiment* (the figure of Goebbels lending much plausibility to this view) – 'es war einfach der Aufstand der unteren (untüchtigsten) Tuis gegen die oberen' (XVII, 34): 'simply the revolt of the lower – or most incompetent – *Tuis* against the higher ones'.

What must first be said openly – it has been implicit in the preceding pages – is that the fierce competition between businessmen (or even between sellers and buyers, shopkeepers and customers, as we have seen) is far more interesting, and provides far richer dramatic material for Brecht, than any kind of sheer ideological contradiction, which at best approaches drama with Mauler's 'two souls' or Joan's agonizing existential choices. Yet it is precisely this set towards business and conspiracy – which ought to be supremely actual once again in an age of insider trading and financial speculation, but still seems to look as antiquated as Hitler or Fordism – that so often entitles Brecht to the contemptuous qualification as a vulgar Marxist or a dialectical materialist, a Marxist functionalist (unless, indeed, for such critics, all Marxism is irrevocably doomed to functionalism in the first place).

It is a characterization that on some days Brecht was proud enough to endorse and to claim for himself: the glorious motto of 'plumpes Denken', for example (XVI, 173: 'crude thinking'), might best be taken as a kind of imperative – namely, to think vulgarly. It is not a bad therapy, particularly for *Tuis*; and I have suggested myself that any hyper-intellectualistic Marxism needs to bear this kind of vulgar *Weltanschauung* at its heart, and vice versa. But then in that case we have to do with a relativism that is based on the nature of the historical situation itself, and no one was as tireless as Brecht in insisting on the ultimate situationality of thought.[26] However, we need to go a little deeper than this, and I will propose that what looks from a distance like a vulgar-Marxist model of crude class interests at work within ideology is in fact a more subtle and negative scheme, in which ideology essentially finds itself judged on the basis of its consequences – or, in German, its *Folgen*, its results, the outcome in practice. Philosophically, it is a position which would mark a Brechtian affiliation with those traditions of contemporary philosophy – American pragmatism, Viennese logical positivism, Korsch's empirical materialism – which are only now beginning to be philologically explored by Brechtian scholarship.[27] But it is a fundamental characteristic of Brechtian slyness – and, indeed, of what we have been so bold as to call the Brechtian 'method' itself – that he does not offer us a positive theory of the consequences and the interests at work in ideology but, rather, a negative one: where the crucial term and leitmotiv (as we have shown above) is indeed the key word 'folgenlos', 'without consequences'. What is thus ideological about a particular work of art or a philosophical school alike is that it should have no consequences, that it should be designed to avoid having consequences.

The point is that the unique unity-of-theory-and-practice makes it impossible for Marxism – or at least, for this Marxism – to have a positive version of this wholly negative or privative phenomenon; we can tell when something intellectual or cultural has no consequences, but it is much more difficult to say when it does have them, because at that point the form or work in question is no longer purely cultural or intellectual, it is part and parcel of *praxis* itself: it can therefore no longer be described in the purely superstructural language of 'thought' or 'art'. Brecht did invent a kind of rough-and-ready stand-in for such a concept: it is the peculiarly attractive notion of 'eingreifendes Denken' or 'conceptual intervention'[28] – a slogan whose energizing resonances remain to be explored afresh for our own time and situation.

As for the past, however, the owl flying in its dusk would probably still find itself equipped with the perhaps antiquated machinery of positive and negative judgements, of those of the progressive and the reactionary. But at that point we find ourselves back in the powerful yet difficult vision of the dialectic offered by the *Communist Manifesto* itself. This is the spirit in which Brecht asks us to offer a particularly timely judgement on the putative progressive features of the great nineteenth-century railroads built (following Gustavus Meyers) by the private enterprise of the robber barons:

Ist die Privatinitiative gut oder ist sie schlecht? Die großen industriellen Werke wurden durch Leute mit Privatinitiative aufgebaut. Sie war also gut. Als die großen Werke standen, war sie unnütz geworden, und die Kollektivinitiative konnte sie abschaffen. Die Arbeiter hatten sie immer schlecht genannt. So war es: je mehr ihr Gutes (in den Werken) hervortrat, desto mehr trat auch ihr Schlechtes hervor. Das Gute bezeichnet das Schlechte als schlecht.

(XXI, 521)

Is private initiative good or bad? The great industrial complexes were built by people on the basis of private initiative. The latter was therefore good. But once these great complexes were already standing, private initiative was no longer necessary and collective initiative could do away with it. The workers always condemned those forms of private property as bad. Here, then, is the answer: to the degree to which the positive dimensions (of such works) becomes visible, to that every same degree their negative or bad dimension can also become perceptible and be registered. What is good in them thus also designates what is bad in them as bad.

What is happening in an account like this is that 'Folgen' or 'consequences' has been replaced as a category of judgement in the historical situation, and in particular in the stream of historical change or development, thereby taking on a degree of dialectical complexity unthinkable in what is so often called 'vulgar Marxism'.

Yet the situation can also be reversed; and over against the model of the railroads, in which something reactionary gradually reveals its productive or progressive dimensions, we may also – particularly in the realm of superstructures, or of the literary and cultural 'classics' – face the opposite one, in which something initially progressive becomes reactionary. This, for example, is what Tatlow is able to show in his luminous discussion of the fragmentary Confucius play: that Brecht had a notion (as Parmalee suggests) of the ways in which classics were once progressive: 'Brecht proposes a successful Confucius who is unhappy about, but eventually accepts, the perversion of his initial reformist intentions: he presides over their perversion with a bad conscience.'[29] In Brecht, Confucius' reforms are idealist, but progressively made: he wishes to improve the peasants' lot by returning to an older set of cultural practices. He fails in the former, but succeeds in the latter. This, then, is the sense in which the classics in general are progressive, yet idealist and subject to misappropriation by the rulers. This, then, is also the sense in which Brechtian satire in general, and this seeming satire of the classics (verse forms, etc.), is rather different from ordinary wholesale ridicule; it wishes to teach a lesson about progressive idealism; it holds to a certain 'moment of truth' (using Hegel's expression) in these same classics whose ineffectuality it must also mock. It wishes to maintain utopian instance in the past, the briefest glimpse, not only of what might have been – since the other classics, those of Marxism, teach that human beings can ask only the questions they are in a position to answer, and that modern revolution and a modern reconstruction of social production is possible only after the thorough development and exhaustion of capitalism (as a saturation of the fulfilled world market) – but also of what is and was intended, what can be remembered, and what once was 'almost'.

17 'Beinah'

Adverbs mark the dissolution of the proverb, as it settles back down to earth in all the multitudinous empiricities of the now. Already Peachum's 'leider' inscribed the mysteries of the linguistic shifter invisibly into the former proverbial proposition: Althusserian imaginary relations transforming what is back into its representations, subject positions, opinions, judgements, places of enunciation gradually showing up across the field, installing themselves on the archaic impersonal verbal object.

'Unfortunately' compounded a subjective judgement, with the secret quoting of another's subject position, yet stamped a definitive pessimism on the world's assessment. Now a different kind of adverb, more optimistic and more hesitant in its very temporality, comes to mark the very climax of the *Chalk Circle*. After the window of opportunity has been successfully exploited, and the doomlike fatality of class history begins once again to settle down upon the hapless inhabitants of Gruzinia, the events we have seen are projected with immense force and yet microscopic clarity into a legendary past. And it is said (after the judgement, when Azdak disappears and is never heard from again) that the people 'did not forget him, and were long mindful still of his judgeship' 'als einer kurzen Goldenen Zeit beinah der Gerechtigkeit' (VIII, 185): 'as a brief golden age of righteousness almost'.

To think of something as a 'golden age' is to rehearse a kind of utopian stereotype; the two words form a single expression, which can then – but not altogether unsurprisingly – be characterized as 'brief', and then specified as one of righteousness – or perhaps we should say, 'of justice'. But what salts the passage and gives this appreciation its savour, preserves its freshness as speech and as the brevity of an intervention in time itself, is the little word 'beinah'/'almost', which keeps all the realistic hesitations and second thoughts of the Grusinians about this worthless drunkard Azdak, and also about the paradox of a golden age that cannot last, at the same time as it expresses the poignancy of loss and the sharp pang for the passage of time itself. But it is with this as with the cranes and the lovers: the verse allows an investment of both antithetical reactions to time and change, which we register on both levels at once, that of fear and loss, that of permanency and celebration. 'Beinah' almost turns the language into meaningless gibberish (as in the romantic refrain of the *Three-Penny Opera*, quoted above, it does or it doesn't, here or there), but suspends itself before doing so, in such a way that we can register the dialectical union of these opposites, their identity or their identity and non-identity, all at once. Yet what 'almost' hesitates before in one long pause is not the quality of the righteousness; it is the span of time, and the utopian regret that tinges contemplation of a 'golden age' that lasted but a season.

Notes

1. Arthur Danto, *Narration and Knowledge* (New York: Columbia University Press, 1985).
2. To a newspaper questionnaire in 1928 – what book made the strongest impression on you in the course of your life? – Brecht answered: 'You're going to laugh: the Bible': 'Sie werden lachen: die Bibel' (XXI, 248).
3. Stéphane Mallarmé, 'Le Tombeau d'Edgar Poe'.
4. Jolles, *Einfache Formen*, p. 157.
5. Karl Marx, the *Grundrisse*, in Marx and Engels, *Collected Works*, vol. 29 (New York: International, 1987), pp. 401, 410.
6. Frigga Haug pertinently suggests that this 'category mistake' offers the most classic embodiment of Ernst Bloch's 'ungleichzeitige Gleichzeitigkeit' ('non-synchronous synchronicity'): see his *Erbschaft dieser Zeit* (1963).
7. See Ernst Bloch's magnificent essay 'Paradoxa und Pastorale bei Wagner', in *Verfremdungen* I (Frankfurt: Suhrkamp, 1962). The same volume contains a lively appreciation of the 'Seeräuberjenny' song from the *Three-Penny Opera*.
8. Jolles, *Einfache Formen*, p. 155.
9. Ibid., p. 156.
10. Ibid., p. 164.
11. Ibid., p. 167.
12. Ibid., p. 170.
13. Ibid., pp. 164–6.
14. Not enough attention has been paid to the pleasures and the fascination of the 'artificial', the false, the sham, what draws attention to itself in its shoddiness precisely as the unreal (and what, thus unanalyzed, takes on the name of 'sheer appearance' in the philosophical tradition). But see Sartre's analysis of Genet's passion for kitsch or 'le toc' (for what is later famously identified by Susan Sontag as 'camp'): *Saint Genet: Comedian and Martyr* (New York: Braziller, 1963), pp. 355–401 ('Strange hell of beauty'), where a passion for the artificial is grasped as driven by a *ressentiment* against that 'reality' which the tawdriness of the artificial and the imitation already goes a long way towards discrediting: the false as an aggressive weapon against the real. And see also, for a related celebration of the false in a more positive spirit, Gilles Deleuze, *Cinéma*, vol. II (Paris: Minuit, 1985), ch. 6: 'Les Puissances du faux'.
15. In Longinus (and in the tradition that follows), the sublime is always identified with a movement of 'elevation and amplification' (sections xi and xii); whereas my proposal suggests the simultaneous possibility of a satiric diminution or lowering so dramatic and prodigious as to evoke sublimity in its own right in turn.
16. Or rather, it is the equivalent on the level of style of what larger shifts the latter determined on the level of plot or narrative perspective: see my 'Generic Discontinuities in SF', *Science-Fiction Studies*, vol. I (Fall, 1973), pp. 57–68. In both instances the shifts and changes inscribe being as a stream of metamorphoses; but they also call for a symbolic meaning to be invested in each specific transformation, each mediation between specific qualities.
17. The famous remarks about photography are thus now in order:

   Die Lage wird dadurch so kompliziert, dass weniger denn je eine 'Wiedergabe der Realität' etwas über die Realität aussagt. Eine Photographie der Kruppwerke oder der AEG ergibt beinahe nichts uber diese Institute. (XXI, 469).

Things have become so complex that a 'reproduction of reality' has less than ever to say about reality itself. A photo of the Krupp factory or the AEG tells us almost nothing about these institutions.

One is tempted to juxtapose Jean-Luc Godard's reflections about the capacity of film to represent labour: in the factory scenes in *Passion*, for example, the shots are compared to pornography – in other words, neither labour nor sex is accessible in any unmediated way; for more about this, see my chapter on *Passion* in *The Geopolitical Aesthetic* (London: British Film Institute, 1993).

18. Translation and original quoted from Patty Lee Parmalee's excellent *Brecht's America* (Miami, OH: Ohio State University Press, 1981), pp. 139–40. Parmalee's topic is not only the America motif in Brecht (as opposed to Lyon's history of his American experience), but also precisely this one of his relationship to Marxism as a storehouse both of representations and of representational dilemmas.

19. Sergei Eisenstein, 'Notes for a Film of Capital' (*October* 2, Summer 1976, pp. 3–38; see also Annette Michelson's commentary on the project, in three instalments, in *October* 2, 3 and 6).

20. Émile Zola, *Les Rougon-Macquart* (Paris: Pléiade, 1967), vol. V, pp. 1293–4.

21. Ibid., p. 23.

22. Theodore Dreiser, *Sister Carrie* (New York: Penguin, 1981), pp. 61–2.

23. For Lukács ('What is Orthodox Marxism?'), see Prologue, Note 29 above. The Gramsci text I have in mind is 'The Revolution against *das Kapital*', in Antonio Gramsci, *Pre-Prison Writings*, ed. R. Bellamy, trans. V. Cox (Cambridge: Cambridge University Press, 1949), pp. 29–42.

24. Parmalee, *Brecht's America*, p. 162.

25. See Part I, Note 19, above.

26. Someone so ill-advised as to have written enthusiastically about both Adorno and Brecht will presumably not be surprised by pressures to choose between them (what they share is evidently a sarcasm, a dialectical cynicism, about the present; what separates them is then the principle of hope). Instead of doing so, however, I recommend Brecht's own version, the parable of the Gordian Knot:

> . . . ach der Mann
> Dessen Hand ihn knüpfte, war
> Nicht ohne Plan, ihn zu lösen, jedoch
> Reichte die Zeit seines Lebens, angefüllt
> Leider nur aus für das eine, das Knüpfen.
> Eine Sekunde genügte
> Ihn durchzuhauen.
>
> (XIII, 353–4)

> . . . Oh, the man
> Whose hand tied it was not
> Without plans to undo it, but alas
> The span of his life was only long enough
> For the one thing, the tying.
> A second sufficed
> To cut it.
>
> (*Poems*, 119)

27. See Prologue, Note 16 above.

28. The *Historisch-kritisches Wörterbuch des Marxismus* (Berlin: Argumentverlag, 1994) has an excellent entry on 'Eingreifendes Denken' by Karen Ruoff Kramer (in Volume III), as well as two enlightening and useful entries on the 'Brecht-Linie' in Volume II.

29. Tatlow, *The Mask of Evil*, p. 402.

Epilogue

18 Modernity

But there is another temporality we need to touch on before concluding, for it is the apparent cancellation of all of this (which was still predicated on the temporality of the feudal, and of peasant experience): even capitalism here could be a sheer merchant activity not at all inconsistent with the trickery of the caravan and the indifference of mercenary armies that sweep back and forth across the subservience of landed populations. What generates another accent in the very concept of the New – now no longer a mere presence to these timeless dialectical reversals, but the eruption of something radically different, the emergence of a *Novum* after which nothing can be the same again – is the modernity of the machine itself, which Brecht also welcomes and celebrates. This, to be sure, is the Brecht of the endorsement of 'the bad new things, rather than the good old things': it is the Brecht of the Lindbergh flight and of the radio plays, a Brecht of cantatas and unison voices, which preside over the conquests of machinery like a Greek chorus whose historical meaning has been violently altered, although it must still be present at the failure and death of individuals – will Lindbergh not fall victim to the force of Sleep, an even greater force than Mist or Snow? And how to come to terms with the death of the fallen aviators (in the *Badener Lehrstück*) or with the sacrifices of the 'Jasager' or the condemned militant of *Die Massnahme*? It is true that machinery is scarcely present at all in the Noh-play starkness of these later and more developed *Lehrstücke*: yet I want to argue that what remains of the modernist/futurist technology here is their very starkness, which emerges from the radio play, and in which the medium of the radio itself stands in for the machine which the disembodied voices cannot convey. Their very purity as disembodiment is that, only apparently inhuman, of the machine as such: the radio takes the relay of the aeroplane; its streamlined effects lie in its abstraction of sheer voice. We do not yet have the kind of analysis of the brief moment of radio that people have so passionately undertaken for cinema on the

one hand, and television on the other; but Brecht's modernism – and the
very modernism of his moment of history in general – is bound up with
radio, and demands the acknowledgement of radio's formal uniqueness
as a medium, of its fundamental properties as a specific art in its own
right, a form in which the antithesis of words and music no longer holds,
but a new symbiosis of these two formerly separate dimensions is
effectuated and rehearsed. To radio can then be attached a productive
nostalgia which is one historicist way of coming to terms with this whole
era (as it has been played out in such varied artifacts as Vargas Llosa's
novel *La tia Julia y el Scribidor*): at one, as well, with the genius of
Welles (of whom one can even say that his very downfall, in *A Touch of
Evil*, is delivered by way of a radio-like interference),[1] and of generations
of pop music for which recording (which will later become autonomous
and a medium in its own right) is a mere surrogate. One man, one
machine: indeed, for anyone who sees it floating modestly among the
airborne crafts of history, from the immense set of wooden slats on
which a single Wright brother once lay to the ominous fightercraft or
the blind, sealed-in, snub passenger planes of the 1930s and 1940s, the
Spirit of St Louis is perfectly proportioned to the human body, as in
some Renaissance golden section. It might indeed be said to be the
Platonic Idea of that other index of modernity contemporaneous with it,
the motor car, for it houses the body and weds its velocity, yet hovers as
a unique exemplar in the undifferentiated element of clouds and mist, a
cross between an automobile and a radio. This mobile being then
organizes a whole complex of themes, as with the horse in classical
society:

> the prehistory of the god Poseidon shows that before reigning over the sea an
> equine Poseidon, Hippos or Hippios, associated, in the mind of the first
> Hellenes as well as of other people, the theme of the horse with a whole
> mythic complex: horse – watery element, horse – underground rivers, infernal
> world, fecundity; horse – wind, storm, cloud, tempest.[2]

This is indeed Brechtian modernity: the Lindbergh flight is not only
new, such a thing has never before been seen; it astonishes the emptiness
of Nature itself, the unpopulated realm of transoceanic altitude, like the
world before the appearance of life: so it is that Mist itself addresses the
foreign body that enters it:

> Ich bin der Nebel. . . .
> 1,000 Jahre hat man keinen gesehen
> Der in der Luft herumfliegen will:

Wer bist du eigentlich?   (III,12)

I am the mist. . . .
For a thousand years has not been seen
One who attempts a flight in the empty air:
Who can you be?

Yet not only the external elements come forward to meet Lindbergh
with as much wonderment as hostility – even an internal element, the
great natural force of Sleep itself, challenges him as a character, thus
making him not some heroic subjectivity but, rather, an element in his
own right, a name. It was therefore ironic that Brecht should have to
have removed this name – whose German ancestry surely added to its
European interest and appeal, like a Central European nation-state
immensely magnified and resonated by the extraordinary space of the
New World – when the aviator rediscovered his own origins the wrong
way, in the Hitler period. The very German title of Lindbergh's autobiographical book *Wir zwei* (We Two), however, underscores the difference
between this modernist symbiosis and the postmodern android or
biological-machine synthesis, equally distinct from the traditional
relationship with tools, of farmer to plough, or handicraft worker. Yet
modernity has meant production, and a crucial problem is raised by the
symbolic production of just such modernist emblems which foreground
the media itself as the technological support of transportation and
communication: the railroad, the combustion engine, the steamship liner
– even, indeed, the radio itself, as it is integrated into the very radio play
of the narrative of the Lindbergh flight. In order to recapture this unique
moment – not yet that of some human dissolution into the computer, yet
marking a reification of labour-power and emergence of the machine as
such out of older forms of properly human bodily toil – we would have
to grasp and perceive the way in which, for one long moment still, this
movement of the machine is precisely at one with production. In the
Lindbergh Flight, this transformation of natural raw material is figured
as an act of *praxis* as transcendence:

        Also kampfe ich gegen die Natur und
        Gegen mich selber.
        Was immer ich bin und welche Dummheiten ich glaube
        Wenn ich fliege, bin ich
        Ein wirklich Atheist.
        Zehntausend Jahre lang entstand
        Wo die Wasser dunkel wurden am Himmel
        Zwischen Licht und Dämmerung unhinderbar
        Gott.   (III, 16)

So I struggle against Nature
And against myself.
Whatever stupidities I may have in my head
When I fly I am
Truly an atheist.
For ten thousand long years there was
At the point where the waters darken against the sky
Irresistibly emerging between the light and the twilight
God himself.

But the modernity of the Lindbergh flight is now the deliberate 'Ver-scheuchung jedweden Gottes, wo / Immer er auftaucht' (III, 17): 'the systematic banishment of any and every god / wherever it seeks to reemerge'. Heroic secularization, then, as the very mark of the Enlightenment project and the reassertion of a new Human Age. Yet the unusual plural of the more definitive title – 'Der Flug der Lindberghs' / 'The Flight of the Lindberghs' – suggests an even greater novelty as far as the modernist conception of the subject is concerned: not merely the replaceability of this actor by all the others, as in the classical *Lehrstück* paradigm, but the plurality of this *actant*, whose words are now to be declaimed by a chorus of boys and girls; to which must be added, in the staged or oratorio-type productions, the designation of the actor who plays the Lindbergh role as 'The Listener', a re-creation of some primal radio situation in which the alleged passivity and receptivity of the radio audience is dramatically reversed, and the act of the hearing of the play is violently redefined as the exploratory *praxis* of the aviator himself as he produces the New by venturing into and struggling with it. Here, too, then, the *Novum* is not some unusual object, as in so many avant-garde conceptions of modernist innovation, but a whole new world of relationships, like the new world of Galileo's physics or the new world of socialist construction, into which writer and reader alike must penetrate by means of daring exploration, and appropriation.

19   Actuality

Have we been able, in the preceding pages, to make a case for the inherent content, not merely of Brecht's 'method' as such, as we have seen it at work in everything from plot construction to the microscopic work of the wordsmith, but also of that included in the dialectic itself, virtually as what defines it and gives it its specificity from other philosophical methods or world-views? It would have to be a defence profoundly related to Hegel's own case for what he called the 'speculative': namely, the way in which the very idea of a concept carries within it its own utopian energy, projects a world 'equal' to the concept in question, at the same time as it passes judgement on worlds that have not yet raised themselves to that level. Change in Brecht would then qualify as a speculative concept of precisely that kind: a purely formal notion that implies and projects its own content by virtue of its unique form. This is not exactly teleology, I would want to argue; although it is certain that it is this aspect of the systems in question which has been caricaturized and discredited under the term teleology in both Hegel and Marxism. The mistake is no doubt in part a confusion between chronology and Hegelian essences or Aristotelian forms: to define the vocation of the world in terms of collective social life and of planned productivity, the reduction of individual labour, and a vision of human control over history, is not to predict any particular sequence of events, and it is certainly not to assert the 'inevitability' of the outcome (history can also 'end', Marx famously reminded us, in 'the ruin of the contending forces').[3] Perhaps it is merely to restore an ideological vision and to make possible again the picture of an alternative future (a task not particularly *folgenlos* or 'without consequences' at the present time). In any case, if the dialectic asserts the primacy of the situation, then one's arguments about change, and one's way of staging it, one's affirmation of it, or call for it, or indeed the demonstration that it is already here, in process, without our knowing it, will be dialectical only if they vary and describe another dimension of the proverbial elephant. The objection, for example, that teleology paralyzes human initiative and encourages a passive or fatalistic surrender to the foreordained is certainly an appropriate one, but not particularly relevant for an already generally passive and fatalistic era (in any case, Marxism has systematically and strategically swung back and forth between the two poles of fatalism and voluntarism).

On the other hand, Marx's structural demonstration, in *Capital*, of the emergence of a new society and a new economy within the old one, of some inner necessity of that emergence which is altogether distinct from a break grounded in either morality or desperation alone – this kind of demonstration might still be useful for us, and produce a very different conception of socialism from the current one.

Yet the celebration of change itself – whether in the form of the Tao or some other chronotope – may be open to all kinds of other doubts and suspicions, particularly in a society whose current economic rhythms perpetuate and thrive on permanent change: capital accumulation, investment and realization, the dissolution of stable firms and jobs into a flux of new and provisional entities, awash in structural unemployment, its cultural infrastructure committed to permanent revolution in fashion and to the imperative to generate new kinds of commodities, when not, in deeper crises, to invent or exploit wholly new production technologies. Indeed, it was precisely this ringing endorsement of the modernist slogans of innovation and novelty by postwar capitalism which did as much as anything else to discredit the modern movement.

The Tao thus stands in some tension with the historical paradigm of the Marxian modes of production, and can perhaps only locally be adjusted to it, an adjustment we can no longer rely on Brecht to provide. Other suspicions, however, will no doubt equally well attach themselves to existential fully as much as to historical time: a way of whistling through the graveyard of individual deaths, besides navigating the uncertainty of the generations and confronting that peculiar thing the theologians called Hope. Brecht did not evade this inevitable dimension of any ideology of change, as interesting sections of *Me-ti* demonstrate:

Und ich sah, daß auch nichts ganz tot war, auch nicht das Gestorbene. Die toten Steine atmen. Sie verändern sich und veranlassen Veränderungen. Selbst der totgesagte Mond bewegt sich. Er wirft Licht, sei es auch fremdes, auf die Erde und bestimmt die Laufbahn stürzender Körper und verursacht dem Meerwasser Ebbe und Flut. Und wenn er nur einen erschräke, der ihn sieht, ja wenn ihn nur einer sähe, so wäre er nicht tot, sondern lebte. Dennoch, sah ich, ist er in bestimmter Art tot; wenn man nämlich alles zusammengetragen hat, worin et lebt, ist es zu wenig oder gehört nicht her, und er ist also im ganzen tot zu nennen. Denn wenn wir dies nicht täten, wenn wir ihn nicht tot nennten, verlören wir eine Bezeichnung, eben das Wort tot und die Möglichkeit, etwas zu nennen, was wir doch sehen. Da er aber doch, wie wir ebenfalls sahen, auch nicht tot ist, müssen wir eben beides von ihm denken und ihn so behandeln wie ein totes Nichttotes, aber doch mehr Totes, in gewisser Hinsicht Gestorbenes, in dieser Hinsicht ganz und gar und unwiderruflich Gestorbenes, aber nicht in jeder Hinsicht.

(XVIII, 73–4)

And I saw that nothing was ever completely dead, not even what had died. The dead stones breathe. They modify each other and cause modifications. Even the allegedly dead moon is in movement. It casts light – however strange – upon the earth and determines the trajectory of falling bodies and causes the ebb and flood of the sea waters. And were the moon even to startle but one person who sees it, nay were even but one person to see it, then it would not be dead but would live. Yet in a certain sense, I saw, it is dead after all; for when one brings together everything in which it can be said to live, that is either too little or is irrelevant, and thus on the whole it is to be called dead. For if we did not do so, if we did not call the moon dead, we would lose a specific characterization, namely, the word dead and the possibility thereby to name something which we in fact see. But since as we have also seen it is also not dead, we are therefore obliged to think both characterizations about it, and to treat it as a dead 'not-dead' thing, which is yet more on the dead side, and in a certain respect a thing which has died, indeed in this respect a thing which has completely and irrevocably died, yet not in every respect.

Thus, if the stream of things is a mixture of dying and regeneration, the thought problems confronting us are dialectical, in the identity of opposites, of negative and positive; and also linguistic, in the logical validity of sentences and the mutual exclusion of their meanings; and also aesthetic, in so far as one aspect of the dead moon's continued life is its perception as *strange* [*fremd*] by even one last living being, its *estrangement* of itself and of that being. Finally, causality intervenes, and intersects the vast sublunary landscape of all that is: raising its own linguistic and dialectical questions.

Brecht was willing to force the issue even more pointedly, as in his suggestion that

> obwohl der Tod des einzelnen rein biologisch für die Gesellschaft uninteressant ist, soll das Sterben gelehrt werden.
>
> (XXI, 402)

> although the purely biological death of the individual is uninteresting to society, dying ought none the less to be taught.

It is probably less a Montaigne-like aspiration than the expression of themes surrounding *Die Massnahme* from this same period. A social Tao, on the other hand, is surely bound up with the issues of technology and modernity raised above, to which we will return in conclusion.

At this point, however, it seems most appropriate to invert the issue by asking not what Brecht's posterity ought to be, but what it has in fact been, and to excavate his now subterranean influence on contemporary thought, an influence which seems to have been forgotten, but is surely the best testimony to his contemporaneity. In other words, the framing of artificial arguments and reasons why Brecht would be good for us today and why we should go back to him in current circumstances seems hypothetical in contrast to the concrete demonstration that we have in fact 'gone back to him' and that his thought is present everywhere today without bearing his name and without our being aware of it.

This is something I want to sketch in for so-called anti-foundationalism and anti-essentialism, by way of passing through some of the great themes of post-structuralism itself. The mediatory figure here has already been mentioned: it is Roland Barthes, whose profound Brechtianism has not often been acknowledged, even though it is responsible for the most original interventions that constituted Barthes's historic significance in the 1950s and were influential in forming what one sometimes thinks of as the poststructural doxa of the 1960s and 1970s. Barthes's inheritance, in those early works, was the Sartrean and existential polemic against nature and against essence, as normative and thereby repressive values. It is not sufficiently recognized today that much of the content of contemporary appeals to 'performativity' and to the anti-normative stance of 'queer theory' is profoundly Sartrean in spirit.[4] Barthes's dealings with 'nature' – with 'human nature' as well as with that metaphysical 'nature' inherent in normative conceptions of the 'meaning of human life' – thus represents a creative and explosive wiring together of the Sartrean philosophical polemics and the Brechtian practical and aesthetic estrangements of the same illusion of stasis and the eternal. The Brechtian origin of some of these themes and positions might help us to recover some of their original political content as well.

In any case, the Brecht we know today includes, but is not completely the same as, the Brecht of Weimar, or of the various exiles (in particular the American one); but he does appear fully, virtually for the first time on the world stage, in the *Théâtre des nations* in Paris in summer 1954: this famous visit, which brought *Mother Courage* from a still war-ruined East Berlin (and the next year, most sumptuous production of them all, the first great *Caucasian Chalk Circle*), no doubt played its part in the universal crystallization of Marxism among French intellectuals. Unlike fellow-travellers like Sartre, in other words, Brecht appeared to be the first genuinely Marxist artist who completed the originality of Marxism and the dialectic as a thought mode with its full originality (beyond the dreary predictabilities of socialist realism) as a new kind of aesthetic.

I have already suggested the significance of inner distance, of the very concepts of distanciation and the split subject, in Brecht's theatrical practice. It remains to assert their philosophical significance and influence in this very Paris in which the ideological crystallization of what we now call structuralism and poststructuralism is taking place (and we have already been able to enlist work of Barthes, well beyond his Marxist period, as testimony for the existence of powerful new aesthetic formulations of these concepts, which Barthes himself found concretely dramatized and acted out in Brecht).

The matter of nature is more obviously central, since it was always the crucial feature in Brecht's own account of the estrangement 'method': to show that what we take to be natural, and thus both 'normal' and 'immutable' all at once, is in reality historical, has come into being by way of a complex human history, and thus has it in it to be done away with by historical action as well. The differentiation on which the V-operation is based and which it reactivates, so to speak, is of a piece with much else in the period: with Lévi-Strauss's influential opposition between nature and culture, for instance, even though the 'synchronic' perspective seems to flatten 'culture' itself back out into something relatively static or stable, very much on the order of that nature to which it was to be opposed in the first place. The general ideological and philosophical discomfort with natural and naturalist foundations throughout this period is, however, clearly staged far more dramatically by Sartrean existentialism, in its pointed onslaught on 'human nature' (essence) and on a metaphysics of the natural. (It was, to be sure, no accident that the proposal to retranslate Lévi-Straussian 'structures' back into forms of human *praxis* is first raised in Sartre's *Critique of Dialectical Reason* [1960], and then, following him in a far more thoroughgoing way, by Pierre Bourdieu's *Outline of a Theory of Praxis* [1972].) But it is surely in Barthes's *Mythologies* that the most usable form of the Brechtian method was developed, and the most influential in the areas of cultural and ideological analysis: Barthes's was a textbook 'application' of the method to a range of social and cultural phenomena, along with a theorization of the objects of estrangement in proto-linguistic terms, which had its own generative influence on the linguistics-based evolution of so-called structuralism itself. (The other dimension of Barthes's early work – which retains its immense historical significance – his work on literary history, as that found lapidary expression in *Writing Degree Zero*, is rather of Sartrean origin.)

But as I have argued above repeatedly, Brecht's was a method, not a philosophical system (hence the appropriateness of extrapolating its consequences out into linguistics, as Barthes did, rather than into this or that reifiable and ontological kind of social theory); and the relationship to nature remained with him a critical one, and something of a two-way street. This is why I must always adduce, as the supreme example of the estrangement-effect, the great moment precisely in this *Chalk Circle* which so electrified its first Parisian audiences, in which Grusha hesitates before taking up the burden of the endangered baby (the overthrown Governor's heir, and thus an obvious target for the conspirators). The singer-commentator's gloss on this hesitation is enough, and it is a whole programme: 'Schrecklich ist die Verführung zur Güte!' (VII, 116): 'Hideous is the temptation of goodness!' For in our traditional views of human nature and its instincts, the notion of temptation (handed down by Christianity and its theologies) normally centres on evil: it is the sinful instincts which have power, and draw us against our will. This means in turn that 'goodness' – here, the cooperative instincts in general, those a Marxian or Rousseauian ideology has always tried to count on – is unmistakably implied to be a relatively weak component of our nature, one perpetually in danger of being subverted by the stronger forces of self-preservation and desire, and whose superficiality is accounted for fairly late in the tradition by the Freudian notion that it is the result of repression and the superego in the first place.

Suddenly Brecht's luminous verse reverses all that ancient tradition of sin and human nature: now it is goodness itself which exerts the baleful force of temptation, which mesmerizes Grusha and is on the point of leading her to do things very much against her own best interests and personal safety. Now the cooperative ideal exerts all the uncanny power of attraction that used to be attributed to vice; and it is the good instincts which seem to have been only momentarily repressed by the process of civilization, and are ready to break out again at the slightest pretext. The reversal is then ratified by the spectacular word 'schrecklich', which designates the horror of such a drive or instinct, and its well-nigh sublime impact on the terrified mortals who witness it, let alone fall victim to its powers. Yet is this not the Aristotelian 'pity and terror' once again? Or at least an *Umfunktionierung* – a radical restructuration – in which it is Grusha's pity that inspires our terror? Yet precisely such restructuration changes everything: for we no longer pity Grusha, as in Aristotelian tragedy, and our own terror – far from reflecting our empathy with the tragic hero – constitutes itself a kind of temptation to some new kind of goodness, namely that of *praxis* itself.

This is Brecht at his most utopian and salvational, and it is significant that it should take place precisely in the context of a proto-philosophical grappling with the issue of nature itself. The argument is then not that a contemporary anti-foundationalism and anti-essentialism emerges directly from these first Brechtian dramatizations of naturality and its dialectical paradoxes, but that Brecht's work centrally feeds the cultural stream which leads to the widespread acceptance of these positions today.

But alongside the matter of nature, we must also shift the rudder in another direction by underscoring the matter of *praxis*, much maligned today under the epithet Prometheanism, which is made to characterize everything from Marx's early poetry to Stalinist industralization and the more general anti-ecological processes of modernization itself. We have dwelt briefly on Brecht's 'modernism', in the sense of his futurist enthusiasm for the new technologies. Now we must add in another characteristic term, namely productivity; it is certainly in evidence in the conclusion of the play just mentioned, the *Chalk Circle*, in which a final transfiguration of the frame story (the struggle for the land between the two kolkhoz) is reached under the moral enunciated by the storyteller:

> Ihr aber, ihr Zuhörer
> ... nehmt zur Kenntnis die Meinung
> Der Alten, daß da gehören soll, was da ist
> Denen, die für es gut sind ...
>
> (VIII, 185)
>
> Know then, ye spectators, the wisdom of the ancients, that things belong to those who use them best and most productively ...

As it may be less clear how this notion of productivity runs through Brecht's entire work, and in order to end with that, we select an unaccustomed reflection on what is normally called literary history.

20   Historicity

It must begin with the well-known historicist conundrum with which Marx broke off his draft Preface of 1857 to the *Grundrisse*, the problem of the value of the art of a different mode of production (ancient Greece) for us today.[5] Brecht first offers a way of estranging what is new by recovering the past of which it was a *Novum*, and inventing a historicity use for that past:

> Eine Verfremdung des Autos tritt ein, wenn wir schon lange einen modernen Wagen gefahren haben, nun eines der alten T-Modelle H. Fords fahren. Wir hören plötzlich wieder Explosionen: Der Motor ist ein Explosionsmotor. Wir beginnen uns zu wundern, daß solch ein Gefährt, daß überhaupt ein Gefährt, ohne von tierischer Kraft gezogen zu sein, fahren kann, kurz, wir begreifen das Auto, indem wir es als etwas Fremdes, Neues, als einen Erfolg der Konstruktion, insofern etwas Unnatürliches begreifen. Die Natur, zu der ja das Auto unzweifelhaft gehört, hat plötzlich das Moment des Übernatürlichen in sich, ihr Begriff ist nunmehr gesättigt damit.
>
> (XXII, 656–7)

An estrangement of the motor-car takes place if after driving a modern car for a long while we drive an old model-T Ford. Suddenly we once again hear explosions; the motor works on the very principle of the explosion. We start feeling amazed that such a vehicle, indeed any vehicle not drawn by animal-power, can move at all; in short we now grasp the automobile by grasping it as something strange, new, as a feat of sheer construction, in short precisely as the unnatural. Nature, to which obviously enough even the automobile belongs, suddenly discloses the moment of unnaturality within itself, and its concept is now saturated with that.

(Willett, 144–5)

So far so good: the New, the *Novum*, is somehow grasped as production and construction, it is always that which is 'against Nature', which must be aesthetically perceived as such in the shock of the V-effect. (Mythically, then, the breakdown of the motor car will be reconstituted into a legendary moment with the founding of *Mahagonny* itself.)

The relationship to art works of the past is thus given here in one form: the content of such works may well itself consist in various estrangements, but in order to experience that more vividly, we must somehow ourselves arrange to estrange the work as a whole (Hegel did this for Marx's Greek classics by positioning them as a conquest after the inarticulate 'sublimity' of his Asiatic pyramids and the like). But a more thoroughgoing theorization sets in when Brecht takes up the most troublesome feature of the historicity problem, at least from the aesthetic perspective: the historicity of feelings and emotions themselves – a subjectivity which has for so long been thought to constitute the principal centre of gravity of the aesthetic anyhow (nor is it any less embarrassing that Brecht's own theatre had so frequently been called intellectualist and accused of wishing to do away with the emotional content of art). Brecht allows for a dialectical relationship between reason and the emotions, and a historical relationship between emotions and interests (recommending, for example, that we compare Kipling with Rimbaud's 'Bateau ivre' – both poetic texts of the greatest importance to him personally – in order to feel the differences 'between French mid-nineteenth-century colonialism and British colonialism at the beginning of the twentieth century'). But then ('as Marx already noticed') he admits:

Schwieriger ist es, wie schon Marx bemerkt, die Wirkung solcher Gedichte auf uns zu erklären. Es scheint, daß Emotionen, welche gesellschaftliche Fortschritte begleiten, in den Menschen lange Zeit fortleben als Emotionen, welche mit Interessen verknüpft waren, und zwar in Kunstwerken verhältnismäßig stärker fortleben, als es angenommen werden könnte, wenn man bedenkt, daß sie doch inzwischen auf Gegeninteressen gestoßen sind. Jeder Fortschritt erledigt einen Fortschritt, indem er eben von ihm fortschreitet, daß heißt über ihn hinwegschreitet, er benützt ihn jedoch auch, und in gewisser Weise bleibt er im Bewußtsein der Menschen als Fortschritt erhalten, wie er im realen Leben in seinen Resultaten erhalten bleibt. Es findet da eine Verallgemeinerung interessantester Arbeit statt, ein laufender Prozeß der Abstraktion. Wenn wir die Emotionen anderer Menschen, der Menschen

vergangener Zeitalter, anderer Klassen usw. in den überkommenen Kunstwerken zu teilen vermögen, so müssen wir annehmen, daß wir hierbei an
Interessen teilnehmen, die tatsächlich allgemein menschlich waren. Diese
gestorbenen Menschen haben die Interessen von Klassen vertreten, die den
Fortschritt führten.

(XXII, 658–9)

It is less easy, as Marx already observed, to explain the effect that such poems
have on ourselves. ... Apparently emotions accompanying social progress
will long survive in the human mind as emotions linked with interests, and in
the case of works of art will do so more strongly than might have been
expected, given that in the meantime contrary interests will have made
themselves felt. Every progress cancels the previous one, insofar as by
definition it moves on further from that one, in other words, it moves across
and away from it; at the same time in a way it also uses its predecessor, so
that this last is somehow preserved in human consciousness as a form of
progress, just as in real life its results live on. We have here a process of
generalization of the most interesting kind, an ongoing process of abstraction.
Whenever the works of art handed down to us allow us to share the emotions
of other people, of people of past ages and of other classes, we must suppose
that in doing so we are sharing interests that are actually universally human.
The dead have here represented class interests that furthered progress.

(Willett, 146–7)

(And he demonstrates this *a contrario* by the example of the fascist art
that cannot be felt to have such effects.) What can be meant by 'progress'
in this sense, and how can it be felt to associate itself with a specifically
historical form of emotion? The example of the imperialist lyric is less
paradoxical than it might seem, since there has been a long debate within
Marxism (and not only within European Marxism) about the progressive
features of imperialism in a Third World or colonial context: that the
antisocial energies of, say, the cannon-song (in *The Three-Penny Opera*)
could be positively evaluated in other contexts we already know from
Me-ti's reflexions. How other kinds of outmoded historical emotions
might still preserve their 'value' seems less clear (although Brecht,
characteristically, presupposes the problem solved in advance: 'when we
share them', he says – the problem arises only if the works of the past
are still alive for us; it is not a matter of historical or philosophical
deduction).

I want to suggest that 'productivity' is the deeper meaning for progress
in Brecht, and that it has to do with activity as such. This association of
production and productivity with activity itself seems the most apt to
redeem the stigmatized word for contemporary values, and is in any case
consistent with Marx's notion of 'living labour', which in its turn then
sheds light back on the 'modernism' of the technologies in which it is

more copiously stored, in the form of what Marx called 'dead labour' or what Heidegger characterizes as a 'standing reserve' [*Bestand*].[6] In general, the struggle between modernist and postmodernist ideologies can be characterized as that between a fetishization of visible reservoirs of energy – machines whose stored labour is still apparent, and to be explosively reactivated, as with the combustion engine – and a ceaseless transmission of electronic signals whose relationship to human energy is problematic and which, rather, offers itself as an immense new element in which human actors might immerse themselves. Brecht's promise invests the V-effect with the capacity to reveal the human productivity latent in even this second, or cybernetic and informational, kind of technology; to disclose it in its turn as a form of production which is at one and the same time a form of activity. And should it be objected that this process amounts to an appropriation of the postmodern, its capture, by the old ideologies of the New, its translations back into a 'new' form of modernism as such, then we must also remember the signal differences between some Brechtian modernism (if that is what it is) and the canonical aestheticizing type. In that case, this evolution would not be a regressive one; and in any event, Brecht's most timely lesson, for an age which has become cautious about the word itself, is that 'progressive' is not to be limited to some stage-like evolution towards a better society, but invoked whenever production and productivity are at stake. It is paradoxical that the current age should be ideologically divided by these two terms: the market rhetoricians celebrating productivity with gusto (even though it is precisely the productivity of finance capital that is in question), while a new post-Marxist orthodoxy systematically denounces the concept of production as unsuited for a communicational and informational age, and in any case redolent of Stalinist productivism and the ecological exhaustion of nature. I have tried to show that the Brechtian conception of activity transforms both versions of the concept and restores a freshness that demands some new characterization. It has its precursors, to be sure: back beyond Marx we may think of Goethe – the non-canonical, heretical Goethe rather than the Goethe of the Weimar court; the Goethe reader and admirer of the unmentionable and still scandalous Spinoza himself, who proclaimed: 'I hate everything that does not heighten and increase my intellectual activity'. 'Intellectual' will now gradually become 'collective', and activity will come to take on a historical dimension: this is the point at which Brechtian productivity takes its place as an exemplary and still actual form of *praxis* itself.

Notes

1. 'A sonorous present, the "voice-off" of the narrator, constituting a veritable radio-phonic centre whose role is fundamental in Welles' – Gilles Deleuze, *Cinéma* II (Paris: Minuit, 1985), p. 152.

2. Jean-Pierre Vernant, *L'Origine de la pensée grecque* (Paris: Presses Universitaires de France, 1962), p. 7. The horse was also, of course, what defined the noble in the Middle Ages, and permitted the emergence of feudal power. But anachronisms are also appropriate in the other direction of time; thus this symbiotic relationship of human being to machine has also been influentially modelled and ideologized in our time under the figure of the cyborg: from a now already burgeoning material, the central text which still stands out is, of course, Donna Haraway, 'A Manifesto for Cyborgs', in *Simians, Cyborgs and Women* (New York: Routledge, 1991).

3. Karl Marx and Friedrich Engels, *The Communist Manifesto*, Part One.

4. For a further development of this proposition, see my article, 'The Sartrean Origin', in *Sartre Studies International*, vol. 1, Issues 1 and 2, 1995, pp. 1–20.

5. Karl Marx, *Grundrisse*, in vol. 42 of the *Werke* of Karl Marx and Friedrich Engels (Berlin: Dietz Verlag, 1983), pp. 44–5.

6. Martin Heidegger, *Gesamtausgabe*, vol. 79: *Bremer und Freiburger Vorträge* (Frankfurt: Klosterman, 1994), p. 28.

Index